Jesus in Nature

A Monastic Christology

Samuel Torvend

LITURGICAL PRESS
Collegeville, Minnesota
litpress.org

Cover art: Icon of the Creation of the Plants, 15th–16th c., Sucevita Monastery, Romania. Used by permission of the Monks of Saint Paul the Apostle Orthodox Monastery.

Library of Congress Cataloging-in-Publication Data

Names: Torvend, Samuel author
Title: Jesus in nature : a monastic Christology / Samuel Torvend.
Description: Collegeville, Minnesota : Liturgical Press, [2025] | Includes bibliographical references and index. | Summary: "In Jesus in Nature, Samuel Torvend uncovers the hidden story of monastic reflection on the presence of Jesus Christ in creation. With frequent references to contemporary life, he offers a comprehensive view of Jesus in his natural world and the various ways in which early medieval monastics discerned the presence of the risen Christ in nature"—Provided by publisher.
Identifiers: LCCN 2025010805 (print) | LCCN 2025010806 (ebook) | ISBN 9798400801686 trade paperback | ISBN 9798400801693 epub
Subjects: LCSH: Nature—Religious aspects—Christianity | Jesus Christ—Person and offices | Monastic and religious life
Classification: LCC BT695.5 .T67 2025 (print) | LCC BT695.5 (ebook) | DDC 232—dc23/eng/20250617
LC record available at https://lccn.loc.gov/2025010805
LC ebook record available at https://lccn.loc.gov/2025010806

"In *Jesus in Nature*, Samuel Torvend provides a characteristically erudite tribute to the cosmic Christology permeating the thinking of Benedict of Nursia, the Venerable Bede, Walafrid Strabo, and Hildegard of Bingen. Erudite, yes, but written in engaging prose that invites readers to consider that nature was not merely scenery and background in the lives of Jesus and these monastic figures but rather was in their eyes charged with the very vitality of God. Readers who take up this invitation will learn from their monastic forebears and find their own appreciation of Christ at work in the cosmos deepened."

— Timothy Brunk, Villanova University

"*Jesus in Nature* impresses in both its depth and breadth. Undertaking something like a monastic *ressourcement*, Samuel Torvend plumbs the depths of the tradition to capture the surprisingly relevant Christologies of medievals like Walafrid Strabo and Hildegard of Bingen. With an eye toward our contemporary ecological crises, Torvend shows how these figures broaden the scope of Christ's saving work to truly cosmic proportions: from the embeddedness of the historical Jesus in a very local ecology to the inseparability of the books of nature and Scripture. This book is a must-read for those of us who want to see how our *sequela Christi* necessarily entails a loving care for creation!"

— Lucas Briola, Saint Vincent College,
Latrobe, Pennsylvania

"Samuel Torvend presents us with an intriguing premise, namely, to craft a Christology through the lens of the environment. He begins by explicating the environmental world Jesus lived in that shaped his stories and worldview, as well as those of Benedict of Nursia, the Venerable Bede, Walafrid Strabo, and Abbess Hildegard of Bingen. Torvend draws a clear line from Jesus, the incarnation of God as expressed through all creation, to the intimate connection among monastic communities and the earth, thus shaping monastic images of who Jesus is for us."

— Laura Swan, OSB

In gratitude for

Deborah Hickey-Tiernan

Fred Speaks

Carol Wesley

In memory of

E. Silas Torvend

Alice Kjesbu Torvend

All beloved gardeners

Contents

Introduction

Every Sunday, in every part of the world, 1.9 billion people gather to hear a story and share an ancient meal. That story concerns Jesus of Nazareth and the command he gave to his first followers to share bread and wine, gifts of the earth and human labor, his Body and Blood. For more than two thousand years, that story has been retold and that meal has been shared in worshiping assemblies throughout the world. Along the way, each generation has reflected on the significance of Jesus of Nazareth and highlighted aspects of his life that respond to their needs and hopes.

Throughout the two millennia of Christian history, the people of God have sought to understand the person and work of Jesus Christ in light of new questions and knowledge within their distinctive cultural contexts. This effort to interpret his meaning in each generation is called Christology, "words about Christ." Christians have focused on the titles given to him in the New Testament, titles rooted in the Hebrew Scriptures, what Christians have commonly called the Old Testament. They have debated his relationship to the God he called his Father, relying on categories drawn from philosophy. They have wondered if he is fully human or fully divine or a union of the two. They have reflected on his role in salvation and the meaning of that term in different cultures. Does he save by liberating from oppression, making satisfaction for human disobedience, or offering God's transformative love? Indeed, much of the language employed in the study of the person and work of Jesus in the first fifteen hundred years after his death and resurrection has been drawn from philosophy, the gift of Athens; and law, the gift of Rome.

This study moves in another direction and uncovers the often-overlooked work of early medieval monastics, who reflected on the significance of Jesus Christ within the framework of the natural world, what the Bible calls the creation. Here we meet Benedict of Nursia, author of the Rule and founder of Western monasticism; the Venerable Bede, monastic historian and student of nature's seasons; Walafrid Strabo, tireless gardener and chronicler of the monastic garden; and Hildegard of Bingen, abbess and mystic, whose visions revealed the verdant Word of God and his greening power throughout the cosmos. These four monastics were adept at "reading" the Book of Nature and the Book of Scripture and, as students of the latter, were conscious of the presence of Jesus in the natural world as recorded in the gospels and other portions of the New Testament.

Thus, this exploration consists of two parts. The first chapter presents the natural world of Jesus' homeland, the Lower Galilee. Here we consider what is rarely undertaken in many studies of Jesus: a portrait of the land and water sources, vegetation and trees, birds, fish, animals, days and seasons, and threats to the ecology of the Lower Galilee at the time of Jesus. The second chapter offers a comprehensive discussion of Jesus within the natural world of his homeland as presented in the gospels: his knowledge of the natural world, his engagement with the natural world, his recognition of struggle with the elements of nature, his use of natural elements in his ministry, and his use of nature as metaphor in his teaching. This chapter concludes with a discussion of early Christian worship and its welcome to the gifts of creation.

The second part of this book presents the distinctive contribution of each monastic to an understanding of Jesus in nature. The third chapter highlights Benedict of Nursia (480–547) and examines the life of Jesus in nature as a model for monastic life. Here we explore the Christocentric character of Benedict's Rule and the images of Christ he favored. We then consider the encouragement Benedict offered for the establishment of a water source and garden in each monastery: the very matrix within which an earth-honoring Christology would come to flourish.

The fourth chapter highlights the Venerable Bede (673–735) and his discussion of light in winter and spring as witnessed in his *On the Calculation of Time* and *On the Nature of Things*. Bede presents an early medieval understanding of the significance of Christmas and Easter: the two preeminent feasts of light in Christianity. Here we encounter Christ as the creator of natural light and the embodiment of light (John 1:1-18). We also discover in Bede's writing the promise of earth's restoration in the resurrection of Jesus Christ.

In the fifth chapter, we meet a Benedictine relatively unknown to most modern readers: Walafrid Strabo (808–849), the quintessential monastic gardener. With Walafrid's *Hortulus* ("Small Garden"), we consider the nutritional, medical, and symbolic purposes of the monastic garden. Walafrid speaks of Christ as rose and lily and thus uses botanical imagery for Jesus. We also note how Paul's discussion of Christ as the firstfruits and the second Adam (1 Cor 15:23, 42-49) was interpreted by early medieval monks and nuns as the image of their own labor in gardens: Paradise being restored on earth.

Much more well-known than Walafrid is the twelfth-century abbess, Hildegard of Bingen (1098–1179), whose writings and music became popular in the second half of the twentieth century. In the first of her three great works, *Scivias* ("Know the Ways of the Lord"), we encounter Christ, the Serene One, suffused with brilliant light; the Sapphire Man, the greening power in the earth, the green wood, and the budding flower; and "the firstborn of all creation" (Col 1:15-20). For Hildegard, salvation is less a matter of owing a debt to God and more the experience of being healed of physical and spiritual wounds by Christ, the verdant power in the earth and in the soul, a healing that employs many elements of the natural world.

The seventh chapter considers how these medieval monastics serve as mentors for contemporary Catholics and other Christians. In light of the global environmental crisis that has deepened since the onset of the Industrial Revolution of the eighteenth century, what wisdom do these monastics offer to us as we worship with elements of the natural world in the sacraments? What suggestions do they offer as we seek to cherish and protect God's creation from further harm? How does their ability to read the Book of Scripture and the Book of Nature challenge and support the needed conversation between science and theology, a conversation often overlooked in our parishes and schools? Here we affirm our participation in the communion of saints and seek to learn within this communion from our sisters and brothers who have gone before us marked with the sign of the cross, the wood of a tree.

In fall 2023, I attended the International Congress of Benedictine Oblates at Sant'Anselmo in Rome, hosted by Abbot Primate Gregory Polan, OSB, a monk of Conception Abbey (Missouri). At the conclusion of the congress, we were honored to participate in an audience with His Holiness, Pope Francis. This study is inspired by his encyclical, *Laudato Si': On Care for Our Common Home* (2015) and his apostolic exhortation, *Laudate Deum: To All People of Good Will on the Climate Crisis* (2023), which was issued only a few days after our audience. *Jesus in Nature* flows from my *Monastic Ecological Wisdom* (Liturgical Press, 2023) and the helpful comments concerning that work from my wonderful colleagues in the Ecology and Liturgy Seminar of the North American Academy of Liturgy. I have been teaching early and medieval monastic history to university students for over twenty-five years: their comments and questions have clarified my own thinking about the riches of the monastic tradition and its relevance to our world.

As an oblate of Saint John's Abbey (Collegeville, Minnesota), I am grateful for the encouragement of Oblate Director Fr. Michael Peterson, OSB, and the monks of the abbey in their support of a sustainable environment. To the nuns of St. Placid Priory (Lacey, Washington), I offer thanks for their hospitality and care for the forested beauty in which they pray and serve. I am grateful for the work of Lucas Briola, Jason Brown, Gordon Lathrop, Martin Marklin, Eleanor Parker, and Gail Ramshaw, and I give thanks for Sean Horner, Rebecca Torvend Rainsberger, and Rex Torvend Rainsberger. To the staff of Liturgical Press, I offer my thanks, in particular to Hans Christoffersen, Monica Bokinskie, Tara Durheim, Stephanie Lancour, Jamie Lauer, Christin Roskos, Angela Steffens, and Michelle Verkuilen, for bringing this book to life.

December 28, 2024
Feast of the Holy Innocents, Martyrs

Part One

1

The Ecology of Jesus' Homeland

In the earliest gospel written, Mark notes that "Jesus came from Nazareth of Galilee and was baptized by John in the Jordan" (1:9). In this short sentence, the author draws our attention to a hill town, a region, and a river that flows from a lake. For most of his life, Jesus, his family, and his first followers lived in the northern part of first-century, Roman-occupied Palestine, in what has been called the Promised Land, the Holy Land, and Israel.[1] The sector where he grew up continues to be called the Galilee: a region that extends from the Mediterranean Sea in the west to the Jordan Valley in the east, and from the Litani River in the north to the Jezreel Valley, or Plain of Esdraelon, in the south.[2]

The Upper Galilee is a mountainous region that includes the majestic Mount Meron (3,992 feet). In the first century of our common era, this northern sector of the Galilee had few towns but numerous villages where vineyards flourished: in

[1] In 63 BCE, the Roman general Pompey conquered the kingdom of Judea, which included southern Galilee. The region became a vassal state, governed by Rome-appointed rulers: first, Herod the Great, and then his son, Herod Antipas—"that fox," as Jesus called him (Luke 13:32).

[2] Galilee comes from the Hebrew *galil*, meaning circular or circumscribed, a district. As the Hebrews became prominent in Canaan after their migration from Egypt, the tribes of Zebulun, Naphtali, Asher, and Issachar were allotted this region. "Jesus left Nazareth and made his home in Capernaum by the sea, in the territory of Zebulun and Naphtali" (Matt 4:13).

certain places, the terrain was treacherous and unfriendly to human habitation. By way of contrast, the Lower Galilee was marked by two prominent mountains (i.e., Tabor and Kamon), hills with thriving villages, fertile valleys, and a large lake. The Lower Galilee is bordered by the Beit HaKerem Valley to the north, the Jezreel Valley to the south, the Sea of Galilee (Lake Kinneret) to the east, and the Zebulon Valley to the west.[3] Jesus spent most of his life here.

Familiar with vast plains and extensive mountain ranges, North Americans may be surprised at the relatively small size of the Lower Galilee: 81 square miles is significantly smaller than the 469 square miles that comprise the city of Los Angeles.

As a child and young man, Jesus would have known his hometown of Nazareth; the larger neighboring Roman city of Sepphoris some three miles away; the newer Roman city of Tiberias on the western edge of the Sea of Galilee (also known as Lake Kinneret or the Sea of Tiberias); the villages of Magdala, Capernaum, and Bethsaida on the western and northern shores of the lake; and Chorazim, to the inland northwest. The topography of the region is marked by limestone, a dolomite rock that serves as a holder for underground aquifers; thus, villages were established around springs or along the shore of the Sea of Galilee, its fresh water fed from the Jordan River and a number of springs in the north. In contrast to the rockier terrain of the Upper Galilee, the fertility of the region rests, in part, on the *terra rossa* soil that holds a strong concentration of minerals which support the growth of trees, plants, and crops. Prior to and during Jesus' lifetime, the hills of Lower Galilee were frequently terraced to grow vines and olive trees that produced wine and olive oil, two staples in the Mediterranean diet.

[3] The region is described as "lower" because its hills are much lower than the mountains of the Upper Galilee.

Water

Concerning the fecundity of the region, the first-century Roman-Jewish historian, Josephus, wrote that "[the] soil is universally rich and fruitful, and full of the plantations of trees of all sorts . . . [The Galilee] produces all kinds of fruits . . . while the olive tree, the vine, and the palm tree are cultivated there. It is also sufficiently watered with torrents, which issue out of the mountains, and with springs that never fail to run."[4] While much of Western Asia and Israel remain arid and dry throughout the year, the Galilee has been the exception for millennia: the region receives over twenty-six inches of rain annually. Agricultural fertility here depends not only on human labor and the quality of the soil, but also on a generous measure of precipitation. Using the Köppen Climate Classification System, the Galilee is considered a Mediterranean Climate in contrast to Desert and Semi-Desert Climates elsewhere in Israel. This classification is based on the following criteria: mild temperatures that fluctuate throughout most of the year between sixty-four and twenty-seven degrees Fahrenheit; precipitation that falls during the wet season of the year, from November to March; and rainfall that averages at least twenty-six to twenty-eight inches each year.[5] Keep in mind that successful plant and crop growth requires mild temperatures as well as early rains that soften the soil in preparation for seeding. For the ancient Israelites, adequate precipitation was a sign of God's generosity: "The LORD will open for you his rich storehouse, the heavens, to give the rain of your land in its season and to bless all your undertakings" (Deut 28:12).

[4] Flavius Josephus, *The Jewish War*, Book 3:42–43, vol. II in the Loeb Classical Library, trans. H. St. J. Thackeray (Cambridge: Harvard University Press, 1927), 589.

[5] Morten Jensen, "Climate, Droughts, Wars, and Famines in Galilee as a Background for Understanding the Historical Jesus," *Journal of Biblical Literature* 131, no. 2 (2012): 311.

Modern Galilee is marked by numerous settlements that depend on sophisticated water systems and extensive irrigation from aquifers and the Sea of Galilee, but such was not the case in the first century; human habitation depended solely on spring water and rainfall.[6] "O God," exclaimed the psalmist, "my flesh faints for you, / as in a dry and weary land where there is no water" (Ps 63:1), a metaphor rooted in the actual experience of the terrain and its weather. Peasant farmers needed ample and fresh spring water, seasonal rains, and mild temperatures for the soil to remain rich and fruitful. Yet agricultural laborers in the Lower Galilee lived in a somewhat precarious situation: with episodic precipitation, the soil could become dry and cracked during an unusually hot summer season, ruining crops and fruit-bearing trees. Water in cisterns was susceptible to stagnation and pollution. Higher summer temperatures produced water evaporation with fewer days of rainfall: evergreen Seattle counts 152 days of rainfall each year; Nazareth has only 60 days. "For seasonal crops to grow, rain is needed not only in the right amount but also at the right time and with the proper dispersal."[7] The Franciscan archaeologist, Bellarmino Bagatti, indicated that first-century Nazareth was supplied with water from three springs.[8]

And then there was the ever-present threat of drought: "How long will the land mourn and the grass of every field wither? . . . the animals and the birds are swept away" (Jer 12:4). Drought, infestation, and hot winds flowing from the

[6] The Roman town of Sepphoris, some three miles northwest of Nazareth, included a sophisticated water system supported by two Roman aqueducts from the springs of two villages—er-Reina and Mashhad—close to Mount Yona, to the northeast of Nazareth. See Zeev Weiss, "Sepphoris," in *Oxford Classical Dictionary*, accessed February 27, 2024, https://doi.org/10.1093/acrefore/9780199381135.013.8039.

[7] Jensen, "Climate, Droughts, Wars," 312.

[8] Bellarmino Bagatti, *Ancient Christian Villages of Galilee*, trans. Paul Rotondi (Jerusalem: Franciscan Printing Press, 2001), 30–32.

eastern deserts produced episodic climate instability and famine—famine that imperiled not only humans but other creatures as well. While Josephus portrayed the Galilee as an Edenic paradise, his observations overlooked the potential peril of the many poor people who lived on the land, depended on agricultural labor for their livelihood, and were at the mercy of weather changes. But then, harmful aridity was not only a threat in ancient Israel: it foreshadowed the drier and hotter conditions that continue to cause extreme drought in western Canadian provinces[9] and a growing number of regions in the United States.[10] It thus appears that the biblical witness as well as contemporary agronomy confirm the simple truth that where there is water, there is life: that plants, crops, and creatures—human and otherwise—are utterly dependent on "living" water.

Trees

Today the distinctive ecology of the Lower Galilee includes some 2,630 species of plants and trees.[11] When Jesus walked there during the first century, however, that number was much smaller: the Bible mentions only 128 species.[12] As Josephus noted, the region was heavily forested, largely with Palestinian oaks (*Quercus calliprinos*) and Tabor oaks (*Quercus ithaburensis*):

[9] See the Canadian Drought Monitor, Government of Canada, accessed February 11, 2024, https://agriculture.canada.ca/en/agricultural-production/weather/canadian-drought-monitor/current-drought-conditions.

[10] See the U.S. Drought Monitor, accessed February 11, 2024, https://droughtmonitor.unl.edu/.

[11] Avinoam Danin, "Flora and Vegetation of Israel and Adjacent Areas," *Bocconea* 3 (1992): 18.

[12] Irene and Walter Jacob, "Flora," in *The Anchor Bible Dictionary* 2, ed. David Noel Freedman (New York: Doubleday, 1992), 803. Paleoethnobotany and first-century literary evidence suggest that the number of species was greater than the 128 mentioned in the Bible.

"The LORD appeared to Abraham by the oaks" (Gen 18:1). In the Galilee, oaks can grow to sixty feet in height, with wood so durable that it was used in the construction of buildings. The box (*Buxus longifolia*), another durable hardwood, carob (*Ceratonia siliqua*), terebinth (*Pistacia palaestina*), and laurestinus (*Viburnum tinus*) species are also found the region.[13]

In the forested regions of the Galilee, an interdependent ecosystem of living organisms thrived. The tree canopy protected the undergrowth that absorbed and preserved precipitation, an undergrowth marked by leaves or needles, acanthus, thistle, wild grasses, bushes, and fallen branches. Forested areas mitigated soil erosion and served as a habitat for many species, from sparrows and foxes to ants, crickets, and wolves. When torrential rain threatened to flood cultivated fields, vineyards, or village homes, the extensive root system of trees and the undergrowth surrounding them stabilized the soil and diminished the possibility of crops being washed away. "The mighty one, God the LORD, / speaks and summons the earth," wrote the psalmist; "every wild animal of the forest is mine" (Ps 50:1, 10). And this: "The trees of the LORD are watered abundantly. . . . In them the birds build their nests (Ps 104:16, 17). Such praise of forests and field trees, however, did not prevent farmers from clearing the land so that crops could be grown: the ancient Galilee was not immune to deforestation, though felling trees for the sake of planting crops and vines was nothing compared to the devastation wrought by invaders, who used clear-cutting as a weapon of intimidation and punishment.

Needless to say, trees were associated with the presence and labor of the divine Creator: "Out of the ground the LORD God

[13] Other trees mentioned in the Bible include the acacia (*Acacia*), Aleppo pine (*Pinus halepens*is), broom (*Cytisus scoparius*), cedar of Lebanon (*Cedrus libani*), cypress (*Cupressus sempervirens*), Mediterranean fir (*Abies spp*), myrtle (*Myrtus communis*), and willow (*Salix acmophylla*).

made to grow every tree that is pleasant to the sight and good for food, the tree of life also in the midst of the garden, and the tree of the knowledge of good and evil" (Gen 2:9). After the mythic flood, Noah received a leaf plucked from an olive tree by a dove, a sign that the waters had receded.[14] Providing shelter from the heat of the day, the hospitality of the oak tree welcomed Abraham and Sarah's three visitors who personified the LORD.[15] Solomon's temple housed the ark of the covenant, over which the divine presence was believed to rest: "He lined the walls of the house on the inside with boards of cedar; from the floor of the house to the rafters of the ceiling, he covered them on the inside with wood; and he covered the floor of the house with boards of cypress" (1 Kgs 6:15). The tree also served as an image of the people of God restored to their homeland after the Babylonian exile: "I myself will take a sprig from the lofty top of a cedar; . . . I myself will plant it on a high and lofty mountain. On the mountain height of Israel I will plant it, in order that it may produce boughs and bear fruit, and become a noble cedar. Under it every kind of bird will live; in the shade of its branches will nest winged creatures of every kind" (Ezek 17:22-23).

In his description of ancient Israel, the author of Deuteronomy wrote of a land filled with "wheat and barley, of vines and fig trees and pomegranates, a land of olive oil and honey" (Deut 8:8). In addition to water sources and forests, the ecology of the Galilee contained trees and plants that bore fruit. Indeed, the first fruit-bearing tree mentioned in the Bible is the fig (*Ficus carica*). Its succulent fruit was eaten raw or used in the creation of sweet cakes and fig wine. The fig tree is short, whereas the sycamore (*Ficus sycomorus*), sometimes called a sycamore fig, is a tall evergreen tree with large green leaves and a somewhat bitter fruit produced several times each year.

[14] Gen 8:11.
[15] Gen 18:1.

The large leaves of this tree were thought to be the first garments of the primal parents, Adam and Eve.[16] Whenever drought or famine spread over the land, poor people sought the fruit of the sycamore. When broken, this tree's leaves produce a white, creamy substance that was used as a dressing for wounds and skin inflammations.

Among the tallest fruit-bearing trees was the date palm (*Phoenix dactylifera*), which could grow to a height of one hundred feet. Its fruit, the date, was one of the few sweeteners available in the first century and was reduced to a syrup; sugar did not reach the Mediterranean until the thirteenth century. When fermented, the date was transformed into wine and vinegar. It was also used in the Galilee and throughout Israel as a laxative. Today we know what ancient Galileans did not: that the date is considered an antioxidant and thus beneficial to heart health.

Three Essential Foods: Olives, Grapes, and Wheat

One might argue that the olive tree (*Olea europea*) was and remains the queen of all trees in Israel and throughout the Mediterranean. This tree and its fruit have been cultivated for over six thousand years and can boast a number of varieties that are over one thousand years old. In her magisterial work, *A History of Food*, Maguelonne Toussaint-Samat speaks of olive oil, bread, and wine—olive, wheat grain, and grape—as the three "sacramental" foods of Mediterranean culture: "Bread and wine, those two pillars of consumption in Western civilization, were joined by oil, which might be described as the light of that civilization. The gift of this trinity was attributed to benevolent and peace-living deities."[17] For the ancient Israel-

[16] Gen 3:7.

[17] Maguelonne Toussaint-Samat, *A History of Food*, trans. Anthea Bell (Oxford: Wiley-Blackwell, 2009), 204.

ites, this tree, the olive, and its oil were gifts given by God: "You anoint my head with oil," proclaims the psalmist of the Lord (Ps 23:5).

The olive and its oil served many purposes: as a fruit to be eaten raw or cooked; as an oil for cooking; as a lubricant for the skin after bathing; as liquid fuel for lamps giving light; and as an offering in the Jerusalem temple. Olive oil and wine were combined as an ointment to treat wounds and inflammation of the skin. As with the fruit of the date palm, modern nutritionists extol the olive's healthy virtues: "Olive oil has the highest percentage of monounsaturated fat, which lowers LDL cholesterol and increases HDL. It has been shown to lower blood pressure and contains plant-based compounds that offer anti-inflammatory and antioxidant properties known to reduce the disease process, including heart disease."[18] The great diversity and life-giving properties of the olive led the psalmist to recognize it as a source of joy: "God, your God, has anointed you with the oil of gladness" (Ps 45:7).

The term "anointed" held considerable significance in ancient Galilee, where olive trees were cultivated on terraced hillsides. The author of Exodus mentions the first form of anointing: "You shall anoint [Aaron] and consecrate him, so that he may serve me as priest" (Exod 40:13). The second mention occurs in the early history of Israel: "The Lord said to Samuel, . . . 'Fill your horn with oil and set out . . . for I have provided for myself a king. . . . Then Samuel took the horn of oil, and anointed [David]" (1 Sam 16:1, 13). There is one instance of a prophet, Elisha, being anointed (1 Kgs 19:16). Thus, priests, monarchs, and prophets were smeared with olive oil and thought to have thereby been anointed by God. The

[18] KC Wright, "The Benefits of Adding a Drizzle of Olive Oil to Your Diet," *American Heart Association News*, September 28, 2022, accessed February 14, 2024, https://www.heart.org/en/news/2022/09/28/the-benefits-of-adding-a-drizzle-of-olive-oil-to-your-diet.

Hebrew term for an anointed person is *mashiaḫ*, whence comes the term *messiah*, and *mashiaḫ* in the Greek of the New Testament is rendered as *christos*: a person marked publicly with olive oil for a mission, a practice that continues in the anointing with chrism, scented olive oil, used in the baptismal ritual of Christians.

Planted on Galilean terraces next to olive trees were vines (*Vitis vinifera*) that produced cultivated grapes (*Vitis vinifera vinifera*). Wild grapes (*Vitis vinifera sylvestris*) grew of their own accord without human intervention. In his song concerning the unfaithfulness of Israel, the prophet Isaiah speaks of viticulture: "My beloved had a vineyard on a very fertile hill. He dug it and cleared it of stones, and planted it with choice vines; he built a watchtower in the midst of it, and hewed out a wine vat in it; he expected it to yield grapes [*Vitis vinifera vinifera*], but it yielded wild grapes [*Vitis vinifera sylvestris*]" (Isa 5:1-2). Here the prophet has offered an accurate description of the vineyards and the winepresses found in the Lower Galilee, including a first-century wine complex recently discovered in Nazareth.[19]

To tend the vineyard, harvest grapes, and produce wine was one of the most labor-intensive forms of agriculture. There was no break, no rest: it was a year-round effort of pruning, fertilizing, and protecting vines and buds; discerning the ripeness of the grapes and harvesting and pressing them; filtering, fermenting, and storing the wine; and then pruning the vines again. After the grapes were harvested in late summer, they were placed on the stone floor of the winepress and crushed by human feet, releasing the juice that flowed from a low point of the winepress floor through a filter into a stone vat for the first fermentation. The juice would then flow through a second

[19] Stephen Pfann, Ross Voss, and Yehuda Rapuano, "Surveys and Excavations at the Nazareth Village Farm (1997–2002): Final Report," *Bulletin of the Anglo-Israel Archaeological Society* 25 (2007): 23, 36.

filter into another vat for the final fermentation: the yeast present in the grape skins provided the chemical reaction that transformed grape juice into wine. The vintner then poured the wine into a goatskin bag or an amphora, a clay or terracotta jug.

While contemporary health care providers urge their patients to drink numerous glasses of water each day, such was not the case in ancient Israel because water often became stagnant or unclean. Drinking wine each day was therefore the normative practice, although wine was also added to water to purify it as a result of the wine's alcohol content. Indeed, watered-down wine was even given to toddlers, though one should keep in mind that the alcohol content of ancient wine was far lower than the wine we drink today. Although Christian temperance movements and conservative Protestants in the United States have decried the use of wine, the many references to wine in the Bible and the archaeological evidence of winepresses in the Lower Galilee and throughout ancient Israel offer another picture. That being said, the widespread use of wine was paired with a warning concerning excess consumption: "The priest and the prophet reel with strong drink, they are confused with wine . . . they err in vision, they stumble in giving judgment" (Isa 28:7). Indeed, the earliest mention of wine in the Bible also includes a cautionary word: "Noah, a man of the soil, was the first to plant a vineyard. He drank some of the wine and became drunk, and he lay uncovered in his tent. . . . Then Shem and Japheth took a garment . . . and covered the nakedness of their father" (Gen 9:20-21, 23).

As with olive oil and wheat, wine was viewed as a gift from God: "You . . . bring forth . . . wine to gladden the human heart, / oil to make the face shine, / and bread to strengthen the human heart" (Ps 104:14, 15)—what Toussaint-Samat called the culinary trinity of Mediterranean life.[20] The goodness of

[20] Toussaint-Samat, *History of Food*, 204.

wine is underscored in Pope Francis's address to Italian vintners: "Dear friends, wine, the land, agricultural skills and entrepreneurial activity are gifts from God, but let us not forget that the Creator has entrusted them to us, to our sensitivity and our honesty, so that we make of them, as the Scripture says, a true source of joy."[21] Indeed, the God of Israel was viewed as the vintner who tended the vineyard: "A pleasant vineyard . . . I, the LORD, am its keeper; every moment I water it. I guard it night and day so that no one can harm it" (Isa 27:2-3). Clearly wine was consumed daily in first-century Israel. It was also used for medicinal purposes as an antiseptic, an anesthetic, and a sedative: "Give strong drink to one who is perishing, and wine to those in bitter distress" (Prov 31:6). "At the head of all healing [is] wine. In a place where there is no wine, herbs are required as medicines."[22] As a people of the Mediterranean, the Israelites were not alone in recognizing the health benefits of wine: the Egyptians, Babylonians, Persians, Greeks, and Romans—all of whom influenced Israel's culture at different times in its history—recognized the healing properties of wine.[23]

The religious use of wine was prominent at the time of Jesus: at the beginning of the Sabbath meal at sunset on Friday, thanksgiving to God was made over a cup of wine: "You are blessed, Lord our God, King of the universe, who [creates] the fruit of the vine."[24] The feast of Booths, commonly called Sukkot,

[21] Pope Francis, "Greeting of His Holiness Pope Francis to the Participants in the Convention Organized by Vinitaly on the Theme, 'The Economy of Francis and the World of Italian Wine,'" January 22, 2024, accessed February 15, 2024, https://www.vatican.va/content/francesco/en/speeches/2024/january/documents/20240122-vinitaly.html.

[22] "Bava Batra 58b," in *The William Davidson Babylonian Talmud*, accessed February 15, 2024, https://www.sefaria.org/Bava_Batra.58b?lang=bi.

[23] Gisela H. Kreglinger, *The Spirituality of Wine* (Grand Rapids, MI: Eerdmans, 2016), 165–68.

[24] In reference to the practice of blessing God over wine, see "Berakhot 33a:35," in *William Davidson Babylonian Talmud*, accessed February 16,

marked the conclusion of the autumn harvest, including the harvesting of grapes: "You shall keep the festival of booths for seven days, when you have gathered in the produce from your threshing floor and your wine press" (Deut 16:13). The springtime feast of Passover was celebrated in homes with wine, unleavened bread, bitter herbs, and roasted lamb: "This month shall . . . be the first month of the year for you. Tell the whole congregation of Israel that on the tenth of this month they are to take a lamb for each family. . . . This day shall be a day of remembrance for you. . . . Seven days you shall eat unleavened bread" (Exod 12:2-3, 14-15).[25] Each of these religious occasions was marked by rejoicing and gratitude: thanksgiving for the creation of the earth and the Sabbath rest; thanksgiving for an abundant harvest; and thanksgiving for freedom from Egyptian slavery: "Wine is very life to human beings. . . . What is life to one who is without wine? It has been created to make people happy" (Sir 31:27).

Three forms of grain dominated life in ancient Israel: barley (*Hordeum vulgare*), durum wheat (*Triticum durum*), and bread wheat (*Triticum aestivum*). The earliest evidence of barley cultivation has been found in the Lower Galilee, next to the southwestern shore of the lake; the remains have been dated to

---

2024, https://www.sefaria.org/Berakhot.33a.35?lang=bi&with=all&lang2=en. Was the blessing of God over wine used in the first century? The Talmud indicates that the *kiddush*—the blessing of God for wine—emerged prior to the first century. For the text of the blessing, see Lucien Deiss, *Springtime of the Liturgy: Liturgical Texts of the First Four Centuries*, trans. Matthew J. O'Connell (Collegeville, MN: Liturgical Press, 1979), 5–6.

[25] These two injunctions—one for lamb, one for unleavened bread—imply two earlier rituals: prayer with the sacrifice of a lamb at the beginning of the lambing season, and prayer for a plentiful grain harvest: both in the spring. These two ceremonies, then, were combined into one feast that celebrated the exodus from Egypt: commemorating God's instruction to paint the blood of a sacrificed lamb on each house's door lintel and the hurried manner in which the Hebrews left with their unleavened bread.

23,000 BCE.[26] Of the three grains, barley was the easiest and cheapest to grow: its roots were shallow and they required less water, thus making it more likely than other grains to survive a drought. Cheaper in price than wheat, barley was used as feed for animals as well as food for the poor: the prophet Elisha commented that barley was sold for half the price of wheat.[27] Given that most people who lived in the Lower Galilee were subsistence farmers and fishers, barley bread was a staple of their diet. The author of 2 Kings narrates the story of Elisha feeding a large group of people with a small number of barley loaves. To their astonishment, they had plenty to eat and there was bread left over.[28] Both barley and wheat seeds were planted in the autumn, but barley matured faster and was harvested in March or April. The feast of Passover coincided with the barley harvest.

Wheat was harvested after barley and was offered in the Jerusalem temple at the feast of Shavuot, fifty days after Passover. Shavuot was also referred to as the feast of Harvest (Exod 23:16). Greek-speaking Jews spoke of this fifty-day period as *pentekoste* (in English, "pentecost"). Given that rainfall and soil conditions determined the timing and location of crop planting, wheat was cultivated in the upper Jordan, Jezreel, and Beit Shean Valleys. Wheat could grow as high as four feet. The ripened grain stalks were cut with a scythe and placed on a threshing floor of stone or beaten earth. A threshing sledge was used to cut the stalks and crush the husks that surrounded the grain. Unneeded stalk was then burned. The husks were placed in a broad winnowing basket and tossed in the air; the wind carried away the lighter chaff, leaving the heavier grain

[26] Dani Nadel et al., "New Evidence for the Processing of Wild Cereal Grains at Ohalo II, a 23,000-Year-Old Campsite on the Shore of the Sea of Galilee, Israel," *Antiquity* 86 (December 2012): 990–1003.

[27] 1 Kgs 7:1.

[28] 2 Kgs 4:42-44.

in the basket. A winnowing fork could also be used. The wheat grain was then stored in a clay jar, a basket, or an underground container and subsequently measured out to be crushed into flour for baking bread.

The consumption of grain—barley or wheat as well as millet or spelt—constituted 50 percent of a first-century Galilean's caloric intake per day.[29] We should not underestimate the role of grains in the diet of the Israelites—a people who worked the land and depended on it for nourishment. Besides bread that was prepared, baked, and consumed on a daily basis, their meals included wine or a fruit juice, goat's milk, fresh or dried figs, pomegranates, lentils, and perhaps a preserved fish sauce called *garum*. Seasonal fruits had to be eaten before they perished. Some vegetables were cultivated or gathered in the wild: onions (*Allium cepa*), leeks (*Allium porrum*)—also considered a poor person's food—beans (*Vicia faba*), cucumbers (*Cucumis melo*), and mushrooms (*Boletus edulis*). But, then, let us keep in mind the small number of references in the Bible to vegetables and the many references to bread, wine, and olive oil. Were vegetables less favored than other produce? If so, it would match the low regard most Americans hold for vegetables: the Centers for Disease Control and Prevention (CDC) report that only 9 percent of US citizens eat a sufficient number of vegetables.[30] As previously noted, the vast majority of those who lived in the Galilee and throughout Israel were subsistence farmers or fishers: poor people for whom bread was the staple of life.

[29] E. P. Sanders, *Judaism: Practice and Belief, 63 BCE–66 CE* (Norwich: SCM Canterbury, 1992), 129.

[30] Centers for Disease Control and Prevention, "Only 1 in 10 Adults Get Enough Fruits or Vegetables," accessed February 17, 2024, https://archive.cdc.gov/#/details?q=https://www.cdc.gov/nccdphp/dnpao/division-information/media-tools/adults-fruits-vegetables.html&start=0&rows=10&url=https://www.cdc.gov/nccdphp/dnpao/division-information/media-tools/adults-fruits-vegetables.html.

With wine, the religious significance of bread was underscored on the Sabbath as the head of the household gave thanks to God over a loaf of bread: "You are blessed, Lord our God, King of the universe, you who have brought bread forth from the earth."[31] An early medieval *haggadah*[32] presents this blessing over *matzah*, unleavened bread, at Passover: "Blessed are You, our Eternal God, Ruler of the world, who causes the earth to bring forth bread. Blessed are You, our Eternal God, Ruler of the world, who has sanctified us by Your commandments and enjoined us to eat unleavened bread."[33]

One might read the Bible as the story of bread. When the primal parents were driven from the Garden of Eden, Adam was told: "By the sweat of your face you shall eat bread until you return to the ground" (Gen 3:19). Abraham and Sarah received the promise of children from whom an entire nation would descend as they offered hospitality to three visitors: "Let me bring a little bread, that you may refresh yourselves" (Gen 18:5). During his exile in Egypt, Joseph became pharaoh's overseer of disaster preparedness: "Joseph stored up grain in such abundance . . . that he stopped measuring it. . . . [Then] seven years of famine began. . . . There was famine in every country, but throughout the land of Egypt there was bread" (Gen 41:49, 54). Joseph's wise planning saved his estranged family from death, and there, in Egypt, they stayed with plenty of bread. Another pharaoh came to power and enslaved the Hebrews in Egypt. Their flight with Moses across the Red Sea led them to the desert, where God provided nourishment: "At twilight you shall eat meat, and in the morning you shall have your fill of bread" (Exod 16:12). Worship in Jerusalem's temple included an offering of bread: "You shall take choice flour, and bake twelve loaves of it. . . . You shall place them in two rows,

[31] Deiss, *Springtime of the Liturgy*, 6.

[32] The text used at the Passover supper.

[33] Michael Shire, *The Illuminated Haggadah* (New York: Stewart, Tabori, and Chang, 1998), 38.

six in a row, on the table of pure gold . . . [before] the LORD" (Lev 24:5-7). King David came from Bethlehem, *Bet Leḥem*, "the House of Bread." The prophet Isaiah condemned the greed of Israel's elites: "Is not this the fast that I choose: to loose the bonds of injustice. . . . Is it not to share your bread with the hungry . . . ?" (Isa 58:6, 7). *Leḥem*, the Hebrew word for "bread," is found 296 times in the Old Testament, highlighting the significance of this humble gift of the earth and human labor.

Fish

The first creation story in the Bible narrates the origin of fish in their great diversity: "Let the waters bring forth swarms of living creatures" (Gen 1:20). Those who live today in Canada and the United States can purchase a "swarm of living creatures," some fifty-nine kinds of fish, from amberjack to wahoo,[34] and a great diversity of shellfish. Though there is little written evidence concerning fish in the Jordan River and the Sea of Galilee, ichthyoarchaeologists—experts in fish remains—suggest that the lake contained a much smaller variety in the first century: nineteen kinds of fish. Prominent among them was the Galilean sardine (*Mirogrex terrae sanctae*), often referred to in the Bible with the generic term, "a small fish." Archaeological evidence suggests that the village of Magdala (in Greek, *Taricheae*), along the western shore of the Sea of Galilee, was a major center of processing and preservation of the sardine through salting.[35] The other prominent fish in the Galilee was tilapia (*Sarotherodon galilaeus* and *Sarotherodon aureus*). Its relatively flat shape and few small bones made it easy to cook with

[34] "Fresh Fish Availability," accessed February 18, 2024, https://www.chefs-resources.com/seafood/fresh-fish-availability-chart/. The varieties of fish exclude the twenty-five most popular species of shellfish available.

[35] James F. Strange, "Magdala," in *The Anchor Bible Dictionary* 4, ed. David Noel Freedman (New York: Doubleday, 1992), 463–64.

a spit, on a flat stone, or in metal pan; it was a popular fish. Other fish included binny or barbels (*Barbus canis; Barbus longiceps*), catfish (*Clarias lazera*), and European eel (*Anguila europaea*). We do well to remember the Levitical code that distinguished between clean and unclean creatures, including fish that were considered kosher or permissible to eat: "These you may eat, of all that are in the waters. Everything in the waters that has fins and scales, . . . such you may eat. But anything in the seas or the streams that does not have fins and scales, . . . they are detestable to you" (Lev 11:9-10). Consequently, catfish and eel, lacking scales, were prohibited.

Historians and biblical scholars remind us that fishing was a labor-intensive profession controlled by the ruling elite in the first century. "Local rulers sold fishing rights to brokers (tax collectors or publicans), who in turn contracted with fishers. The fishers received capitalization along with fishing rights and were therefore indebted to brokers . . . at the bottom of the industry were the hired laborers who contracted with fishers."[36] A romantic view of fishing on the Sea of Galilee, one that has often been promoted in Christian communities, is corrected when we consider that fishers were not autonomous, successful, and contented entrepreneurs: "Ever at the mercy of the brokers (toll collectors) who financed their operations, first-century fishermen were far from middle class. They had no control over their activities because of storms or unfavorable conditions and were nearly always in debt."[37] This is to suggest that fishers were among the working poor. At the same time, a nostalgic view of fish and fishing merits a bracing correction when one considers the 139 fish species in the United

[36] K. C. Hanson and Douglas E. Oakman, *Palestine in the Time of Jesus: Social Structures and Social Conflicts* (Minneapolis: Fortress Press, 1998), 106.

[37] John Pilch, *The Cultural Dictionary of the Bible* (Collegeville, MN: Liturgical Press, 1999), 188.

States now threatened with extinction due to pollution, deforestation, and urban development.[38]

Those who fished on the Sea of Galilee or by the Jordan River employed different methods. A gill or trammel net was a long net supported with floats that caught larger fish who could not swim through the netting: "Put out into the deep water and let down your nets for a catch" (Luke 5:4). The net was frequently placed at night and then hauled to the shore in the morning. A dragnet was a net of great length with cork on the top and weights on the bottom that was drawn into the water, forming a semicircle; each end was then drawn by the fishers toward the shore. Once ashore, the haul would be separated by the type of fish caught. The book of Ezekiel refers to this kind of net: "People will stand fishing beside the sea from En-gedi to En-eglaim; it will be a place for the spreading of nets; its fish will be of a great many kinds, like the fish of the Great Sea" (Ezek 47:10). A third form was the circular cast net that was thrown into the water, sinking below. The fishers would then dive into the water and haul the net into the boat. On the other hand, someone fishing alone employed hook and line. When the prophet Isaiah spoke of the doom that would afflict Egypt, he wrote: "Those who fish will mourn; / all who cast hooks in the Nile will lament" (Isa 19:8).

Readers of the New Testament recognize the prominence of fish and fishing in the gospels; after all, the adult Jesus made his home in Capernaum, a fishing center on the northwestern shore of the Sea of Galilee, and a number of his disciples were drawn from the fishing industry in that town.[39] But there is little mention of Galilean fish and fishing in the Old Testament,

[38] U.S. Fish and Wildlife Service, "FWS-Listed U.S. Species by Taxonomic Group—Fishes," accessed February 20, 2024, https://ecos.fws.gov/ecp/report/species-listings-by-tax-group?statusCategory=Listed&groupName=Fishes. See also "Threats to Birds," accessed February 21, 2024, https://www.fws.gov/library/collections/threats-birds.

[39] Matthew writes that Jesus made his home in Capernaum; see 4:13.

though we know that the Galilee's salted sardines were transported to Jerusalem and sold at the city's Fish Gate (Neh 3:3). Were fish available in Nazareth? Perhaps preserved sardines but little else. Keep in mind that Nazareth rests nineteen miles from the shore of the Sea of Galilee, and the fastest form of transport was a donkey: no truck or car delivery. There was no ice or refrigeration to keep fish or any other foodstuff from spoiling.

Birds

"God created . . . every winged bird of every kind. And God saw that it was good. God blessed them, saying, . . . 'Let birds multiply on the earth'" (Gen 1:21, 22). In 1962, Rachel Carson published *Silent Spring,*[40] her classic work on the dangers of pesticides to all creatures, from birds to human beings—a book that gave birth to the environmental movement in the United States. The book's title was inspired by the thought of birdsong going silent should the chemical pollution of air, water, and soil continue unabated. In the Bible, however, there is no silencing of birdsong; rather, it is welcomed and praised: "You make springs gush forth in the valleys; / they flow between the hills . . . By the streams the birds of the air have their habitation; / they sing among the branches" (Ps 104:10, 12). "The flowers appear on the earth; / the time of singing has come, / and the voice of the turtledove / is heard in our land" (Song 2:12).[41]

As a geographical midpoint between Africa and Europe, the land of Israel has long been a way station for birds migrating between the two continents. Indeed, flying from Europe

[40] Rachel Carson, *Silent Spring* (New York: Houghton Mifflin, 1962). For Carson's commitment to the natural world, see Linda Lear, *Rachel Carson: Witness for Nature* (New York: Houghton Mifflin, 1997).

[41] The turtledove (*Streptopelia arenicola*) is now an endangered species.

over the plains and mountains of Lebanon and Israel to the African continent was much easier than soaring over the waters of the Mediterranean Sea. Birds with heavy bodies and long wingspans could float on the warm air currents over the land during the day, riding the breeze until it cools. They then could glide down, expending very little energy until they reached the next warm thermal current.[42] Today, the Hula Valley, the Jordan Valley, and the shoreline around the Sea of Galilee are prime sites to see the many species that travel this route.

The Sea of Galilee drew a great variety of birds, including great cormorants (*Phalacrocorax carbo*), European shags (*Gulosus aristotelis*), great crested grebes (*Podiceps cristatus*), purple herons (*Ardea pupurea*), and whiskered terns (*Chlidonias hybridus*). In the hills surrounding Nazareth, there were doves (*Streptopelia senegalensis*), eagle owls (*Bubo bubo*), red-throated pipits (*Anthus cervinus*), house sparrows (*Passer domesticus*), and red-rumped swallows (*Hirundo daurica*). Among the nations of the Middle East, modern Israel has the largest number of bird species—591.[43] Some 25 bird species are mentioned in the Bible—and of that number, some were considered unclean for consumption: "These you shall regard as detestable among the birds. They shall not be eaten . . . the eagle, the vulture, the osprey, the buzzard, the kite of any kind; every raven of any kind; the ostrich, the nighthawk, the sea gull, the hawk of any kind;

[42] Edwin Firmage, "Birds," in *The Anchor Bible Dictionary* 6, ed. David Noel Freedman (New York: Doubleday, 1992), 1144.

[43] Of that number, thirty-four species are considered endangered or critically endangered: see the *Israeli Red List of Threatened Breeding Birds* at https://redlist.parks.org.il/en/aves/. According to the North American Bird Conservation Initiative Committee (NABCI), the United States and Canada have lost three billion breeding birds since 1970—a loss of one in four birds. In 2022, seventy bird species were in danger of becoming extinct: NABCI, *State of the Birds Report: United States 2022*, ed. Gus Axelson (Cornell, NY: Cornell University, 2022): 3–4.

the little owl, the cormorant, the great owl, the water hen, the desert owl, the carrion vulture, the stork, the heron of any kind, the hoopoe, and the bat" (Lev 11:13-19).[44] For those who grew grapes and olives, the challenge was to prevent birds from eating the fruit before it ripened: hungry birds were considered a menace.

We should be mindful of the ways in which a variety of birds played significant roles in the lives of human beings. Noah sent a dove to search for land at the conclusion of the great flood; it returned with an olive branch in its beak.[45] Wandering through the wilderness after their escape from Egypt, the Hebrews were given quail as nourishment.[46] In the midst of drought and famine, ravens brought food to the prophet Elijah.[47] These stories serve as images of providential care. At the same time, birds were considered models of virtue. Jeremiah praised storks for their faithfulness to their mates.[48] Job praised the eagle for its strength and fearlessness.[49] The psalmist described the sparrows and swallows who found a safe and secure dwelling place to raise their young in Jerusalem's temple.[50]

Animals

"God made the wild animals of the earth of every kind and the cattle of every kind and everything that creeps upon the ground of every kind. And God saw that it was good" (Gen 1:25). From the adder (*Vipera berus*), a venomous snake, to the

[44] See Ralph Bulmer, "The Uncleanness of the Birds of Leviticus and Deuteronomy," *Man* 24, no. 2 (June 1989): 304–21, on the various and conflicting reasons for designating a group of birds unclean.

[45] Gen 8:6-11.

[46] Exod 16:13-15.

[47] 1 Kgs 17:2-6.

[48] Jer 8:4-7.

[49] Job 39:27-28.

[50] Ps 84:3.

wolf (*Canis lupus*), some 120 different kinds of animals are mentioned in the Bible.[51] As an adult, Jesus called the fishing center of Capernaum his home, but as a child and young adult, he lived in Nazareth, a small hamlet with terraced agriculture and pasture fields. What pilgrims and tourists experience today in the sprawling modern city of Jesus' youth was a creation of the late nineteenth century, when European Christians began to build churches and shrines at the sites associated with Jesus, his mother Mary, and his followers (e.g., Peter of Capernaum, Mary of Magdala). Prior to this incredible and recent activity to transform it into a holy city, Nazareth was a sleepy farm community.

As a small village, first-century Nazareth had vineyards and olive trees. Archaeologists have discovered underground grain silos in the town's soft limestone bedrock. Here, then, were the three fundamental foods of Mediterranean culture: grapes for wine, olives for olive oil, and grain for bread. How, then, were fruit and grain transported from vineyards, orchards, and fields to presses and threshing floors? Oded Borowski notes that in the Near East, the first animal to be domesticated for use in labor was the donkey (*Equus africanus*).[52] "They loaded their donkeys with their grain" (Gen 42:26). "The . . . donkeys that till the ground will eat silage, which has been winnowed with shovel and fork" (Isa 30:24). As a work animal, the donkey carried grapes and olives as well as exhausted laborers. In other Mediterranean cultures—Egyptian, Persian, Greek, and Roman—a camel, horse, or elephant was used to transport generals and monarchs. But it seems that in Israel, the donkey

[51] The dietary code of Leviticus offers a catalog of animals not to be eaten: "The camel . . . rock badger . . . hare (rabbit) . . . pig . . . the weasel, the mouse, the great lizard according to its kind . . . and whatever moves on its belly" (11:4-7, 29, 42).

[52] Oded Borowski, *Every Living Thing: Daily Use of Animals in Ancient Israel* (Walnut Creek, CA: AltaMira Press, 1998), 28. Let us also note that the term "donkey" was coined in the late eighteenth century. The biblical term for this animal is "ass."

and its cousin, the mule, served this royal purpose: David, Solomon, and Absalom all rode on these beasts of burden.[53] Writing of Jerusalem's restoration after the Babylonian exile, the prophet envisioned the advent of the nation's ruler in a similar manner: "Lo, your king comes to you; triumphant and victorious is he, humble and riding on a donkey, on a colt, the foal of a donkey . . . he shall command peace to the nations" (Zech 9:9, 10). As first-century Galileans knew well, with the horse comes war; with the donkey, the promise of peace.[54]

Oh, the poor goat! Its reputation was not the best in ancient Israel. If a goat escaped the domesticated herd, it often wreaked havoc on the land, destroying trees by climbing, breaking branches, chewing away the bark, and eating leaves and twigs to their nubs. Goats (*Capra hircus*) were known to destroy vegetation by crushing and eating bushes, hedges, and crops.[55] So detrimental were goats to olive tree orchards that sharpened spikes were planted in the base of the trees to prevent goats from climbing and eating the leaves and fruit. Indeed, the misbehavior of the goat inspired the vision of Daniel who saw "a male goat . . . coming across the face of the whole earth. . . . It ran with savage force. I saw it approaching the ram [a male sheep]. It was enraged against it and struck the ram . . . [who] did not have power to withstand it; it threw the ram down to the ground and trampled upon it" (Dan 8:5-7). On the other hand, the domesticated goat provided milk and meat; its hair was woven into cloth. On the Day of Atonement, two goats were presented before the priests, one offered to God as puri-

[53] 1 Kgs 1:33; 1 Kgs 1:38-39; and 2 Sam 18:9. The texts refer to the mule, the offspring of a male donkey and a female horse.

[54] The horse was the preferred animal that the Roman cavalry rode into the Galilee to quell uprisings against the empire in 6 CE, 67 CE, and 132 CE.

[55] It seems that goat behavior has not changed in the last two thousand years, as reports of goats damaging forests, business offices, and homes continue to emerge in the United States.

fication for the people and one sent into the desert signifying the removal of their sins (Lev 16:6-10). Thus, the term "scapegoat" entered our vocabulary, signifying a person or group wrongly blamed for a catastrophe, great or small.

The examination of faunal remains—the bones of animals discovered in archaeological excavations—reveals that sheep (*Ovis aries*) were a dominant group of domesticated animals in Nazareth during the Hellenistic-Roman period, which includes the first century.[56] Thus we can safely assume that the pasture fields around Nazareth were one of the primary feeding grounds for sheep and lambs. Not the brightest animals on God's green earth, sheep were tended by shepherds and dogs (*Canis lupus*) that the shepherds trained to keep the sheep together and moving in a particular direction. Sadly, both shepherds and dogs were frequently viewed in a negative light: shepherds slept with and smelled like their sheep, came into contact with the sheep's manure and bloody flesh wounds, and at times allowed their flocks to graze in someone else's fields, thus committing the crime of trespassing. Other than those trained for herding, most dogs roamed in packs, were viewed as scavengers, and were considered highly aggressive: "Dogs are all around me; / a company of evildoers encircles me" (Ps 22:16).[57] The well-known Psalm 23 offers a more benevolent view of the shepherd.

Similar to goats, sheep were raised for their milk and meat: "These are the animals you may eat: the ox, the sheep, the goat" (Deut 14:4). Lamb was and is a popular food in eastern Mediterranean cultures. Indeed, roasted lamb was central to

[56] Nimrod Maron, "Faunal Remains from Nazareth," *'Atiqot* 98 (2020): 94. Maron's Table I indicates sheep counted as 77 percent of animal remains in the Hellenistic-Roman period.

[57] 2 Sam 9:30-37 narrates the death of Queen Jezebel, whose body was scavenged by wild dogs, an incident repulsive to modern readers but one that was not uncommon in ancient Israel due to fear of infection and ritual uncleanliness incurred by touching corpses.

the feast of Passover, the annual spring commemoration of the angel of death *passing over* homes marked with the blood of a lamb: "They shall eat the lamb . . . roasted over the fire with unleavened bread and bitter herbs" (Exod 12:8). The wool of the sheep provided warmth on cool days. In the pastoral economy of the Lower Galilee, a large flock of sheep was a sign of wealth: "There was a man in Maon, whose property was in Carmel. The man was very rich; he had three thousand sheep and a thousand goats" (1 Sam 25:2).

A constant threat to sheep, goats, and other small animals was the wolf (*Canis lupus arabs*), often found hunting in packs. In his condemnation of the injustice and violence of the people and their leaders, the prophet Ezekiel compares them to wolves: "Its officials . . . are like wolves tearing the prey, shedding blood, destroying lives" (Ezek 22:27). The prophet Habakkuk speaks of wolves waiting for dusk (Hab 1:8), a reference to their practice of attacking a flock of sheep under cover of darkness. Indeed, the God of Israel is likened to a shepherd who saves the flock from being ravaged, an allusion to the carnivorous wolf who preyed on livestock. No wonder the psalmist prayed for protection: "Do not deliver the soul of your dove to the wild animals" (Ps 74:19).

What other animals were present in first-century Nazareth? Maron found slight evidence of chickens (*Gallus gallus domesticus*)—roosters or hens, we do not know—and cattle (*Bos taurus*): possibly oxen, bulls (male), cows (female), and heifers (young female cows).[58] There are but two mentions of chickens in the Old Testament, and those two are open to interpretation, for the term used is "fowl," a generic expression that includes chickens, ducks, geese, turkeys, and partridges. The gospels of the New Testament are slightly more explicit about chickens.[59] We know that the crowing of a rooster—the cockcrow—served

[58] Maron, "Faunal Remains from Nazareth," 95.
[59] For example, see Luke 11:11-12; Luke 13:34; Luke 22:34.

as a living wake-up call.[60] Chickens were kept for their eggs and for human consumption, though meat was not a regular part of the peasants' diet.[61] The ox was a beast of burden used to push a grinding stone or pull a hoe to break up soil to prepare it for planting. In the absence of oxen, the cow could serve the same function as a laboring animal. Though North Americans drink milk taken from cows or plants such as almonds or soybeans, those who lived in the ancient Galilee and throughout Israel relied mostly on goat's milk.

When Moses encountered the burning bush at Mount Horeb, the author of Exodus reports this promise made by the Lord: "I have observed the misery of my people who are in Egypt; I have heard their cry on account of their taskmasters. Indeed, I know their sufferings, and I have come down to deliver them . . . and to bring them . . . [to] a land flowing with milk and honey" (Exod 3:7, 8). One of the most common sweeteners in Israel was honey, created by the honeybee (*Apis mellifera anatoliaca*). Domestication of the honeybee began in Egypt and consequently spread northward into Israel. Honey is mentioned at least fifty times in the Old Testament. In the contest between Saul and his son, Jonathan, we read of honey dripping from a honeycomb.[62] Having been freed from Egyptian slavery and brought into a land of milk and honey, the psalmist notes that those who continue to keep the covenant with God will be fed "with the finest of the wheat, / and with honey from the rock" (Ps 81:16). Honey from a rock and not a honeycomb? Could it be that this psalm verse suggests the

[60] "These Eighteen blessings have no appointed order. Each blessing is recited at the appropriate time and occasion. For example . . . When he hears the cock crow, he recites the blessing, 'Who hast given the cock intelligence.'" *Mishneh Torah, Prayer and the Priestly Blessing*, chapter 7, accessed February 19, 2025, https://www.sefaria.org/Mishneh_Torah%2C_Prayer_and_the_Priestly_Blessing.7?lang=bi.

[61] 1 Kgs 4:23 and Neh 5:18.

[62] 1 Sam 14:25-26.

transformation of stony and sandy soil—its rockiness—into a fertile orchard soil in which sweet things—honey—could thrive? Or is the use of "rock" a reference to God: "The Lord is my rock" (Ps 18:2), who provides sweetness to God's people?

Days and Seasons

"God said, 'Let there be light'; and there was light. And God saw that the light was good; and God separated the light from the darkness. God called the light Day, and the darkness he called Night. And there was evening and there was morning, the first day" (Gen 1:3-5). Often unknown to many is the biblical and Jewish keeping of time that obtains among the majority of Christians in the world: the "day" begins at sunset and ends at sunset twenty-four hours later.[63] The psalmist speaks of the day divided into three parts: "I call upon God . . . evening and morning and at noon" (Ps 55:16-17). The Roman calendar used in Israel in the first century named days of the week after the gods of the empire: *dies Solis* (the day of the Sun god: Sunday); *dies Martis* (the day of Mars, the god of war: Tuesday); *dies Veneris* (the day of Venus, goddess of love: Friday). By way of contrast, the Israelites named the days after numbers, reflecting the order of their creation in Genesis 1: *Yom Rishon* (the first day: sunset Saturday to sunset Sunday); *Yom Revii* (the fourth day: sunset Tuesday to sunset Wednesday); *Yom Shabbat* (the seventh day: sunset Friday to sunset Saturday).

The day was not calculated by the market or the government, but rather by the setting, rising, and zenith of the sun. In a culture that believed the earth was flat, the sun "rose" into the sky from the east, heralding light, and "set" in the west,

[63] Three examples: Sunday begins with Sunday Evening Prayer I at sunset on Saturday evening and concludes with Sunday Evening Prayer II at sunset on Sunday; Christmas begins at sunset on December 24; Easter begins with the lighting of the new fire at sunset on Holy Saturday. The Christian keeping of the day does not begin with midnight or sunrise.

announcing darkness. Of course, this sense of time assumed keen observation of movement in the sky, something diminished if not lost today among many urban dwellers, whose sense of time is usually shaped by a digital phone or watch that offers only the current moment.[64] Among first-century Jews, the times for prayer were linked to careful observation of the heavens—dawn, sunrise, noon, dusk, darkness, moon, and stars: *Ma'ariv*, Evening Prayer; *Shacharit*, Morning Prayer; and *Minchah*, Afternoon Prayer. Labor in the fields, the home, and the market was suspended in order to pray. In this regard, the function of prayer was to recognize that time itself and the celestial bodies governing the sense of time are not simply a human construction but a creation and gift of God.

The Amidah, or Eighteen Benedictions of Jewish prayer, also give thanks for the seasons of the year: "Blessed are You, Lord our God: You are a helper, a savior and a shield. Blessed are You, the Shield of Abraham. You are mighty forever . . . You cause the dew to descend [in summer]. You cause the wind to blow and the rains to fall [in winter]."[65] For those who live in regions of North America that have four distinct seasons of the year, it will be helpful to consider the weather in the Los Angeles and Santa Clara Valleys of California as mirrors of weather in ancient and modern Israel: two seasons, a cooler one and a warmer one. In the time of Jesus, the Galilee experienced a mild rainy season from October to March or April, with most of the rain falling from November to February. John Pilch notes that travel—walking or riding on a donkey or mule—was treacherous during the wet winter season.[66] The second season was marked by mild and dry weather from

[64] In contrast to an analog watch, on which one can observe the sweep of "hands" around the numbers of the hours, seeing the time elapsing: past, present, and future.

[65] *Siddur Tehillat Hashem*, trans. Nissen Mangel (New York: Kehot Publication Society, 2004), 45.

[66] Pilch, *Cultural Dictionary of the Bible*, 181.

April or May to September, with warmer and mostly cloudless days during which grapes and olives ripened on vine and tree. Barley and wheat were harvested in the spring, and grapes and olives were harvested in late August or early September.

In Israel's agricultural economy, all life depended on a steady supply of water to irrigate crops, orchards, and grazing fields. "If you will only heed his every commandment . . . loving the LORD your God, and serving him with all your heart and with all your soul—then he will give . . . the early rain and the later rain, and you will gather in your grain, your wine, and your oil" (Deut 11:13-14). The author's mention of "early rain" indicates precipitation in late autumn, and the "later rain," precipitation in early spring. For those who have no connection to rural agricultural life—more than 80 percent of Canadians and Americans now live in an urban setting[67]—it might be a challenge to imagine the slow process of plowing, seeding, waiting for rain, and hoping, with some or considerable anxiety, for the right amount of rain: an unexpected torrential downpour could destroy crops and budding fruit, and the absence of rain wreaked havoc in regions that had few natural springs. It is little wonder that the psalmist called upon the Most High to protect the land from "the pestilence that stalks in darkness, / or the destruction that wastes at noonday" (Ps 91:6).[68] And yet the capricious nature of weather—destructive forest fires with toxic smoke, blistering heat in summer, or atmospheric rivers bringing torrential rains, flooding, and increasingly violent hurricanes—alerts North Americans to the power of global warming and its disastrous effects.

[67] Rural and small-town population in the United States peaked in 1940 at 57 percent; as of 2023, it had shrunk to only 14 percent.

[68] Note that both the *Roman Missal* ("Masses and Prayers for Various Needs and Occasions") and the *Book of Blessings* ("Rogation Days") provide prayers for rain.

We should keep in mind that no one lives in a generic ecology (e.g., "the West Coast" or "rural Canada") but rather in a local one (e.g., the Simi Valley of California, the Fraser River Lowland of British Columbia). The same holds for Jesus and his family: they lived in Nazareth among the hills of the Lower Galilee, north of the plain of Esdraelon, not far from the Roman city of Sepphoris. In an agricultural economy, there was constant engagement with terrain, water sources, cultivated and wild vegetables, grain fields, fruit-bearing trees, farm animals, predatory insects and animals, forests, the warming or burning sun, mild or torrential rains, and the fear of drought and infestation. Life was guided by the rising and setting of the sun; by dry and wet seasons; by plowing, seeding, tending, protecting, harvesting, and storing produce; and by caring for and guarding flocks of sheep or goats. The local ecology in which Jesus lived was not mere backdrop but rather the very fabric of life inhabited by all Galileans. And thus it was that *this* ecology shaped Jesus' life and work.

2

Jesus in the Natural World

The authors of the gospels were intent on seeing Jesus in his local ecology, the Galilee, and in other regions of Israel as well as in Jerusalem. Even though none of the gospel writers lived in Israel, as far as we can tell, they described his knowledge of the natural world and his engagement with it in great detail. This should surprise us because the gospels were directed largely to communities of early Christians who lived in densely populated cities: Damascus, Antioch, Ephesus, Rome. Yet Jesus' engagement with the natural world was captured in each gospel: from hillsides where he prayed, to the many animals who appear in his sayings and stories. One gains the clear impression that the evangelists wanted their urban communities to recognize the importance of his earthy nature and his affinity for the natural world.

Perhaps they portrayed him in such a manner because they were eager to correct what they considered false views of Jesus that emerged after his death and resurrection: that he was an incorporeal spirit masquerading in a human body, that he was nothing more than a miracle worker who defied the laws of nature, or that he was a "heavenly" teacher who imparted a secret knowledge with which his followers could escape their "earthbound" bodies into an immortal and immaterial future. By way of contrast, Luke places the birth of Jesus at a specific time: "In those days a decree went out from Emperor Augustus that all the world should be registered. This was the first registration and was taken while Quirinius was governor of Syria"

(Luke 2:1-2). And he offers a specific location: "[In] the city of David called Bethlehem . . . [Mary] gave birth to her firstborn son and wrapped him in bands of cloth, and laid him in a manger" (Luke 2:4, 7). From a different though complementary perspective, John makes a similar claim in one short sentence: "The Word became flesh and lived among us" (John 1:14).

It would seem, then, that matter and materiality actually mattered to the writers of the gospels: "The trajectory of these books [the gospels] is toward a 'sarcophilic' Christianity,[1] toward a community that loves and honors the 'flesh,' [and] the conditions of the creation within which it lives. . . . The activity of God takes place in the midst of the actual places and circumstances of *this* world."[2] Thus, we can read, sing, study, teach, and pray the gospels and letters through the "lens" of materiality: that is, we can look for the natural world and its significance in the life and public ministry of Jesus and his followers. Why? The materiality of the earth and the earthy matter of his bodily existence were not overlooked. Or say it this way: When we read the gospels with "ecological" eyes, through an ecocentric lens, the natural world begins to appear in abundance—not as a mere backdrop to the life of Jesus and his followers but rather as an important actor in their lives.[3] This is a different way of encountering the central text of Chris-

[1] "Sarco," from the Greek *sarx*, "the flesh," and "philic" from the Greek *philia*, "love for." Thus, love of the flesh.

[2] Gordon Lathrop, *Holy Ground: A Liturgical Cosmology* (Minneapolis: Fortress Press, 2003), 130; emphasis mine.

[3] Consider these studies that employ an ecological perspective in exploring the gospels: Dong Hyeon Jeong, *Embracing the Nonhuman in the Gospel of Mark* (Atlanta: SBL Press, 2023); Elaine M. Wainwright, *Habitat, Human, and Holy: An Eco-Rhetorical Reading of the Gospel of Matthew* (Sheffield, UK: Sheffield Phoenix Press, 2016); Michael Trainor, *About Earth's Child: An Ecological Listening to the Gospel of Luke* (Sheffield, UK: Sheffield Phoenix Press, 2017); Susan Miller, "'I Came That They May Have Life, and Have It Abundantly' (John 10:10): An Ecological Reading of John's Gospel," *Expository Times* 124, no. 2 (2012): 64–71.

tian faith and life, different in the sense that it expands beyond an androcentric, or solely human focus to an ecocentric, or creation focus that includes humans; other creatures; the earth with its soil, minerals, water, air, sunlight, vegetation, mountains, forests, and plains; and the creating Word who became flesh in Jesus of Nazareth: "All things came into being through him, and without him not one thing came into being" (John 1:3).

Jesus' Awareness of the Natural World

What, then, do we know of Jesus' awareness of the natural world as presented by the gospel writers? Let us keep in mind that he lived in an agricultural economy and grew up in a village that produced grapes for wine and wheat and barley for bread. As an adult, he lived in close proximity to the Sea of Galilee (Lake Kinneret) and was familiar with fish and the fishing industry. As a child and an adult, he celebrated a number of religious festivals every year, festivals with requisite rituals aligned to the cycles of the natural seasons and harvests, communal festivals mandated in Exodus 23:14-17: Passover, or *Pesach*, in early spring, coinciding with the barley harvest, spring herbs, and the start of the lambing season; Weeks, or *Shavuot*, what Greek-speaking Jews called Pentecost, in late spring with the conclusion of the wheat harvest; and Ingathering, or *Sukkot*, in autumn, a festival celebrating the harvest of grapes, olives, and other fruits. In celebrating these festivals, he encountered not only the produce of the land but also the challenging labor to produce barley, herbs, lamb, wheat, grapes, olives, and fruits: staples in the diet of Mediterranean cultures—an intense labor involving soil, field, rain, and sun.

But let us not forget that he and his Galilean followers kept the weekly Sabbath, *Shabbat*, from sunset Friday to sunset Saturday, commemorating the conclusion of God's labor to bring forth the creation as set forth in the first chapter of Genesis, a day of rest not only for humans but for the whole creation: "You shall not do any work—you, or your son or your daughter, or your male or female slave, or your ox or your donkey, or any of your livestock, or the resident alien in your towns, so that [all] . . . may rest as well as you" (Deut 5:14). We should not underestimate the significance of this day, for it asked faithful Jews to remember and give thanks for the first act of God: the creation of the cosmos, an activity marked by God's grace and peace; an activity that honored each element in and of itself. In this regard, the earth and its many creatures appear as pure gift in which "humans are essential . . . but so are the other parts of creation."[4]

At the same time, the Sabbath served and continues to serve as a commemoration of God's liberating the Hebrews from harsh labor as slaves in Egypt. It does this by setting aside one day each week when there is freedom from labor and the consequent stress or fatigue it can produce. While one reads of contemporary Christians taking a "sabbath" from work, what is frequently forgotten in this appropriation of a Jewish practice is its clear call to seek liberation for that which is oppressed in the present moment. Sabbath is not only the opportunity to give thanks for God's creation, but also the occasion to consider what or who is suffering in the world with the intention to alleviate such suffering. No wonder, then, that on the Sabbath, Jesus heals a man, freeing him from his infirmity,[5] and also defends his own followers, who plucked and ate grain to free themselves from hunger.[6]

Toward the beginning of Mark's gospel, the earliest gospel written, Jesus is asked why his disciples do not fast as do the followers of John the Baptist and the Pharisees. He responds in an enigmatic fashion that nonetheless indicates his knowl-

[4] Richard Bauckham, *The Bible and Ecology: Rediscovering the Community of Creation* (Waco, TX: Baylor University Press, 2010), 15.

[5] See Mark 3:1-6; Luke 6:6-11; Matt 12:9-13.

[6] Mark 2:23-28; Luke 6:1-5; Matt 12:1-2.

edge of winemaking: "No one puts new wine into old wineskins; otherwise, the wine will burst the skins, and the wine is lost, and so are the skins, but one puts new wine into fresh wineskins."[7] There is to be no fasting, for something new and wondrous is emerging that asks for feasting; there is no pouring of new and still fermenting wine into an old wineskin, for the new growth will burst the older container.

In another parable, Mark reveals the potential for harsh economic conditions. "A man planted a vineyard, put a fence around it, dug a pit for the winepress, and built a watchtower; then he leased it to tenants and went to another country" (Mark 12:1). At the conclusion of the grape harvest, the owner sends employees and then his son to collect the owner's share of the produce. In each case, the collector is beaten or killed because the tenants hope to keep the produce for themselves. What will the owner do, asks Jesus. Why, he will give the vineyard to others.[8] Here we recognize Jesus' knowledge of the wine industry, the physical elements needed for a winery, the crushing impoverishment of laborers that could lead to violence, and the perils of absentee landowning—a common practice in first-century Israel. Wine, we know, was the daily drink for Galileans, a beverage with a light alcohol content, one that appears at the Last Supper and later flows into the eucharistic meal of Christians.[9]

In one his most famous parables, Jesus demonstrates his knowledge of the risks involved in producing a grain harvest: "Listen! A sower went out to sow" (Mark 4:3). Some seed fell on a path, where it was eaten by the birds. Other seed fell on rocky ground, where it was scorched by the sun. Other seed fell among thorns that choked it. And yet more seed fell into

[7] Mark 2:22.

[8] Mark 12:2-9.

[9] For an enchanting exploration of wine in Christian sacramental and health practice, see Gisela H. Kreglinger, *The Spirituality of Wine* (Grand Rapids, MI: Eerdmans, 2016).

good soil, where it brought forth abundant grain.[10] Although Jesus offers an interpretation of the parable regarding the "sowing of the word," the use of such imagery was possible only because he observed the process and risks involved in the sowing of seed during the months of October and November, the primary planting season in Israel.

Matthew's gospel includes Jesus demonstrating his knowledge of common herbs as he responds to religious leaders who criticized him: "Woe to you . . . hypocrites! For you tithe mint, dill, and cumin, and have neglected the weightier matters of the law: justice and mercy and faith" (Matt 23:23). Although herbs were used to flavor food, they were valued primarily for their medicinal qualities. And herbs—bitter herbs—were an integral and edible element in the Passover ritual: tasting the bitterness of slavery.[11]

Matthew includes a parable drawn from the Galilean fishing industry, in which Jesus compares the kingdom of heaven to a net thrown into the sea, a net which "caught fish of every kind" (Matt 13:47). This was the dragnet, a net of great length with floating cork on its top and weights on the bottom that was pulled by fishers to the shore, where they separated the diverse catch into different piles in preparation for the market.[12] Jesus then notes that "good" fish—saleable fish—are put into baskets while "bad" fish—unmarketable fish—are thrown out. Mark and Matthew write that although Jesus grew up in Nazareth, he made his home in Capernaum, a fishing village by the Sea of Galilee.[13] Indeed, all four gospels recount his calling of followers who were engaged in the Galilean fishing industry.[14]

[10] Mark 4:3-8.

[11] "In the second month on the fourteenth day, at twilight, they shall keep [Passover]; they shall eat it with unleavened bread and bitter herbs" (Num 9:11).

[12] See chapter 1, page 21.

[13] Matt 4:13. See also Mark 2:1.

[14] Mark 1:16-20; Matt 4:18-22; Luke 5:1-11; John 1:35-42.

Would they not have shared knowledge of their trade with Jesus?

Luke mentions Jesus describing God's care for birds and flowers: "Consider the ravens: they neither sow nor reap, they have neither storehouse nor barn, and yet God feeds them. . . . Consider the lilies, how they grow: they neither toil nor spin; yet I tell you, even Solomon in all his glory was not clothed like one of these" (Luke 12:24, 27). Or this: when the Pharisees and Sadducees sought to test Jesus by asking him to produce a sign from heaven, he responded with this rather caustic observation: "When it is evening, you say, 'It will be fair weather, for the sky is red.' And in the morning, 'It will be stormy today, for the sky is red and threatening.' You know how to interpret the appearance of the sky, but you cannot interpret the signs of the times" (Matt 16:1-3).

New wine in new wineskins, the layout of a Galilean winery, absentee land ownership, sowing seeds of grain, cultivated herbs, dragnet fishing, birds in the air, lilies in the fields, and redness in the sky: all these indicate Jesus' astute awareness of his local ecology. Indeed, we do not find abstract conceptualization or abstruse commentary on Scripture but rather a fundamental grasp of the natural world, its processes, and the labor within it. Of course, contemporary preachers, catechists, biblical scholars, and everyday readers of the gospels have sought to grasp the meaning of Jesus' parables and sayings, and understandably so. And yet the search for their significance—their spiritual meaning for today—can lead one to overlook what they so clearly present: the natural world in all its diversity and Jesus' presence in and knowledge of that world.

What Did He Encounter in the Natural World?

When he narrates the birth of Jesus, Luke writes that "[Mary] gave birth to her firstborn son and wrapped him in bands of cloth and laid him in a manger" (Luke 2:7). Although today we find many churches and parochial schools using a manger made of wood for Christmas pageants and the nativity crèche at the altar, archaeological evidence suggests that ancient mangers—feeding troughs for domesticated animals—were made of stone containing an indentation where the feed was placed. This, then, was Jesus' first encounter with the natural world: with a stone "crib" and a "cushion" of grasses, grains, or plants—fresh feed for animals. We are right to imagine that as a newborn infant, he received nourishment from his mother's breast and then, as a toddler, was fed softened bread, mashed vegetables, and perhaps a simple porridge.

As an adult, Jesus was a walker—with a few exceptions, such as crossing the Sea of Galilee in a fishing boat and entering Jerusalem on a donkey. For the vast majority of his life, he encountered the natural world by walking along beaten pathways or roads in the Galilee: he was close to the earth, not above it on a horse or in a carriage. He did not speed by in a train, automobile, or airplane, missing the surrounding fields or mountains, the nearby lakes or vineyards. Such walking, the slowest means of transportation, allowed him and his followers to observe more closely the local ecology through which they moved. In reading the Gospel of Luke, for instance, we discover many and diverse elements of the natural world in the life of Jesus.

Weather patterns, days, and times of day: the Sabbath (4:16; 23:54); daybreak (4:42); the close of day (9:12); lightning (9:29); an overshadowing cloud (9:34); the middle of the night or dawn (12:38); clouds and rain; south winds and scorching heat (12:54-55); Passover (22:1); darkness over the land (23:44); early dawn (24:1); evening (24:29); and the third day (24:46).

Earth elements: the river Jordan (3:3; 4:1); the wilderness (4:1; 7:24); a stone (4:3); the brow of a hill (4:29); a deserted place (4:42; 5:16); Lake Gennesaret (5:1); deep water (5:4); fishing nets (5:4); new wine (5:37); climbing up a mountain (6:12; 9:28);

good trees, good fruit (6:43); walking through grain fields (6:1); thorns and grapes (6:44); a flooding river (6:49); a reed shaken by the wind (7:24); ointment (7:37-38); sowing seed (8:4-8); sailing in a boat (8:22); wind and raging waves (8:23-24); five loaves of bread and two fish (9:13); walking on a road (9:57); dust clinging to one's feet (10:11); oil and wine (10:34); daily bread (11:3); yeast (12:1); crop storage (12:13-21); lilies (12:27); the grass of the fields (12:28); a fig tree (13:6-9; 21:29-33); mustard seed (13:18-19); salt (14:34); a mulberry tree (17:6); a sycamore tree (19:4); a vineyard (20:9-19); wine, the fruit of the vine (22:18); bread (22:19; 24:30); the Mount of Olives (22:39); a rock-hewn tomb (23:53); and spices with ointments (23:56).

Other creatures: sheep (2:8; 15:1-7); turtledoves (2:24); swine (8:33; 15:15); foxes and birds (9:58); lambs and wolves (10:3); snakes and scorpions (10:19); fish, snake, egg, and scorpion (11:11-12); sparrows (12:6); ravens (12:24); a hen and her brood (13:34); a fatted calf (15:23); a colt (19:30); lambs (22:7); a crowing cock or rooster (22:60); and broiled fish (24:42).

Reading the gospels through an ecological lens allows us to recognize the presence of God's creation in Jesus' life and the lives of his followers who would continue his movement after his resurrection. There is no *ecomisos*, hatred of the earthly environment, but rather affectionate engagement with it. Real things, the created things of ordinary experience, were not overlooked by the gospel writers. Indeed, a number of significant events in Jesus' life—events that Christians would eventually keep as solemnities or feasts forming the liturgical year—underscore Jesus' place *within* the creation:

His birth, at which he was placed in a common feed trough for animals

His baptism in the waters of the Jordan River

His testing for forty days in the wilderness with wild animals

His preference for deserted places to commune with God

His teaching by a lake, a hillside, in grain fields, and near vineyards

His transfiguration on a mountaintop

His entrance into Jerusalem on a donkey, with branches and palm fronds marking his path

The identification of his self-giving life with bread and wine, fruit of field and vine

His prayerful suffering and arrest in the Garden of Gethsemane

His crucifixion, his being "lifted up" on the wood of a tree at a place called Golgotha

Mary Magdalene's encounter with him as a gardener outside the garden tomb

The sending forth of the Holy Spirit as tongues of fire

In these various events, the gospel writers draw one's attention to the natural world as the earthly places where Jesus lived and where his public ministry took place. We find no string of ethereal sayings, no esoteric teaching for incorporeal souls—though the temptation has been great in the history of Christianity to forget or intentionally overlook the down-to-earth nature of his life. We who hear or read these stories within our own local ecologies encounter the One who embraced his particular environment: from hilltops to vineyards, in the early morning and at dusk, with sparrows and lambs, crowing roosters and fish. Is it any wonder, then, that early and medieval Christian artists produced murals, frescoes, sculpture, and illuminated pages filled with nature's images drawn from the gospel page? "Jesus lived in full harmony with creation. . . . He was far removed from philosophies which despised the body, matter, and the things of this world. . . . [He] worked with his hands, in daily contact with the matter created by God."[15]

Such a view of his engagement with the natural world, however, should not lead one to assume that the Galilee was an Edenic paradise. Drought and its disruption of agricultural life were not uncommon. Jesus spoke of earthquakes, famine, and plagues[16]—inscribed in the Old Testament and experienced in Mediterranean cultures. Torrential rains produced flooding that ruined grainfields, vineyards, and homes.[17] Raging waves could swamp fishing boats.[18] He knew of diseased trees that failed to bear fruit.[19] Domesticated animals were frequently subject to predation.[20] Did the annual Passover narration of the escape from slavery in Egypt not include the recital of invasive and destructive species—frogs, gnats, flies, and locusts—species that could overwhelm crops and herds?[21] Although Jesus praised the flowers of the field, he also experienced the torture of twisted thorns fashioned as a crown for his head.[22] Without scientific knowledge, an eclipse of the sun was viewed as an ominous omen: "When it was noon, darkness came over the whole land until three in the afternoon" (Mark 15:33). Indeed, the Hebrew word for eclipse is *likui*, meaning "defect."

For those who work in herding and agriculture today, none of this will come as a surprise: such labor is marked by the risk of natural threats to crops and cattle. Farmers, vintners, and ranchers live daily with the awareness that destructive weather, extreme temperatures, invasive species, drought, and flooding

[15] Pope Francis, *Laudato Si': On Care for Our Common Home* (Rome: Libreria Editrice Vaticana, 2015), no. 98.

[16] Luke 21:11.

[17] Matt 7:24-27.

[18] Mark 4:39.

[19] Luke 13:6-9.

[20] John 10:12.

[21] Exod 8:1-32; 10:1-20.

[22] Mark 15:17.

bring damage, if not ruin. Yet in our world today, something has shifted: various species of fish, birds, insects, animals, seeds, and flowers are becoming extinct due to human action: deforestation, pollution, and the accelerated warming of the planet. The followers of Jesus may have feared the power of the natural world to produce chaos; now one wonders if the natural world is alarmed "by our irresponsible use and abuse of the goods with which God has endowed [the earth]."[23]

How Was the Natural World Present in Jesus' Public Life?

At the beginning his gospel, Mark notes that Jesus was baptized in the waters of the Jordan River by John the Baptist, a man of the wilderness who was clothed in camel's hair and survived on a diet of locusts and wild honey.[24] In the waters of the Jordan, Jesus was washed into public life as the anointed agent of God, a *mashiya* or messiah, a term often used to describe those consecrated with olive oil for a public task, a practice that continues among sacramental Christians in the use of chrism (fragrant olive oil) at baptisms and ordinations. But there is more: this is the river through which the Hebrews passed after their forty-year journey in the wilderness, walking through this body of river water as they had passed earlier through the waters of the Red Sea.[25] Thus, the waters of the Jordan were suffused with the memory of and the hope for liberation from oppressive suffering, a new existence made possible by God's presence.[26] To enter the waters, then, was a

[23] Pope Francis, *Laudato Si'*, no. 2.

[24] Mark 1:6. See John Binns, "John the Baptist: Desert and Diet," *Theology* 127, no. 1 (2007): 13–21.

[25] Exod 14 and Josh 3.

[26] In 2 Sam 19, David crosses the Jordan and returns to his kingdom; in 2 Kgs 2, Elijah strikes the Jordan with his cloak, the water recedes, and he and Elisha cross on dry ground.

washing into the creative and liberating work of God in this world. Some may be surprised to read that the baptismal font in some medieval churches was called "the Jordan," its consecrated waters welcoming infants and adults into this same creative and liberating work of God.[27]

From the waters of the Jordan, Jesus entered a bone-dry wilderness—a desolate place—and was with Satan, wild beasts, and angels.[28] In that trio, Satan appears as the opponent and angels appear as friends of the righteous person. Between them are the wild animals. But why does Mark alone mention wild animals? Perhaps the evangelist had Isaiah in mind when he narrated the baptism of Jesus and the presence of animals with him: "A shoot shall come out from the stump of Jesse. . . . The spirit of the Lord shall rest on him. . . . With righteousness he shall judge the poor, and decide with equity for the meek of the earth. . . . The wolf shall live with the lamb, the leopard shall lie down with the kid, the calf and the lion and the fatling together, and a little child shall lead them" (Isa 11:1, 2, 4a, 6). In his baptism, Jesus was marked by the spirit of the Lord as the One "who decides for the oppressed" and as a friend to wild animals. Taking his cue from Isaiah, Mark may well be suggesting that in the kingdom of God, Jesus enacts peace between humans and animals, a restoration of the peace found in the Garden of Eden, an allusion to the first *'adam* or "earth creature."[29] There is no domination of animals and no

[27] "Severus, patriarch of Antioch, and Sophrinus, patriarch of Jerusalem, both record that the baptismal font is called the Jordan." Kilian McDonnell, OSB, *The Baptism of Jesus in the Jordan: The Trinitarian and Cosmic Order of Salvation* (Collegeville, MN: Liturgical Press, 1996), 77. See also Robin M. Jensen, *Baptismal Imagery in Early Christianity: Ritual, Visual, and Theological Dimensions* (Grand Rapids, MI: Baker Academic, 2012), 185.

[28] Mark 1:12-13.

[29] Modern English translations of Gen 2–3 use the term "man" or the proper name "Adam" for the original Hebrew *'adam*. But *'adam* is not a proper name, and thus the term can be translated as "earth creature."

forming them into pets for human amusement. Jesus is simply there with them in a peaceful manner.[30]

Throughout the gospels, we find that Jesus frequently sought solitude to pray in a deserted place or on a hilltop. In the culture of ancient Israel, the distinction was made between a village, town, or city—the habitable realm—and deserted places or wilderness—uncultivated land in which wild animals lived.[31] We read that he prayed in such places early in the morning or in the evening, before daily labor began and after it ended. It seems that Jesus did not fear the "uncultivated" or potentially "wild" spaces of the earth. In fact, he sought them out and considered them an ideal place to be in communion with God. Did his presence on a deserted hillside suggest that God is also present in what appear to be inhospitable places?

Mark narrates a story of Jesus' presence in another potentially dangerous location: the Sea of Galilee.[32] For those trained in modern science, oceans, fjords, rivers, and lakes become chaotic and threatening to humans when towering waves are created by the friction between the surface of the water and wind. As wind blows over the water, the continual disturbance creates a crest: the stronger the wind, the larger and more volatile the cresting wave. For those who lived around the ancient Mediterranean, however, wind and bodies of water were

[30] Bauckham, *Bible and Ecology*, 127. His *peaceful* presence among wild animals stands in stark contrast to the Roman imperial passion for animal slaughter in the thousands, which took place in coliseums throughout the empire. Concerning imperial animal slaughter as entertainment, see Micah Kiel, *Apocalyptic Ecology: The Book of Revelation, the Earth, and the Future* (Collegeville, MN: Liturgical Press, 2017), 68–71. For the contemporary practice of animal degradation, see Mary McGann, RSCJ, "The Corporate Industrial Food System: Origin, Goals, Outcomes," in *The Meal That Reconnects: Eucharistic Eating and the Global Food Crisis* (Collegeville, MN: Liturgical Press, 2020), 59–76.

[31] Bruce J. Malina and Richard L. Rohrbaugh, *Social-Science Commentary on the Synoptic Gospels*, 2nd ed. (Minneapolis: Fortress Press, 2003), 146–47.

[32] Mark 4:35-41; also Matt 8:23-27 and Luke 8:22-25.

thought to be controlled by spirits and thus immune to human control. Consequently, when the disciples panic as waves begin to swamp the boat, they beg Jesus to do something—anything! Jesus speaks to the waves and the wind, saying, "Peace! Be still!" (Mark 4:39). And here is Mark's point: All becomes calm as the wind and water acknowledge God's sovereignty over the creation expressed through the command of Jesus. Again, there is peace.

John the Baptist appears a second time in Mark's gospel as a man imprisoned by Herod Antipas, the ruler of the Galilee. John had been arrested because he condemned an illicit marriage entered into by Herod and his brother Philip's wife, Herodias. At a sumptuous birthday feast, Herodias's daughter, prompted by her mother, asked for the head of John—that is, she asked for his execution by decapitation. Herod acceded to the request, and John's head was then brought into the banquet room on a serving platter.[33] Set next to this story of a gruesome death, Mark juxtaposes the story of Jesus feeding five thousand followers.[34] Again we find Jesus in a deserted place, this time with a great crowd, as the day begins to wane. His disciples want to send the people away, but Jesus says, "You give them something to eat" (Mark 6:37). They find only two fish and five loaves of bread. Then Jesus blesses God for these gifts of the field and lake with gestures and words that will be repeated at the Last Supper and will become, in time, the gestures and words offered at every Mass.[35] There is more than enough to eat, with ample food left over.

[33] Mark 6:14-29.

[34] Mark 6:30-44, with parallels in Matt 14:13-21; Luke 9:10b-17; and John 6:1-15.

[35] When the priest lifts the bread and then the chalice, he says, "Blessed are you, Lord God of all creation, for through your goodness we have received the bread we offer you: fruit of the earth and work of human hands, . . . for through your goodness we have received the wine we offer you: fruit of the vine and work of human hands." See *The Roman Missal*, Third Typical Edition (2011), Liturgy of the Eucharist.

To many modern readers of this story, the transformation of five loaves of bread and two fish into a meal that could feed five thousand seems fantastical. Thus we find various "explanations" that attempt to make sense of this miracle (e.g., the crowd shared the food they already possessed). Others view the story as "proof" of Jesus' divinity: Who else but God could make such meager rations extend to five thousand hungry people? Yet both views seem to miss the point: With the corrupt and paranoid rulers in the kingdoms of this world, death is served on a platter in order to silence the truth; in the kingdom of God, however, life and its nourishment are served—and served to overflowing. With Herod, death; with Jesus, life. What we recognize in this story are the gifts of the earth, the very means through which God nourishes and sustains life. But there is more when we look to Isaiah: earth's food is abundant, more than enough to sustain *all* creatures, not only humans, for "the calf and the lion and the fatling together" (Isa 11:6b).

What we witness in these stories of Jesus at peace with wild animals, preserving the lives of his frightened followers in a storm on the sea, and feeding hungry people in a deserted place is his recognition of their bodily existence and the powerful presence of the natural world. He does not overlook the material nature of life. And then there is this: each action reveals the nature of the kingdom of God in which we see the promise of peace between humans and other creatures, in which threatening aspects of the natural world dissipate, in which all creatures are nourished. This process has begun but is not yet complete. Those who encounter Jesus' gospel are invited to look not only to the present but also to the future, when "[Christ's] kingdom will have no end,"[36] a kingdom that is coterminous with the whole creation.

[36] *Roman Missal*, Creed.

The Natural World in Jesus' Stories and Sayings

It should come as no surprise that Jesus' immersion in an agricultural economy would lead him to draw on images from his agrarian context: we find very few, if any, images from an urban setting. His employment of nature images was at the service of his primary message: "[He] came to Galilee proclaiming the good news of God and saying, 'The time is fulfilled, and the kingdom of God has come near'" (Mark 1:14-15). "[Jesus said to the crowd,] 'I must proclaim the good news of the kingdom of God . . . for I was sent for this purpose'" (Luke 4:43). "Jesus began to proclaim . . . 'The kingdom of heaven has come near'" (Matt 4:17).[37] Again we need to recognize that in the history of Christianity, the kingdom of God has been frequently interpreted as a reality present for humans alone or for the soul alone.[38] But is that so: that God guides, governs, or leads life only for humans, or only for the immaterial soul? Here we suggest that reading New Testament texts using an ecological lens opens one to a larger vision that includes not only humans in their earthy, bodily existence, but all other dimensions of the world created and sustained by God, the "maker of heaven and earth, of all things visible and invisible."[39] Consequently, the stories, parables, and the sayings of Jesus reveal different aspects of God's presence with creation—frequently in contrast to the economic, political, and social "kingdoms" of this world.

Indeed, Jesus likens the kingdom of God to an agricultural season: "The kingdom of God is as if someone would scatter seed on the ground, and would sleep and rise night and day, and the seed would sprout and grow, he does not know how.

[37] Matthew uses the term "kingdom of heaven" instead of the "kingdom of God."

[38] Other images for kingdom include commonwealth, dominion, realm, and reign.

[39] *Roman Missal*, Creed. "At that time Jesus said, 'I thank you, Father, *Lord of heaven and earth*'" (Matt 11:25); emphasis mine.

The earth produces of itself, first the stalk, then the head, then the full grain in the head. But when the grain is ripe, at once he goes in with his sickle, because the harvest has come" (Mark 4:26-29). Jesus' ability to speak of the process of seeding, sprouting, growing, and harvesting would not be possible without careful observation of the sower's labor in the field. There is human labor, but there is also the earth, the soil that produces *of itself*: "the sower does not know how." Is this not an allusion to the mystery of the reign of God: that it asks for human engagement and at the same time recognizes that human initiative is made possible only by what God has already created: soil, water, and sun, which act together in a wondrous yet unseen fashion? And more: human impatience in the modern drive to achieve "results" as quickly as possible is countered by the processes of the natural world at work beyond human control. In the growth of the kingdom of God "on earth as it is in heaven" (Matt 6:10), there is human labor, but the farmer, gardener, baker, vintner, and herder know that the possibility of growth rests with another power. Patience is needed.

Consider, then, the people who were associated with Jesus: peasant fishers, farmers, vintners, and herders who lived in an oral, rural culture in which literacy was non-existent.[40] "He went throughout Galilee" writes Mark,[41] and spent the vast majority of his time among poor people who labored on lake or land: "Images from nature become meaningful to an audience in constant relationship with nature in their daily activities, with its experience of pathos and joy. It brings to their perception in down-to-earth fashion the close connection between the work of nature and divine activity."[42] In fishing,

[40] See Meir Bar-Ilan, "Illiteracy in the Land of Israel in the First Centuries C.E.," in *Essays in the Social Scientific Study of Judaism and Jewish Society*, ed. Simcha Fishbane, Alain Goldschläger, and Stuart Schoenfeld, 46–61 (New York: Ktav, 1992).

[41] Mark 1:39.

[42] V. G. John, "Kingdom of God and Ecology: A Parabolic Perspective," *Bangalore Theological Forum* 34, no. 1 (June 2002): 97.

tending small plots of land, and herding sheep or goats, Jesus' audience came into intimate contact with the rhythms of gestation, birth, growth, maturation, diminishment, and death present throughout creation. They were familiar with summer flowers, animal stillbirths, greening vines, predatory insects, the smell of fresh herbs, the blood and viscera of fish, the taste of baked bread, enervating humidity, hunger, and dark soil—the "pathos and joy" of laboring in soil and sea. For his Galilean compatriots, their lives and labor took place under this psalmodic canopy: "The earth is the LORD's and all that is in it, / the world, and those who live in it" (Ps 24:1).

Jesus spoke of salt, which was used as a preservative, flavoring, and disinfectant. Salt was harvested from the Mediterranean and Dead Seas by pouring saltwater into stone pits or containers, letting the water evaporate, then collecting the dried salt. "Salt is good," says Jesus, "but if salt has lost its saltiness, how can you season it? Have salt in yourselves, and be at peace with one another" (Mark 9:50). Not to be taken literally, the salt in oneself refers to the bond of friendship marked by peace and compassion for others. In Matthew's Sermon on the Mount, Jesus says to his audience of farmers and fishers, "You are the salt of the earth" (Matt 5:13), suggesting that those who dwell in the kingdom of heaven are valued by God: he invites them not to lose their "saltiness" as salt does when mixed with other minerals, producing an unpleasant taste. Indeed, these sayings flowed into the ancient Christian process of baptismal formation, when catechumens received salt as a symbolic preservative of their faith and when infants received a few grains of salt on their lips just prior to their baptism, a sign of their calling to be the salt, the presence of Christ, in society.[43]

Set next to salt, we find yeast, one of the earliest domesticated microorganisms that converts carbohydrates into bubbling

[43] The placing of salt on an infant's lips also served as an apotropaic, a protection against evil.

carbon dioxide, which expands the dough to which it is added. Luke presents us with two different interpretations of yeast. "When the crowd gathered by the thousands . . . [Jesus] began to speak first to his disciples, 'Beware of the yeast of the Pharisees, that is, their hypocrisy' " (Luke 12:1). Here Jesus exhorts his followers to let their actions conform to their words. The failure to reflect in deed what is spoken can "bubble up," as it were, and contaminate one's witness to the dominion of God.

On the other hand, Jesus makes a startling claim when he speaks about a woman mixing yeast with dough: "To what should I compare the kingdom of God? It is like yeast that a woman took and mixed in with three measures of flour until all of it was leavened" (Luke 13:20-21). In Jerusalem's temple, unleavened bread was offered by male priests as a pleasing sacrifice to God. Keep in mind that every trace of leaven, or yeast, had to be removed from every Jewish home before the celebration of Passover with its holy, *unleavened* bread. But here Jesus teaches that in the reign of God, a peasant woman, a laywoman—not a male priest—makes the offering, and the offering is leavened bread—not unleavened bread. It would seem, then, that common expectations are turned upside down in the reign of God: "The dominion of God has no outsiders."[44] In this realm, there is no hierarchy, no separate, "sacred" food because food itself is a gift from God. Would this not surprise peasant farmers listening to Jesus, people who were thought to be on the lowest rung of society, outsiders living and laboring at a distance from urban and elite culture, a culture in which only men, not women, served as priests in the temple? And then this: Jesus' praise of leaven continued for hundreds of years in the Latin West, where Christians used yeasty bread

[44] For an enlightening discussion of this yeasty parable, see Gordon Lathrop, *Holy Things: A Liturgical Theology* (Minneapolis: Fortress Press, 1993), 24–27.

in the Eucharist, a practice continued without change among Eastern Orthodox Christians.[45]

Other parables and sayings indicate Jesus' familiarity with the natural world: a mustard seed that grows into a tree where the birds find a home (Mark 4:30-32); a Galilean vineyard (Mark 12:1-12); a fig tree that foretells the coming of summer (Mark 13:28); caution concerning dogs and swine (Matt 7:6); caution concerning false prophets: wolves dressed in sheep's clothing (Matt 7:15); foxes with holes, birds with nests, and nowhere for the Son of Man to lay his head (Luke 9:58); sending his followers, his lambs, among wolves (Luke 10:3); the power to tread on snakes and scorpions (Luke 10:19); a Samaritan who uses wine and olive oil to dress wounds (Luke 10:34); a foolish landowner who builds large barns, failing to share his produce, only to die (Luke 12:13-21); Jesus as the mother hen, who desires to gather her brood (Luke 13:34); lost sheep (Luke 15:1-7); the son who suffers famine, becomes a pig feeder, and receives a welcoming feast with a fatted calf (Luke 15:11-32); bread (John 6:35-40); light (John 9:1-11); shepherd (John 10:1-18); way (John 14:1-7); and vine (John 15:1-8).

How Did Jesus View the Natural World?

As one author notes, Jesus walked lightly on the earth.[46] He did not have a possessive view of the land as one frequently finds among those who own property, whether they be individuals, families, governments, or corporations. Living as God's servant in the household of creation, he refused to use

[45] Robert Cabié, *The Eucharist*, ed. A. G. Martimort, trans. Matthew J. O'Connell (Collegeville, MN: Liturgical Press, 1986), 77, 132–33. Only in the eleventh century did the use of unleavened bread become widespread.

[46] Celine Mangan, "Jesus in His Environment," *Today's Good News*, accessed April 14, 2024, https://www.goodnews.ie/environment.shtml.

earth's gifts for personal profit or social status. This was in contrast to Rome's imperial mandate to dominate and control land and water for the benefit of the elite: the more land, the greater one's wealth and social standing. In Jesus' life, we see none of what imperial Rome sanctioned during the first century: pollution, deforestation, toxic mining, and animal slaughter as entertainment.[47] Instead, we witness his recognition that human beings are not the earth's owners who can do with it whatever they please—from clear-cutting forests to dumping sewage and other harmful material into rivers. In light of his biblical heritage, he recognized that human beings are renters on the earth, and temporary ones at that: "The LORD spoke to Moses, saying: 'The land is mine; with me you are but aliens and tenants'" (Lev 25:23). Given that many of us live in a culture that nurtures acquisitiveness and praises conspicuous consumption, one has to wonder if walking lightly on the earth is even possible.[48] To his followers, ancient and modern, he says: "Take care! Be on your guard against all kinds of greed; for one's life does not consist in the abundance of possessions" (Luke 12:15).

This biblical and Christian claim will be hard to accept for those who view humans as the sole possessors of the earth and for those who consider the environmental crisis a hoax or a problem to be solved by someone else.[49] For the world's

[47] See Samuel Torvend, *Monastic Ecological Wisdom: A Living Tradition* (Collegeville, MN: Liturgical Press, 2023), 5–9; Micah D. Kiel, *Apocalyptic Ecology*, 57–88; Filip Havlíceki and Miroslav Morcinek, "Waste and Pollution in the Ancient Rome Empire," *Journal of Landscape Ecology* 9, no. 3 (2016): 33–49.

[48] For the intentional "training" and manipulation of North Americans to become mass consumers during the twentieth century, see the 2002 BBC documentary, *The Century of the Self*, June 20, 2016, accessed April 17, 2024, https://www.youtube.com/watch?v=DnPmg0R1M04.

[49] According to a study produced by the University of Michigan, nearly 15 percent of Americans claim that global warming is a hoax while 26 percent believe that climate change is "normal" and thus harmless:

1.4 billion Catholics guided by church and papal teachings[50] and the Eastern Orthodox, Anglican, and mainline Protestant communions who also hold that "[the] heavens belong to the Lord your God, [and] the earth with all that is in it" (Deut 10:14), creation is a primary revelation of God's active presence, God's love of diversity, and "the foundation of all God's saving plans . . . that culminate in Christ."[51] The praise of God as the maker of heaven and earth thus makes a claim on those who worship the God revealed in Jesus Christ: "Do not damage the earth or the sea or the trees" (Rev 7:3).

The gospel writer indicates that Jesus spoke of heaven as the throne of God and the earth as God's footstool.[52] He offered public thanks to the "Lord of heaven and earth" (Matt 11:25).[53] Thus he spoke of God as the Creator who is engaged with the entire creation in all its materiality, its physical matter. Indeed, when his disciples asked him how to pray, he offered this petition: "Your will be done, on earth as it is in heaven" (Matt 6:10): note that the direction is *toward the earth*. There is no hint of an

Nayiri Mullinix, *Michigan News*, University of Michigan, February 14, 2024, accessed April 17, 2024, https://news.umich.edu/nearly-15-of-americans-deny-climate-change-is-real-ai-study-finds/. According to studies by the Pew Research Center, a large percentage of Americans claim that the climate crisis is of great concern to them, but those who actually engage in activities to diminish the crisis remain quite small: Alec Tyson, Cary Funk, and Brian Kennedy, "What the Data Says about Americans' Views of Climate Change," accessed February 19, 2025, https://www.pewresearch.org/short-reads/2023/08/09/what-the-data-says-about-americans-views-of-climate-change/.

[50] For example, the biblical texts and actions of the Mass and Liturgy of the Hours, *Catechism of the Catholic Church*, and papal teachings on care for creation.

[51] *Catechism of the Catholic Church*, 2nd ed. (United States Catholic Conference—Libreria Editrice Vaticana, 1997), no. 280.

[52] Matt 5:34-35.

[53] Cf. Luke 10:21; see also Ps 146:5-6: "Happy are those whose help is the God of Jacob, / whose hope is in the Lord their God, / who made heaven and earth."

ecophobic spirit eager to escape the earth but rather an abundant focus on the cultivation of life in *this* world, God's world. What Jesus professes is his faith in the divine Creator of the cosmos, the earth, and all its creatures. His use of the term "father" expressed his intimate and trusting relationship with the One who brought him and all other creatures into existence through the natural process of germination, growth, and birth. Indeed, early and medieval Christians speak of this process as the very one through which the Word of God became flesh in Jesus: the finite and earthy matter of this world is capable of holding and revealing the presence of the infinite and the divine.[54]

But there is more. Jesus also speaks of God as the One who cares for and supports life on this earth: "Look at the birds of the air: they neither sow nor reap nor gather into barns, and yet your heavenly Father feeds them" (Matt 6:26). Perhaps in Jesus' words we hear an echo of Psalm 104: " O Lord my God, . . . You make springs gush forth in the valleys; / they flow between the hills. . . . By the streams the birds of the air have their habitation; / they sing among the branches" (Ps 104:1, 10, 12). In the household of creation, all creatures find sustenance in God's earth. No wonder the psalmist speaks of the creation offering praise: "Let the heavens be glad, and let the earth rejoice; / let the sea roar, and all that fills it; / let the field exult, and everything in it. / Then shall all the trees of the forest sing for joy" (Ps 96:11, 12). Earlier interpreters of these texts claimed that such exuberant praise from non-human creatures was a rhetorical device to underscore the notion that the heavens and the earth are God's: "Fields don't exult! Trees don't sing!" Yet recent studies suggest that animals, fish, birds, and trees communicate in languages that humans are only beginning to understand. Is it possible, then, to imagine that God's suste-

[54] John 1:1-18.

nance of earth's flora and fauna actually elicits a response—not only from humans but also from other creatures?[55]

We know well that earth's creatures need sustenance to live. Bats and frogs consume mosquitoes; dolphins search for fish, shrimp, and octopus; birds dine on seeds, berries, and insects; raccoons eat just about anything; and humans partake of food and drink in great variety. Given creatures' need for food, one can view the earth and its diverse organisms from a utilitarian perspective, that is, the earth's flora and fauna serve but one purpose: they are consumable goods, nothing more. Apart from their usefulness, their "utility," they have no other value. They are useful for one thing only: nourishment for the food chain. Given this perception of the creation, it is not difficult to see how flora and fauna can be objectified, treated as nothing more than commodities to be purchased and consumed. In a culture shaped by consumerism, the drive for commodification is ever-present. What matters most is securing profit for those who produce product. Thus, we witness the destruction of the Amazon Rainforest, home to a rich diversity of plants and animals unknown in other parts of the world, a region that holds 50 percent of all rainforests in the world. "Why not cut down the forest?" say some. "The demand for beef in China and the United States must be met." And so the

[55] See "Dolphin Communication 2024," accessed March 17, 2024, https://dolphins.org/communication; Frankie Adkins, "Boops, Hums and Farts: The Mysterious World of Fish Communication," April 19, 2024, accessed April 19, 2024, https://www.bbc.com/future/article/20240418-boops-hums-and-farts-the-mysterious-world-of-fish-communication; Peter Wohlleben, *The Inner Life of Animals: Love, Grief, and Compassion: Surprising Observations of a Hidden World*, trans. Jane Billinghurst (Vancouver, BC: Greystone Books, 2017); Toshitaka N. Suzuki, "Wild Birds Use an Ordering Rule to Decode Novel Call Sequences," *Current Biology* 27, no. 15 (August 2017): 2331–36; Peter Wohlleben, *The Hidden Life of Trees: What They Feel, How They Communicate: Discoveries from a Secret World*, trans. Jane Billinghurst (Vancouver, BC: Greystone Books, 2016).

widespread deforestation of this priceless ecology paves the way for cattle ranching.[56]

Luke's Jesus presents another perspective: "Consider the lilies, how they grow: they neither toil nor spin; yet I tell you, even Solomon in all his glory was not clothed like one of these" (Luke 12:27).[57] Here the flora of the fields are praised for their beauty: they serve no economic purpose. They simply exist in their loveliness. "Look at the birds of the air; they neither sow nor reap" (Matt 6:26): they do not labor and yet they are valued by their divine Creator, who feeds them daily through the agency of the natural world. They possess intrinsic worth as one of God's creations apart from their ability to do anything, to be useful. How odd that must sound to Christians and others who insist that charitable contributions to people challenged by poverty should be given only to those who are able to work, to those who can demonstrate their usefulness: a punitive view not shared by Jesus. "The concept of intrinsic value reflects the perspective that nature has value in its own right, independent of human uses. Intrinsic value opens us up to the possibility that nature has value even if it does not directly or indirectly benefit humans. Intrinsic value is viewed from an ecocentric standpoint."[58] Of course in an androcentric world where all things find their value or purpose in serving humans alone, the gifts of the natural world are easily commodified for human use. If they don't serve human need or desire, what possible value do they possess? In an ecocentric world, however, the lily, fish, tree, bird, and rainforest share a common value as God's creations. Humans are thus called to

[56] Sasha Chavkin, "How an American Meat Broker Is Fueling Amazon Deforestation," *Associated Press*, November 3, 2023, accessed April 26, 2024, https://apnews.com/article/brazil-china-amazon-deforestation-beef-climate-trade-2a7a9a4310b6abca727dabb596e2e84d.

[57] See also Matt 6:28-29.

[58] Anne W. Rea and Wayne R. Munns Jr., "The Value of Nature: Economic, Intrinsic, or Both?," *Integrated Environmental Assessment and Management* 13, no. 5 (2017): 953.

recognize them as companion creatures to be respected for their distinctive nature.

Trust in the God who alone possesses heaven and earth; gratitude for God's continuing care of creation, a gratitude voiced not only by humans but also by other creatures[59] and earth's flora; rejection of any abuse of God's creation; and praise for the intrinsic value of all creatures: these flow from Jesus' view of the natural world, a view shaped by the experience of his local ecology, the festivals of his religion, and his subsequent drawing on images from land and sea in his parabolic proclamation of the kingdom of God, a dominion or commonwealth frequently at odds with the degrading and death-dealing practices found in the kingdoms of this world.

It was in that contrast and conflict between the kingdom of Caesar—a man who claimed to be the lord of heaven and earth and the slaveholding master of the world—and the kingdom of God announced and embodied by Jesus that the gospel writers lead us to Jerusalem, the place of his suffering and death. Yet even in that horrific death, the natural world was present. He was arrested during the celebration of Passover, the commemoration of freedom from slavery, from a system of degrading domination in which the gifts of the earth served one purpose: the glorification of the ruler. Before his arrest, while sharing bread and wine, fruit of the field and vine, with his disciples, he identified his life's purpose as one who serves. He was arrested in a garden at night. After his interrogation, a crown of thorns was placed in mockery on his head. Once again, he was led to a desolate place, where he was nailed to the wood of a tree. He was offered sour wine to slake his thirst.

[59] The author of Revelation notes that it is four animals, not a human cantor or chorus, who lead the heavenly assembly in praise, singing a canticle that eventually enters into the Christian liturgy as the Sanctus, or Holy, Holy, Holy: "The four living creatures, each of them with six wings, are full of eyes all around and inside. Day and night without ceasing they sing, 'Holy, holy, holy, the Lord God the Almighty, who was and is and is to come' " (4:8).

Darkness covered the land: the light of the sun failed. He died at the ninth hour of the day. He was placed in a rock-hewn tomb in a garden.

On the first day of the week, a Sunday, Mary Magdalene comes to the garden tomb and thinks she is speaking with a gardener who is, to her utter astonishment, Jesus risen from the dead. In another account, the faithful women bring spices to dress his body. The earth quakes as a heavenly messenger appears, directing them to the Galilee. In the scenes that follow, his materiality is underscored: he invites Thomas to touch his wounds; he breaks bread with two disciples in Emmaus; he asks his disciples for something to eat; standing by the Sea of Galilee, he instructs them on how they might gain a greater catch of fish; he offers them bread and broiled fish; he invites them to feed his sheep; and he promises them the outpouring of the Holy Spirit, who renews the face of the earth.[60]

It was after the resurrection that his Jewish and Gentile followers began to see the crucified and risen Jesus not only in relationship to his local ecology but also to the world.[61] That is, *they recognized continuity between his earthly life in the natural world and his risen presence with creation*. How, then, did they speak of him? Consider these images: the new Adam or new earth creature (1 Cor 15:22),[62] the creating Word of God (John 1:1-3),[63] "the Lamb of God" (John 1:29),[64] "the light of the world" (John 8:12),[65] "the firstborn of all creation" (Col 1:15-16),[66] "the bright morning star" (Rev 22:16),[67] the gatherer of all things in heaven and earth (Eph 1:10), the sustainer of all things (Heb 1:3), and "the great shepherd of the sheep" (Heb

60 "When you send forth your spirit, they are created; / and you renew the face of the ground" (Ps 104:30).

61 Mangan, "Jesus in His Environment."

62 See also Gen 1:26.

63 See also Gen 1:1-31.

64 See also John 1:36; Rev 5:6.

65 See also John 9:5.

66 See also Rom 8:29.

67 See also 2 Pet 1:19.

13:20).[68] This continuity between the life of Jesus in the natural world and his risen presence throughout all creation, indeed, the cosmos, led early Christian communities to worship him as God's agent of creation, through whom "all things came into being" (John 1:3) and as the One in whom "all things hold together" (Col 1:17).

At the same time, a number of these images portrayed his followers in the emerging Christian communities of the Mediterranean: "You are God's field" (1 Cor 3:9); "a new creation" (2 Cor 5:17); "You, a wild olive shoot" (Rom 11:17); "You are the salt of the earth" (Matt 5:13); "You are the light of the world" (Matt 5:14); "Children of light" (Eph 5:8); "One flock" (John 10:16); "The branches [of the vine]" (John 15:5); and "The assembly of the firstborn" (Heb 12:23).[69] Drawing on the horticultural life of Israel, these diverse images were planted, so to speak, in the urban cultures in which many of the early Christian communities emerged in the first century.

The Natural World in Early Christian Practice

Such earthy metaphors reflect the presence of the natural world in early Christian worship. The *Didache*, one of the earliest sources other than the New Testament, describes the liturgical practices of one Christian community. Those to be initiated are baptized in "living" or running water, preferably in a river or spring, the memory of Jesus' baptism in the Jordan flowing into the community's practice.[70] At the celebration of

[68] See also John 10:11.

[69] See the still-helpful work of Paul S. Minear, *Images of the Church in the New Testament* (Louisville: Westminster John Knox Press, 1960), especially the following two sections: "Minor Images of the Church" and "The New Creation," 28–65 and 105–35.

[70] *Didache*, 7.1, in Lucien Deiss, *Springtime of the Liturgy: Liturgical Texts of the First Four Centuries*, trans. Matthew J. O'Connell (Collegeville, MN: Liturgical Press, 1979). "In those days Jesus came from Nazareth of Galilee and was baptized by John in the Jordan" (Mark 1:9).

the Eucharist, the one who leads at table gives thanks to God "for the holy vine of David, your child, which you have revealed through Jesus."[71] The thanksgiving includes a reference to "the bread broken that was first scattered [as seed] on hillsides."[72] God is referred to as the "almighty master who has created everything."[73] The worshiping assembly is exhorted to "take all the first fruits of vintage and harvest, and of cattle and sheep, and give these first fruits to the prophets."[74] The assembly gathers on the Lord's Day, Sunday, the day of Christ's resurrection.[75] The author of the *Didache* exhorts the Christian assembly to be aware of false prophets: "Sheep will turn into wolves."[76] The final encouragement in this early Christian manual invites the assembly to look for the Lord "coming on the clouds of the sky."[77]

Other sources indicate that olive oil was used to mark the newly baptized: "We are anointed with blessed unction, following that ancient practice by which, ever since Aaron was anointed by Moses, there was a custom of anointing them for priesthood."[78] After they have been welcomed into the assembly, the freshly baptized receive milk and honey. Here the memory of the exodus is evoked with the promise of a "good and broad land, a land flowing with milk and honey" (Exod 3:8)—the "land" now a reference to Jesus Christ present in the

[71] *Didache*, 9.2. "I am the vine, you are the branches. Those who abide in me and I in them bear much fruit, because apart from me you can do nothing" (John 15:5).

[72] *Didache*, 9.4. "A sower went out to sow his seed" (Luke 8:5).

[73] *Didache*, 10.3. "The God who made the world and everything in it . . . is Lord of heaven and earth" (Acts 17:24).

[74] *Didache*, 13.3.

[75] *Didache*, 14.1.

[76] *Didache*, 16.4.

[77] *Didache*, 16.7.

[78] Tertullian, *On Baptism*, edited and translated with introduction and commentary by Ernest Evans (London: SPCK, 1964), 4.

Christian community.[79] The *Apostolic Tradition* includes a blessing for cheese and olives: "Sanctify this solidified milk, just as you also bring us together in your love. Let this fruit not leave your sweetness, this olive which is a symbol of your abundance, which you made to flow from the tree."[80] The bishop is instructed to bless these fruits: the grape, fig, pomegranate, pear, apple, blackberry, peach, cherry, and plum.[81] In addition, the bishop blesses flowers, in particular the rose and the lily.[82] Among Christians in Armenia, Cappadocia (modern Turkey), and Constantinople (modern Istanbul), laurel leaves were formed into crowns that were placed on the heads of the bride and groom: the verb "to marry" in Greek being "to crown." [83] In Egypt and Ethiopia, early Christians placed floral wreaths on the heads of the newly baptized.[84]

Widely used in many cultures—such as those of China, India, Persia, Greece, and Rome—incense entered Christian use in the late third or early fourth century, a practice reflected

[79] Tertullian, *On the Crown*, 3. "Like newborn infants, long for the pure, spiritual milk, so that by it you may grow into salvation" (1 Pet 2:2); "O Christ Jesus, you are the heavenly milk pressed from the sweet breasts of a young mother, full of the graces of your wisdom. Our tender lips seek to be nourished by the spiritual milk." Clement of Alexandria, "Hymn to Christ the Teacher," in Deiss, *Springtime of the Liturgy*.

[80] *Apostolic Tradition*, 6.2–3, in Deiss, *Springtime of the Liturgy*. See Andrew McGowan, "Food and Drink in Early Christian Rituals," in *Ascetic Eucharists: Food and Drink in Early Christian Ritual Meals* (Oxford: Oxford University Press, 1999), 95–106, 115–17.

[81] *Apostolic Tradition*, 32.1.

[82] *Apostolic Tradition*, 32.2. "I am a rose of Sharon, a lily of the valleys" (Song 2:1). Sharon is a valley in the Lower Galilee. The red rose will come to be identified with Jesus and the martyrs; the white rose with enlightenment and purity.

[83] Jean Evenou, "The East: The Rite of Crowning," in *The Sacraments*, vol. III in *The Church at Prayer*, ed. A. G. Martimort (Collegeville, MN: Liturgical Press, 1988), 192–95. In time, floral crowns became metal crowns embedded with precious jewels.

[84] Robert Cabié, "The Coptic and Ethiopian Rites," in *Sacraments*, vol. III in *Church at Prayer*, ed. Martimort, 83.

in the Scriptures: "The four living creatures and the twenty-four elders fell before the Lamb, each holding a harp and golden bowls full of incense" (Rev 5:8).[85] Although many contemporary Christian communions impose ashes on the forehead during the Ash Wednesday liturgy, their first use among Christians appears in the second century as a sign of repentance at any time during the year: "With regard to the dress and food [of the person who is repentant], [the penitent] is to lie in sackcloth and ashes."[86] Here we are reminded of Jesus' warning: "Woe to you, Chorazin! Woe to you, Bethsaida! For if the deeds of power done in you had been done in Tyre and Sidon, they would have repented long ago, sitting in sackcloth and ashes" (Luke 10:13).

The early Christian welcoming of the natural world into its common life included the work of artists. Consider the late-second-century catacombs of Priscilla in Rome, which includes a variety of images: a shepherd with sheep and goats, birds singing in trees, peacocks strutting, trees filled with greening leaves and buds, vases filled with fruits, loaves of bread, a whale with the prophet Jonah, and a mother with her newborn infant. One interpretation suggests that these images were intended to focus one's attention on heaven as an Edenic paradise or as signs of the resurrection to new life, an interpretation focused on the future.[87] After all, the catacombs formed a vast

[85] The Spanish nun, Egeria, in her fourth-century travel memoir, indicates that incense was used at Sunday evening vespers in the Anastasis, the Church of the Resurrection, in Jerusalem: "Censers are brought in so that the whole basilica of the Anastasis is filled with incense." *Pilgrimage* II.1, in *The Pilgrimage of Egeria*, trans. Paul F. Bradshaw and Anne McGowan (Collegeville, MN: Liturgical Press, 2018).

[86] Tertullian, *On Repentance*, IX, in *The Ante-Nicene Fathers: Fathers of the Second Century*, ed. Alexander Roberts, James Donaldson, and A. Cleveland Coxe, trans. Sydney Thelwall (Buffalo, NY: Christian Literature Publishing, 1885).

[87] Sandro Carletti, *The Catacombs of Priscilla*, trans. Alice Mulhern (Vatican City: Pontifical Commission for Sacred Archaeology, 1982).

network of tombs for Christians who placed their hope in "the resurrection of the dead and the life of the world to come."[88] Another and compelling interpretation suggests that these images presented early Christians as a community marked by generous hospitality (meal scenes), peace and safety in the midst of a violent culture (a praying woman, mother and infant, rescue scenes), and trust in the crucified and risen Christ as guardian and guide in this world (a young shepherd carrying sheep or goat),[89] an interpretation focused on the present.

The flowing water of a river, scented olive oil, a cup of milk mixed with honey, leavened bread, a cup of wine mixed with water, an offering of cheese and olives, roses and lilies, fragrant incense, ashes, pomegranates and almonds, floral crowns, gathering at sunrise and sunset, a shepherd carrying a baby goat, trees filled with greening leaves: does this look like an earth-escaping, matter-degrading practice? No, not at all. What we witness in the practice and art of early Christians is an *ecophilic* spirit marked by love for the things of this earth, a love shaped by Jesus, the material presence of God in the world. Indeed, it was his presence in the natural world of the Galilee and his affectionate regard for creation that soon flowed into early Christian practice. At the heart, then, of Christian faith and life was the conviction that the risen Christ, the first fruits of creation,[90] was with the assembly through the gifts of the created world, the One whose earth-embracing Presence would come to be called the Mystery of the Incarnation, God with the world in the flesh.[91]

[88] *Roman Missal*, Creed.

[89] Graydon F. Snyder, *Inculturation of the Jesus Tradition: The Impact of Jesus on Jewish and Roman Cultures* (Harrisburg, PA: Trinity Press International, 1999), 91–98.

[90] 1 Cor 15:23.

[91] John 1:14.

Part Two

3

Benedict of Nursia: Prefer Nothing to the Love of Christ

Born into a wealthy family in Nursia,[1] Benedict was sent to the Eternal City as a young man to receive a liberal education.[2] From his Rule written later in life, we gain the impression that he was an avid reader of the Bible. And yet at the time he was studying in Rome, the emerging capital of the Christian West, not a single school was devoted to the study of sacred Scripture.[3] Did such a lacuna in Christian education distress the pious student from a small provincial town? Benedict's biographer, Gregory, is silent on the matter. He does make clear, however, that Benedict was disgusted with his fellow students: all males from elite families who engaged not in study but in debauchery—young men, "masters," who were quick to command the servants who waited on them.

[1] Modern Norcia, some 110 miles north by northeast of Rome.

[2] Gregory the Great (540–604), monk, bishop, and Benedict's hagiographer, writes that Benedict left his parents for "liberalibus litterarum studiis." *Dialogues: Tome II*, ed. Adalbert de Vogüé, OSB, trans. Paul Antin, OSB, vol. 260 in *Sources Chrétiennes* (Paris: Éditions du Cerf, 1979), II.1.1.

[3] In 535, thirty years after Benedict's departure from Rome, a monk, Cassiodorus, wrote to Agapetus, bishop of Rome, urging him to establish a school where the Christian Scriptures could be studied: "I was sad that the Divine Scriptures had no public teachers . . . I urged Agapetus to collect subscriptions [donations] and establish Christian schools in the city." Peter Llewellyn, *Rome in the Dark Ages* (New York: Praeger, 1971), 33. Despite Cassiodorus's plea, however, no teachers were engaged and no school was founded.

What Gregory does not mention is that the church in Rome had become thoroughly Romanized after Christianity was made the state religion in 381.[4] "As Rome turned ever more Christian, the Church turned Roman." [5] Indeed, the church had become quite wealthy, "its economic interests wed to those of the great landholding families . . . and the hierarchy of the Church [had] been penetrated by educated patricians and by intellectuals linked to their circles."[6] Did the opulence of the newly constructed basilicas as well as the imperial and political trappings of the senior clergy meet with Benedict's skepticism? And what of the nasty rivalry between candidates who were vying for the office of bishop?[7] Was Benedict reminded of Jesus' admonition to his disciples who sought worldly positions of honor: "The kings of the gentiles lord it over them; and those in authority over them are called benefactors. But not so with you; rather, the greatest among you must become like the youngest and the leader like one who serves" (Luke 22:25-26).

[4] The Christian emperor, Theodosius (347–395), with his co-emperors Gratian and Valentinian II, issued the decree *Cunctos populous*, "To all the people," in February 380. This decree of fewer than two hundred words significantly influenced the Western church for the next fourteen hundred years because it made Nicene Christianity the one legitimate religion of the Roman Empire. See "Theodosius I (379–395) on Catholic and Heretic," in *Documents of the Christian Church*, 4th ed., ed. Henry Bettenson and Chris Maunder (Oxford: Oxford University Press, 2011), 23.

[5] Richard Krautheimer, *Rome: Profile of a City, 312–1308* (Princeton: Princeton University Press, 2000), 39.

[6] Krautheimer, *Rome*, 39.

[7] In November 498, the archdeacon Symmachus was elected Rome's bishop at the church of St. John Lateran. On the same day, a rival candidate, the archpriest Laurentius, was elected bishop at the church of St. Mary Major. Reports of violent clashes between the supporters of the two clerics and their use of disinformation made for high tension in the city. See Jeffrey Richards, *The Popes and the Papacy in the Early Middle Ages, 476–752* (London: Routledge and Kegan Paul, 1979), 55–99.

"Abandoning his literary studies," writes Gregory, "and leaving behind his home and family inheritance, he sought to please God."[8] Having cast aside his social status, wealth, the possibility of marriage and children, and what would have been a promising secular career, Benedict walked into the valley of Sublacus within the Simbruini Mountains, what Gregory called a lonely wilderness some forty-five miles east of Rome.[9] There he became a hermit, living in a cave within the rock face of Mount Taleo, above the Anio River. His sudden departure from Rome brings to mind the immediate withdrawal of the first followers of Jesus from their labor as fishers: "[Jesus] said to them, 'Follow me, and I will make you fish for people.' *Immediately* they left their nets and followed him" (Matt 4:19-20, emphasis added). Divesting himself of social privilege, Benedict's vocation began to emerge in the cave, hidden from the world.[10] In the Subiacan Valley, he experienced solitude,[11] temptation,[12] and threats to his life for his fidelity to God.[13] And there he eventually welcomed those inquirers who were attracted to him and his way of life.[14]

[8] *Dialogues* II.1.1.

[9] Present-day Subiaco received its name from the Latin *Sublaqueum*, "under the lake," a reference to the damming of the Anio River (in Italian, Aniene) by the emperor Nero, who desired artificial lakes next to his summer villa.

[10] The cave, the Sacro Speco, is surrounded by a monastic complex dating to the twelfth and thirteenth centuries.

[11] Gregory, *Dialogues*, II.1.1.

[12] Gregory notes that Benedict was tempted to lust after a woman, that is, to objectify and use another human being for one's personal pleasure (*Dialogues*, II.2.1–5)

[13] The lazy and corrupt monks of Vicovaro attempted to poison him (*Dialogues* II.3.1–13); the priest Florentius sought to poison him (*Dialogues* II.8.1–3) and sent naked dancers to tempt him (*Dialogues* II.8.4–9).

[14] Gregory writes that Benedict's reputation for holy wisdom spread afar, and pious families in Rome began to send their sons to join him (*Dialogues* II.3:14). In time, Benedict established twelve monasteries in the Subiacan Valley, with twelve monks in each monastery: note the biblical allusion to the twelve disciples (*Dialogues*, II.3.13).

His sojourn in what Gregory called a *deserta*, a deserted place, was not without precedence in biblical and early Christian history. In the wilderness, Moses received the divine name and his vocation to lead his people out of slavery under pharaoh.[15] Once freed from their cruel masters in Egypt, the Hebrews traveled through the desert region of the Negev for some forty years.[16] Having escaped from the homicidal Queen Jezebel, the prophet Elijah found refuge in a deserted place where, outside a rocky cave, he received his commission from God.[17] The prophet John lived in the wilderness and from there came to the Jordan River, where he baptized Jesus.[18] After his baptism, Jesus was driven by the Holy Spirit into the wilderness, where he was tested.[19] In a deserted place, Jesus fed a large and hungry crowd, an event inspired by God's feeding of the starving Hebrews in the wilderness.[20] And in a desolate place, Jesus was crucified.[21] In imitation of Jesus' repeated withdrawals to deserted places to pray, Antony, the progenitor of monastic life in Egypt, withdrew to an empty fort in the wilderness and lived there in solitude for some twenty years.[22]

At some distance from the life of village or city, with its many voices tugging for one's attention, the wilderness becomes a place of revelation in which God speaks; a place of refuge in which one can become invisible; a place of solitude, prayer, and refreshment; and certainly a place in which one can receive a calling, a new direction to take in one's life. Thus, one antidote to the overwhelming power and frequent distrac-

[15] Exod 3.
[16] Num 14:1-34.
[17] 1 Kgs 19:1-18.
[18] Mark 1:1-11.
[19] Mark 1:12-13.
[20] Mark 6:30-44; Exod 16.
[21] Mark 15:22.
[22] St. Athanasius, *The Life of St. Antony*, trans. Robert T. Meyer (Westminster, MD: Newman Press, 1950), 30.

tion of modern social media and urban noise is entering a *deserta*, a place of silence and solitude, so that one's own voice and the voice of God might be heard. Indeed, psychologists and spiritual directors indicate that the increasing use of social media, earbuds, and loud sounds in urban and suburban areas accelerates biological and psychological damage to humans and other creatures.[23] Was Benedict's withdrawal from urban life also a withdrawal from its noise and its many competing distractions? His distance from clamorous urban life and his experience of silent solitude in the Subiacan Valley thus stands within a larger tradition of temporary separation from the commotion of this world's kingdoms, a practice exemplified by Moses, Elijah, John the Baptist, Jesus, and Antony.

Jesus Christ the Monk

In Benedict's life, we witness the call to follow Jesus. In the history of early monasticism in the West, this following was called the *sequela Christi*, the "going after" Christ, being led by Christ, and imitating the life of Christ. Jesus left his home in Nazareth. He was baptized in a river and then entered the wilderness, where he was offered the power and status of this world's kingdoms, yet refused them. He gathered disciples into his movement. He claimed no possessions or property and renounced the temptation to seek material prosperity. He frequently conversed with his heavenly father in an uninhabited place. He embodied humility, being down to earth, and

[23] Joanna Silberner, "A Healthy Dose of Quiet," *Scientific American* 330, no. 5 (May 2024): 58–65; Andrew B. Newberg et al., "Effect of a One-Week Spiritual Retreat on Dopamine and Serotonin Transporter Binding: A Preliminary Study," *Religion, Brain & Behavior* 8, no. 3 (March 2017): 265–78; for the history of silence in the Christian tradition and monastic silence in particular, see Diarmaid MacCulloch, "The Triumph of Monastic Silence," in *Silence: A Christian History* (New York: Penguin, 2013), 53–104, with attention to Benedict in 92–95.

hospitality, serving those in need.[24] He prayed in one garden before his arrest and crucifixion and was raised to life in another one. Note the significance of the landscape: river, wilderness, deserted place, mountainside, and garden. In these significant moments of Jesus' life, the natural world was not mere backdrop but served as a prominent actor.

Consequently, we recognize that Benedict saw in Jesus the model for his life. Indeed, Jesus exemplified virtues and practices fundamental to Benedict's vision of monastic spirituality: leaving one's home and place of privilege; entering the wilderness (a rocky, forested ravine); creating monastic communities; praying with others and in solitude; renouncing all claims to personal property and possessions in a community of equitable sharing; leading a life of humble service to other monastics; and offering hospitality to strangers, pilgrims, and the poor.[25] At times, the parallels between the life of Jesus and the life of Benedict are striking, though we should recognize that Gregory clearly sees Benedict's life as an imitation of Christ's. As the distinguished scholar Jaroslav Pelikan points out, Benedict and his monks came to see Jesus as the ideal monk and thus patterned their lives after his. At the same time, they slowly but surely transformed the image of Jesus into that of a monastic: the monk who presided over Christian faith and life in the West for close to a thousand years.[26]

[24] The root of humility is *humus*, the dark, organic soil of the earth. To be humble is not to be subservient or sheepish but rather to know oneself as a creature—not the Creator—who is grounded in the soil along with all other creatures.

[25] Dariusz Kasprzak, OFM Cap, "Monastic Exegesis and the Biblical Typology of Monasticism in the Patristic Period," *Theological Research* 2, no. 1 (2014): 98.

[26] Jaroslav Pelikan, "The Monk Who Rules the World," in *Jesus Through the Centuries: His Place in the History of Culture* (New Haven: Yale University Press, 1985), 110. Concerning one thousand years: from the third century with the origins of monasticism in Egypt's desert to the thirteenth century with the emergence of urban, mendicant orders. For this image,

We find a similar regard for Jesus the monk in early medieval Ireland and Britain—in particular, the seventh-century monastic commentary on the Gospel of Mark. Written perhaps by an Irish abbot for his monks,[27] *The First Commentary* claimed that monastic life was an imitation of the life of Christ and that Christ was the ideal monk:

> The monastic life . . . represented the apex of Christian aspirations in the Insular world.[28] For nearly all, it must have seemed the surest road to salvation. . . . Commenting on Mark 1:45 ("but he was in the desert places") the first Markan commentator writes:
>
> > Certainly Jesus was not made known to all those who in wide-open places serve their own praises and wishes. However, he does show himself to those who go out into the desert places which the Lord chose for prayer and for feeding the people, who forsake the love of the world and who give up everything they possess so that they may say, "The Lord is my inheritance" (Ps. 119:57).[29]

Notice that the commentator highlights prayer and feeding people, *ora* and *labora* (prayer and work), as the primary marks of Jesus and the monastic life. And consider the commentator's allusion to Jesus' exhortation: "If any want to become my followers, let them deny themselves and take up their cross and follow me. For those who want to save their life will lose it, and those who lose their life for my sake, and for the sake of

---

see also Columba Marmion, OSB, "The Following of Christ," *Christ: The Ideal of the Monk* (Brewster, MA: Paraclete Press, 2014; 1926), 23–42.

[27] See *The First Commentary on Mark: An Annotated Translation*, trans. and ed. Michael Cahill (New York: Oxford University Press, 1998), 4–7.

[28] Insular: a reference to the Irish and British islands.

[29] Cahill, *First Commentary on Mark*, quoted in Michael W. Herren and Shirley Ann Brown, *Christ in Celtic Christianity: Britain and Ireland from the Fifth to the Tenth Century* (Woodbridge, England: Boydell Press, 2002), 141.

the gospel, will save it. For what will it profit them to gain the whole world and forfeit their life?" (Mark 8:34-36). For those attracted to the monastic life, the *sequela Christi* was amply guided by the gospels, guided by Christ, the first monk, who went out into deserted places to commune with God and offered the bread of life to the hungry.

Of course, other figures came to represent the monk: Adam and then Eve, living in Paradise and serving as the gardeners of God's creation; the prophet Elijah, who separated himself from the world and was noted for his prayerful dependence on God; John the Baptist in the wilderness, eschewing material gain, a sort of spiritual "wild man" living on honey and locusts; and the first community of Christ's followers in Jerusalem who, according to Luke, were steadfast in communal prayer and shared all things in common so that no one was in need. In these biblical figures, Benedict and his followers found inspiring and challenging models for their way of life.[30] Yet none of them eclipsed Jesus, who captured the imagination of the student, hermit, monk, and abbot from Nursia.

Christ in the Rule

Having established twelve monasteries in the Subiacan Valley, Benedict moved in 525 to a deserted mountaintop close to the town of Casinum, overlooking the Valle Latina, some seventy miles southeast of Subiaco. Over a four-year period, he established a monastery on the mountain plateau. Again, we recognize the significance of the natural location in which Benedict and his monks lived, for the mountain was considered a place of meeting and revelation. At Mount Horeb, Moses

[30] Concerning the early and medieval use of biblical models for monastic life, see García M. Colombàs, "Bibbia e monachesimo," in *Dizionario degli Istituti di Perfezione*, vol. I, ed. Guerrino Pelliccia and Giancarlo Rocca (Rome: Edizioni Paoline, 1974), 1448–58.

encountered God and God's passion for those who suffer under tyrants in the kingdoms of this world.[31] At Mount Sinai, God's covenant with the Hebrews was sealed with Ten Commandments and a meal.[32] At an unnamed hillside in the Galilee, Jesus offered his Sermon on the Mount, a teaching which influenced Benedict and monastic leaders in the Latin West.[33] On Mount Tabor, the disciples encountered the transfigured Christ.[34] On the hill called Golgotha, Jesus met his death,[35] and on a Galilean mountain, the risen Christ commanded his followers to go out into the world, teaching, baptizing, and thus making disciples in all nations.[36] On the acropolis of Casinum, Benedict found refuge and, as Gregory notes, a place in which the presence of God was manifested in Benedict's power over sickness, hunger, dissimulation, and death.[37] It was here in 529 that he began to write a *regula*, or rule, that would come to shape monastic and church life in Western Europe for the next seven hundred years.

At the beginning of the Rule, wherein he sets forth his vision of monastic life, Benedict invites the reader to take up obedience to our "true King, Christ the Lord."[38] One is called to pray

[31] Exod 3.

[32] Exod 19.

[33] Matt 5–7.

[34] Matt 17:1-8.

[35] Mark 15:21-24.

[36] Matt 28:16-20.

[37] Gregory's narrative includes stories of Benedict healing a boy from leprosy (*Dialogues* II.26), trusting God's provision of grain and olive oil in a time of famine (*Dialogues* II.21, 29), recognizing monks who failed to keep monastic practice (*Dialogues* II.18, 19, 20), and raising a boy from death (*Dialogues* II.11).

[38] RB Prol. 3. "Lord (*Dominus*) clearly refers to Christ, as it often does in RB even when it is used alone. Although it cannot be held that every appearance of *Dominus* in RB refers to Christ, nevertheless that is the case throughout the Prologue." Terence Kardong, OSB, *Benedict's Rule: A Translation and Commentary* (Collegeville, MN: Liturgical Press, 1996), 9.

to Christ before every good work,[39] listen for the voice of Christ speaking,[40] embrace the gospels as the guide for one's life,[41] translate Christ's teaching into action,[42] praise the Lord who is working in and through one's life,[43] and share in the sufferings of Christ so as to dwell in his kingdom.[44] Benedict is less inclined to invoke the name of the Person of the Trinity whom Jesus called father; rather, the Rule has a distinctly Christological tone. Indeed, Benedict writes, "prefer nothing to the love of Christ."[45]

When he mentions Christ, Benedict draws on a variety of images that reflect his early medieval cultural and religious context. He speaks of Christ as the Lord (*dominus*), thus underscoring his recognition of Christ's divinity and that he alone is One who guides Christians in their spiritual journey: no other "lord" can claim this role. In contrast to *The Rule of the Master*, which refers to Jesus nineteen times as king (*rex*),[46] Benedict employs the metaphor only four times. No doubt the inspiration for this image was Jesus' preaching of the kingdom or reign of God, his primary message; his preaching focused not so much on a place or location but rather the experience of God guiding or ruling one's life. Indeed, Benedict speaks of the kingdom of God as a metaphorical tent in which the monk, nun, and oblate offer praise for the grace of Christ working in them.[47]

[39] Timothy Fry, OSB, ed., *The Rule of Saint Benedict in Latin and English with Notes* (Collegeville, MN: Liturgical Press, 1981), Prol. 4.

[40] RB Prol. 19.

[41] RB Prol. 21.

[42] RB Prol. 35.

[43] RB Prol. 30.

[44] RB Prol. 50.

[45] RB 4.21.

[46] *The Rule of the Master* (RM) antedates Benedict's Rule. Contemporary scholarship suggests that Benedict borrowed heavily from and revised RM for his own purposes. See Kardong, *Benedict's Rule*, 26, and RB 79–83.

[47] RB Prol. 22, 29.

Another rich metaphor, this one from the world of herding, draws our attention to Jesus, who is quoted in the Gospel of John saying, "I am the good shepherd" (John 10:11). Such an image was not lost on Benedict, for he was familiar with its various meanings. The shepherd was the one who cared for the sheep, a prized animal in Mediterranean cultures. The shepherd lived with the sheep, day in and day out. The shepherd, male or female, guided the sheep to pastures where they grazed on grass, clover, and herbaceous flowering plants. The shepherd tended to the wounds of the sheep, released them when they were caught in a thicket, and sought and found them when they went astray: "Which one of you, having a hundred sheep and losing one of them, does not leave the ninety-nine in the wilderness and go after the one which is lost until he finds it?" (Luke 15:4). Given that sheep tend to be docile creatures, they often were attacked by more powerful predators: birds of prey, wild dogs, feral hogs, wolves, and jackals. Thus, the shepherd spent considerable energy on protecting the sheep: "I am the gate. Whoever enters by me will be saved, and will come in and go out and find pasture. The thief comes only to steal and kill and destroy" (John 10:9-10).

It might seem reasonable that modern readers, unfamiliar with shepherding, would dismiss the image as antiquated or simply sentimental—fluffy lambs on Easter cards—and yet the image of the shepherd came to symbolize the political leader or ruler who governed a region or nation: "[God] chose his servant David, / and took him from the sheepfolds; / from tending the nursing ewes he brought him / to be the shepherd of his people Jacob, / of Israel, his inheritance. / With upright heart he tended them, / and guided them with skillful hand" (Ps 78:70-72). Here we encounter the notion that the ruler or governor has responsibility for the people and that the leader's care for the people will be judged by the degree to which the leader sees to their welfare, ensuring that they have the basic elements needed to live. No wonder, then, that the prophetic voice was heard when the monarch—the political leader—abused his or her authority, overlooked the good of the people, or produced their misery: "Ah, you shepherds of Israel who have been feeding yourselves! You eat the fat . . . but you do not feed the sheep. You have not strengthened the weak, you have not healed the sick, you have not bound up the injured, you have not brought back the strayed, you have not sought the lost, but with force and harshness you have ruled them" (Ezek 34:2, 3-4). To anyone in the world today who has suffered under incompetent or injurious leadership, the ancient critique can seem freshly alive.

In his Rule, Benedict employs the image of the shepherd as an apt metaphor of the abbot. There are the sarabaites who have no shepherd: "They pen themselves up in their own sheepfolds, not the Lord's. Their law is what they like to do, whatever strikes their fancy."[48] And then there are the cenobites "who belong to a monastery, where they serve under a rule and an abbot."[49] Benedict speaks of the monastic community as a *grex*, a flock, whose souls are entrusted to the care of the *pastor*, the shepherd.[50]

He also notes that "Christ is the sole master of his flock. He therefore has plenary authority over [the abbot]."[51] Consequently, the abbot-shepherd will be held accountable for the monastic community: "Let the abbot always remember that at the fearful judgment of God, not only his teaching but also his disciples' obedience will come under scrutiny. The abbot must, therefore, be aware that the shepherd will bear the blame wherever the father of the household finds that the sheep have yielded no profit."[52] The shepherd bears responsibility for the

[48] RB 1.8.

[49] RB 1.2.

[50] RB 2.32.

[51] André Borias, OSB, "Le Christ dans la Règle de Saint Benoit," *Revue Bénédictine* 82 (1972): 122.

[52] RB 2.6-7.

flock in the same way that a parent bears responsibility for the welfare of the household. Thus, Benedict writes that "the abbot must always remember what he is and remember what he is called, aware that more will be expected of a man to whom more has been entrusted. He must know what a difficult and demanding burden he has undertaken."[53]

Benedict stands within the biblical and historical tradition that employed the image of a shepherd as a way of describing persons who are charged with caring for others. That care, however, was met with a high degree of accountability to Christ, the One who called the flock into existence.[54] At the same time, we do well to remember that the use of such an image was made possible by the careful observation of real sheep and their shepherd, the entire tradition grounded in a good measure of animal husbandry. Thus, this particular dimension of the natural world entered into the discourse of Benedictine monasticism and the life of the church for hundreds of years.

The Work of God

In the Rule, Benedict makes clear that ecclesial and monastic life is nourished in common prayer, the Work of God, in praying what has come to be called the Liturgy of the Hours or the Divine Office.[55] The number of times to gather for prayer was inspired by Jewish practice: "The Prophet says: Seven times a day have I praised you. We will fulfill this sacred number of seven if we satisfy our obligations of service at Lauds, Prime, Terce, Sext, None, Vespers, and Compline, for it was of these

[53] RB 2.30-31.

[54] See Borias, "Christ dans la Règle," 122, who notes that in contrast to RM, wherein the abbot has a greater degree of unquestioned authority, Benedict insisted on a delegated authority and accountability to the monastic community.

[55] "Office" from Latin *officium*, a service, ceremony, or duty.

hours during the day that he said: Seven times a day have I praised you (Ps 118[119]:164)."[56] These hours included and still include a selection of psalms, an excerpt from Scripture, a biblical canticle assigned to particular hours, intercessory prayer, and the Lord's Prayer. These seven times of common prayer constituted the *ora*, or prayer, of the monastic community. That Benedict devotes thirteen chapters in the Rule to the Divine Office indicates the significance of this singular dimension of monastic life.

In addition to praying the psalms, Benedict indicates that an Ambrosian hymn should be sung, a reference to the lyrics created by the fourth-century bishop, Ambrose of Milan. Here again Jesus Christ appears, cloaked in images of the natural world. In one of the hymns of authentic Ambrosian origin, he is referred to as the *lucifer*, the bringer of light, who releases the heavens from darkness, an allusion to the morning star who arises just before dawn.[57] This image will appear as the fifth antiphon in the well-known Great O Antiphons of Advent, dating from the sixth century: "O Rising Dawn, Radiance of the Light eternal and Sun of Justice."[58] As natural and metaphysical light, Christ shines in human senses, guides those who are lost, and warms the repentant with forgiveness. Here we find the commingling of the sun's natural light with the light of Christ.[59] But, then, for Ambrose and Benedict, the sun's light is one of *God's* creatures, not simply a celestial object of

[56] RB 16.1-3. Lauds, at first light; Prime, at 6:00 a.m.; Terce, at 9:00 a.m.; Sext, at 12 noon; None, at 3:00 p.m.; and Vespers, at 6:00 p.m. Compline was kept prior to retirement for the night. See RB 8.1-2.

[57] 2 Pet 1:19.

[58] "Magnificat Antiphon for December 21" (the Winter Solstice), in *Benedictine Daily Prayer: A Short Breviary*, 2nd ed., ed. Maxwell Johnson, OblSB (Collegeville, MN: Liturgical Press, 2015), 1337.

[59] *Aeterne rerum conditor* ("Eternal Maker of all things"). Translations of Ambrosian hymns are drawn from Brian P. Dunkle, SJ, *Enchantment and Creed in the Hymns of Ambrose of Milan* (Oxford: Oxford University Press, 2016), 221–24.

scientific inquiry. And the agent of this creation was and is the Word of God revealed in Jesus Christ. From this perspective, the sun and its light appear as a visible sign of the light of Christ, a natural sacrament. In another Ambrosian hymn, Christ is called the bright splendor and perfect morning who floods the earth with light.[60] We cannot help but see the inspiration of the hymn prologue in the Gospel of John at work in these Christological images: "All things came into being through him . . . and the life was the light of all people . . . we have seen his glory, the glory as of a father's only son" (John 1:3-4, 14).

In a hymn appointed for the *hora tertia*, the third hour of common prayer at nine in the morning, Ambrose speaks of the cross as "Christ's triumph," an echo of John's interpretation of the crucifixion as an act of victory over the forces of evil.[61] Christ's ultimate triumph over the powers of diminishment, degradation, and death is now offered through his grace to parish and monastic communities through the sacred mysteries, the sacraments. In yet another hymn,[62] Ambrose directs praise to God and thanksgiving for God's creation. He does not countenance what one discerns in some contemporary forms of Christian rhetoric: that God is present in all things and not greater than all things, that the universe is God. Ambrose was not a pantheist. If anything, he would be a pan*en*theist: God is present to and with all of creation but not restricted by it, thus highlighting both the transcendence as well as the immanence of the divine. He maintains the helpful distinction between the Creator and the creation and yet refuses to separate them. The natural world—sun, moon, stars, clouds, light, and darkness—is the ever-flowing gift of the Triune God. No wonder the call to praise God and give thanks for creation

[60] *Splendor paternae gloriae* ("Splendor of the Father's glory")
[61] *Iam surgit hora tertia* ("Now dawns the third hour").
[62] *Deus creator omnium* ("O God, creator of all things").

begins Morning Prayer as light grows across the sky: "O come, let us sing to the LORD; / let us make a joyful noise to the rock of our salvation! . . . In [God's] hand are the depths of the earth; / [and] the heights of the mountains" (Ps 95:1, 4). Such psalmodic praise is coupled with Ambrosian thanksgiving for Christ, the "Light of light" and the "light's living Spring."[63] Amid the psalms of Israel sung or spoken at each of the seven hours, there is the figure of Christ, the firstborn of all creation and the creator of all things.[64]

What should be noted, furthermore, is that the gathering for common prayer was not determined by a work schedule or the demands of the market but rather by the natural rhythms of the day and the seasons: the rising, zenith, and setting of the sun; the growing and waning of the moon and the darkness of night; the longer hours of daylight in summer and the shorter hours in winter; the solstices and equinoxes that signal the changing seasons of the year and the transformation of air and land. In a way that may be a challenge for contemporary urban dwellers to experience, ancient and medieval Christians were more than familiar with the natural rhythms of each day and of the seasons: one's very sense of time was shaped by terrestrial and celestial movements.

Is it any different today? Are not the feasts and seasons kept by millions of Catholics and other Christians throughout the world formed by earth's natural and changing seasons? Consider the chilling of the air and the dying of summer's greenness in the Northern Hemisphere with the November remembrance of one's beloved dead at All Souls; the return of light amid winter's darkness at the solstice with the keeping of the birth of the Light, Jesus Christ; the cold and frequently cloudy days that accompany the beginning of Lent; the emergence of early green growth with the lambing season at the

[63] *Splendor paternae gloriae* ("Splendor of the Father's glory").

[64] Col 1:15-16.

vernal equinox and the keeping of Easter, the feast of the Lamb; the wheat harvest in late spring and the ingathering of believers at Pentecost; the greatest measure of daylight in June that marks the Nativity of John the Baptist, the one who with the daylight will decrease as the months progress; the flourishing of floral gardens throughout summertime; the ripening of grapes and their harvest in August as the church celebrates the "gathering" of the Mother of God, her assumption into heaven; and the olive harvest at the autumnal equinox with the preparation of sacramental oils.

All these turn toward the birth, public life, death, and resurrection of Jesus Christ, a grace-filled way of keeping time so different from the relentless competition of the market and its addiction to profit and unfettered growth, its division of people into "productive winners" and "unproductive losers." The daily keeping of common prayer thus continues to serve as a time devoted to rest with God, the opportunity to renew one's fundamental identity as a child of God whose value is not in serving the acquisitive god of wealth but as a beloved creature endowed with the image of God. Benedict envisioned a common life of equals in the "tent of the kingdom of God,"[65] guided by a common sharing of all things and nourished by common prayer. Thus daily prayer and labor, *ora et labora*, were attuned to the celestial elements of the sky, drawing one into contemplation of the cosmos: to the changing pattern of light during the day, to the night sky adorned with glittering lights, to the growth and decline of the moon in the course of a month, and to the One who "determines the number of the stars; / [and] gives to all of them their names" (Ps 147:4). For contemporary Christians who labor in "the world," the keeping of daily prayer in some form serves as a potent reminder that one's life flows from and is sustained by the "true light, which enlightens everyone" (John 1:9).

[65] RB Prol. 22.

Water and Garden

Benedict lived the majority of his life in a rural setting, at a distance from city and town life. He was well acquainted with the local ecologies of the Subiacan Valley and the acropolis of Casinum, a familiarity that becomes clear in Gregory's *Dialogues*, his hagiography of Benedict created in the 590s. As a wise and pragmatic reformer of Christian faith and life, Benedict recognized that monastic communities, founded in deserted places, would need to be self-sufficient. Keep in mind that there were no department stores, no grocery chains, and no construction outlets in early medieval Italy. If a monastic community were to survive and flourish, its members would bear responsibility for the basic elements of life: water, food and drink, shelter, light, clothing, medicine, and warmth in winter. As communities in which the sacraments were celebrated, there was need of grain for bread, grapes for wine, olive oil for anointing, water for ablutions, oil for lamps, beeswax for candles, and vellum for texts. Thus Benedict writes, "The monastery should, if possible, be so constructed that within it all necessities, such as water, mill and garden are contained, and the various crafts are practiced."[66]

From this instruction, monastic communities began their engagement with the local ecology, the distinctive natural world in which they set down roots, an engagement that has endured for fourteen hundred years. Let us remember that a monastery might be located in a ravine, on a mountaintop, or in a forest or a remote plain, each location producing its own opportunities and challenges. Consider for a moment the distinctive ecologies in which a number of contemporary monastic communities are located: the sandstone cliffs and ponderosa pine trees of the Chama Canyon in northern New Mexico (Monastery of Christ in the Desert); the low, rolling

[66] RB 66.6.

hills, fertile plains, and many lakes of central Minnesota (Saint John's Abbey and Saint Benedict's Monastery); the viticultural region of California's Central Valley, marked by an abundance of vineyards and wineries (Abbey of Our Lady of New Clairvaux); the forested Camas Prairie of north-central Idaho (Monastery of St. Gertrude); and the tropical region of central Florida, not far from the Green Swamp (St. Leo Abbey). Benedict lived in a rock cave on Mount Taleo, established twelve monasteries in the lush Subiacan Valley, built a monastic complex on a barren acropolis overlooking the fertile Latin Valley, and offered advice on the establishment of a monastery at Terracina along the Mediterranean coastline, each ecology different than the others.

The need for water, paramount among all creatures human and otherwise, drew monastic communities to rivers and springs: Sta. Scholastica by the Anio in Subiaco, Montecassino by the Liri in Casinum, San Vincenzo by the Volturno in Molise, Sta. Maria by the Farfa in Rieti, Sacra di San Michele by the Doria Riparia in Sant'Ambrogio di Torino—to name a few. Indeed the quest for a regular supply of water often determined where a monastic community would be established. No water, no life. Consequently, the flow of water into the community frequently determined the spatial ordering of the monastic complex and became the means through which an apparently deserted site could be transformed into a garden, an orchard, a grain field, or a vineyard.[67] The absolute need for water and its many uses—from washing and cooking to ritual ablutions and sprinkling—entered the life of the monastic community: water as a gift from God,[68] that assuages

[67] Weiqiao Wang and Jiang Feng, "Water as a Common Reference for Monastic Lives and Spaces in Cistercian and Han Buddhist Monasteries," *Frontiers of Architectural Research* 12, no. 1 (February 2023): 86.

[68] Gen 1:9-10.

thirst,[69] produces growth in fields and sustains creatures,[70] provides a home for fish,[71] cleanses what is dusty or dirty,[72] and refreshes what is dry.[73] It is a living thing, filled with life-giving energies that sustain metabolism, photosynthesis, and respiration.

In his critical study of water use in early medieval Italy, Paolo Squatriti notes that Benedictine communities built aqueducts when their water source was at some distance from the monastery.[74] They created channels for the water to enter holding cisterns, from which it would then flow through pipes to the kitchen, lavatory, entrance to the oratory, and infirmary.[75] Concerns about wasting water led monks and nuns to recycle it: water used for cooking or handwashing was then used to flush refuse out of the latrines.[76] Water was guided using gravity to the mill, where its pressure turned the wheel that ground grain into flour for daily bread and eucharistic bread. In some monasteries, large tanks were built underground to hold water in the event of a drought. A fountain, laver, or cistern provided

[69] John 4:7. Let us note the skepticism with which some early medievals viewed drinking water—thus the preference for wine, as noted begrudgingly by Benedict in RB 40.6.

[70] Ps 104:10-13.

[71] Gen 1:21.

[72] Gen 18:4; John 13:5.

[73] Isa 44:3.

[74] Paolo Squatriti, *Water and Society in Early Medieval Italy, AD 400–1000* (Cambridge: Cambridge University Press, 1998), 20–21.

[75] "The sick may take baths whenever it is advisable, but the healthy, and especially the young, should receive permission less readily" (RB 36.8). Kardong and Squatriti note that the aversion to bathing found in other monastic rules stemmed from the widespread Greek and Roman practice of public bathing in the nude as a form of socializing and personal pleasure. Benedict has no axe to grind on bathing: it can be helpful for one's health.

[76] Squatriti, *Water and Society*, 33–34. See also Lawrence Wright, *Clean and Decent: The Fascinating History of the Bathroom and the Water Closet* (New York: Viking Press, 1960), 24–32.

water for floral beds and medicinal herbs. Cisterns external to the monastery collected rain and snow for the irrigation of crops and orchards.[77]

Historians of the medieval period note that due to their self-sufficiency, monastic communities became expert in the use of water and made advances over what they had inherited from Roman water systems. At the same time, monks and nuns had access to the biblical and patristic commentaries on water and recognized its symbolic significance, something that can be easily overlooked when scientific analysis becomes the sole frame of reference for engaging a natural element of the earth.[78] Benedict writes that "the abbot shall pour water on the hands of the guests, and the abbot with the entire community shall wash their feet,"[79] a practice inspired by the hospitality of Abraham and Sarah and the humble act Jesus offered his disciples.[80] Here the image of Jesus the servant is invoked, the One who did not come to be served but rather to serve others.[81] Indeed, Benedict grounds monastic hospitality and service to the poor and pilgrims in this saying recorded in Matthew:

[77] For a detailed study of monastic water systems from the early to the high Middle Ages, see Roberta J. Magnusson, *Water Technology in the Middle Ages: Cities, Monasteries, and Waterworks after the Roman Empire* (Baltimore: Johns Hopkins University Press, 2001).

[78] Cardinal Walter Kasper, "The Symbol of Water in the Biblical, Patristic, and Liturgical Tradition," in *The Adriatic Sea: A Sea at Risk, A Unity of Purpose*, ed. Neal Ascherson and Andrew Marshall (Athens: Religion, Science and the Environment, 2003), 159.

[79] RB 53.12-13.

[80] When three visitors approach Abraham, he says to them, "My lord, if I find favor with you, do not pass by your servant. Let a little water be brought, and wash your feet, and rest yourselves under the tree" (Gen 18:3-4). In John's account of the Last Supper, he writes that "Jesus . . . got up from supper, took off his outer robe, and tied a towel around himself. Then he poured water into a basin and began to wash the disciples' feet and to wipe them with the towel that was tied around him" (John 13:3, 4-5).

[81] Mark 10:45; Matt 20:28; Luke 22:27; John 13:14-15.

> "'I was thirsty and you gave me something to drink, I was a stranger and you welcomed me'. . . . Then the righteous will answer him, 'Lord, when was it that we saw you . . . thirsty and gave you something to drink? And when was it that we saw you a stranger and welcomed you?' . . . And the king will answer them, 'Truly I tell you, just as you did it to one of the least of these who are members of my family, you did it to me.'" (Matt 25:35, 37-38, 40)

In Matthew's gospel, Jesus invites his disciples to offer "a cup of cold water to one of these little ones" (Matt 10:42), a practice continued in the monastery with care for kitchen servers, the sick, and the poor. The call to serve each other in the monastery was no small thing: recall that persons from positions of social privilege and accustomed to being waited on by servants entered a community in which their status was turned on its head, where they were drawn to serve others, including those who in the dominant society were believed to be of much lower social status. The call to serve others was thus an instance of status reversal: something of considerable challenge to those who ordered the allegedly "lowly" others around: "The brothers should serve one another."[82] Slaking the thirst of someone in need; giving a cup of cold water to the sick or poor: What did Benedict call the monastery and monastic life? "A school for the Lord's service."[83]

Of course water is needed for the growth of creatures and crops. Consequently, Benedict mentions the need for water and for a garden in the same instruction. With no grocery stores or food delivery services, the monastic community needed to grow or gather its food supply, as well as medicinal herbs and

[82] RB 35.1.

[83] RB Prol. 45. Kardong notes that *dominici schola servitii* ("school of the Lord's service") denotes the Lord's service to his followers as well as "mutual aid, [for] mutual service is the primary way cenobites serve the Lord." *Benedict's Rule*, 22.

flowers used in the infirmary to treat the sick or injured. And yet we rarely find gardens enclosed solely within the monastery: grain fields, vineyards, orchards, and larger garden plots were established outside the monastic complex. Indeed, "garden" could serve as a term for fields, vineyards, or orchards.

The modern words "*garden*" and "*yard*" are descendants of the Indo-European *gher*, an "enclosure."[84] A garden was and is a space enclosed or set apart for cultivation. Indeed, we know that gardens have been in existence for close to twenty-three thousand years, with the earliest evidence found along the Sea of Galilee.[85] Benedict inherited a rich tradition of gardening from Mesopotamian, Israelite, and Roman horticulture, though we need to point out that his proposal for a monastic garden had more to do with subsistence gardening—the cultivation of vegetables, fruits, flowers, and herbs to feed a family or monastic community from day to day and week to week. He was, no doubt, mindful of the gardens mentioned in the Bible:

The *first* garden, planted by God, "a well-watered place," filled with trees containing various fruits: "The Lord God planted a garden in Eden, in the east. . . . A river flows out of Eden to water the garden, and from there it divides and becomes four branches" (Gen 2:8, 10).

A *royal* garden, prominent in elite, monarchical societies in which the wealthy had sufficient resources to hire gardeners: "[King] Ahab said to Naboth, 'Give me your vineyard, so that I may have it for a vegetable garden, because it is near my house' " (1 Kgs 21:2).

[84] Robert Claiborne, *The Roots of English: A Reader's Handbook* (New York: Times Books, 1989), 111.

[85] Ainit Snir et al., "The Origin of Cultivation and Proto-Weeds, Long Before Neolithic Farming," *PLoS One* 10, no. 7 (July 2015), accessed July 4, 2024, https://journals.plos.org/plosone/article?id=10.1371/journal.pone.0131422.

A *lover's* garden, in which spouse and espoused, beloved and lover meet: "Awake, O north wind, and come, O south wind! Blow upon my garden that its fragrance may be wafted abroad. Let my beloved come to his garden, and eat its choicest fruits" (Song 4:16).

A garden of *prayer* and *betrayal* experienced by Jesus the night before his crucifixion: "[He] went with them to a place called Gethsemane; and he said to his disciples, 'Sit here while I go over there and pray. . . .' [Then] Judas, one of the twelve, arrived; with him was a large crowd with swords and clubs" (Matt 26:36, 47).[86]

A garden of *new life* where the risen Christ appears to the Magdalene: "Mary stood weeping outside the tomb. As she wept, she bent over to look into the tomb. . . . she turned around and saw Jesus standing there, but she did not know that it was Jesus. Jesus said to her, 'Woman, why are you weeping? Whom are you looking for?' Supposing him to be the gardener, she said to him, 'Sir, if you have carried him away, tell me where you have laid him, and I will take him away.' Jesus said to her, 'Mary!' She turned and said to him in Hebrew, 'Rabbouni!' (which means Teacher)" (John 20:11, 14-16).

As noted in the Rule, a garden was needed to provide food, herbs, and flowers for the monastic community. By necessity, however, monastics' skill in gardening increased as communities grew in size and responded to the needs of pilgrims and the poor, who saw the monastery as one of the few places of refuge and healing in a chaotic era. The idealized plan of the ninth-century Monastery of St. Gall indicates medicinal herb, vegetable, fruit, and cloister gardens.[87] In addition, then, to its

[86] John 18:1 refers to this place as a garden.

[87] Walter Horn and Ernest Born, *The Plan of St. Gall: A Study of the Architecture and Economy of, and Life in, a Paradigmatic Carolingian Monas-*

practical use as a source of food and medicine, the garden came to be a place where, in imitation of Jesus, members of the monastic community could pray. And then, in the allegorical interpretation of the Song of Songs, two very human lovers came to represent the spiritual union of Christ and the soul (*anima*).[88] Thus, the cloister garden, reserved for members of the monastic community with no mundane distractions, served as a site in which monk or nun could contemplate the presence of the divine lover in the soul.

Benedict knew well the natural world in which he lived during his sojourns in the Subiacan Valley and on the acropolis of Montecassino.[89] He recognized that monastic prayer as set forth in the Rule is guided by the natural cycle of the day and of the earth's seasons. His pragmatism led him to recognize the need for water, mill, and garden. Gregory's life of the hermit and monastic leader narrates frequent encounters between Benedict and the elements of the natural world: water, olive oil, grain, bread, wine, birds, rain, rivers, lakes, and mountains.

At the same time, the figure of Jesus Christ was prominent in his life. The Rule is suffused with the presence of the One who is Lord, shepherd, and servant. He speaks of monastic life as a school for the Lord's service, a continuation of Jesus' life of care for others. He invites his followers to sing Ambrosian hymns in which Christ is portrayed using images drawn

---

tery, trans. Charles W. Jones, 3 vols. (Berkeley: University of California Press, 1979), I.14.7. For a more recent study of the monastery and its garden inventory, see Barbara Schedl, *Der Plan von St. Gallen: Ein Modell europäischer Klosterkultur* (Vienna: Böhlau Wien, 2014), 123–24.

[88] For Bernard of Clairvaux's interpretation of the text, see *Sermons on the Song of Songs*, 4 vols., trans. Kilian Walsh, OCSO, and Irene M. Edmonds (Collegeville, MN: Liturgical Press, 1971–80); concerning Bernard's emphasis on Christ and the soul, see E. Ann Matter, *The Voice of My Beloved: The Song of Songs in Western Medieval Christianity* (Philadelphia: University of Pennsylvania Press, 1992), 123–50.

[89] See Samuel Torvend, *Monastic Ecological Wisdom: A Living Tradition* (Collegeville, MN: Liturgical Press, 2023), 53–74.

from the natural world: the bright splendor of the morning, the "Light of light," and the "living Spring."

In these various ways, Benedict created the matrix that would enable his followers to engage and honor the natural world as God's first gift of grace created through the Word of God,[90] "the firstborn of all creation,"[91] and the gatherer of all things in heaven and earth.[92] While Benedict held to a high Christology, one that emphasized the divinity of Christ, he considered the monastic community an earthly and very human embodiment of Christ's presence, a presence he wrote that could also be discerned everywhere in creation. No wonder he offered his followers this advice: the love of Christ must come before all else.[93]

[90] John 1:3.
[91] Col 1:15-16.
[92] Eph 1:10.
[93] RB 4.21.

4

The Venerable Bede: A Sun to Illuminate the Whole Earth

Over one hundred years after the death of Benedict, a young boy named Bede was offered as an oblate to the monastery of St. Peter's at Monkwearmouth on the River Wear, not far from the coastline of northeastern England.[1] St. Peter's was founded in 674 by Benedict Biscop, an Anglo-Saxon monk who was strongly influenced by the Rule of Benedict. In 684, Benedict established a second monastic house, St. Paul's, a few miles north of St. Peter's in the village of Jarrow. The two houses eventually became the double monastery of Monkwearmouth-Jarrow. Bede's name—*Baeda* in his native tongue—reflects his Anglo-Saxon heritage, a name that means "to bid, encourage, or command." Beginning his monastic life in Monkwearmouth, Bede moved to the monastery at Jarrow where Ceolfrith was the abbot and served as one of his mentors.

In a world that had no internet, telephone, postal service, or reliable transportation system, the expansion of Benedictine life from Montecassino in central Italy to northeastern England, fifteen hundred miles apart, might seem miraculous. One either walked or a rode a mule to travel that long distance. But then it is helpful to remember that Benedict's monks and nuns constituted a stable and self-sufficient community, capable of living

[1] The name of the site is a mouthful: it refers to the monastic house (Monk) where the river (Wear) opens (Mouth) into the North Sea.

in remote areas with little external support. Gregory of Rome, both monk and pope, was well aware of the strength found in a monastic community that was anchored apart from urban life. In 594, he sent a group of monks led by Augustine, a Benedictine, to plant the seeds of Christian faith and life in England. From Augustine's monastery in southeastern England, monastic life spread slowly northward, from Canterbury to Ely, Peterborough, Ripon, and then to the kingdom of Northumbria, home of the double monastery at Monkwearmouth-Jarrow. Elements of Benedictine life began to shape the Christian spirituality of the English: a liturgical practice marked by simplicity and a lack of ostentation; the contributions of the musical and visual arts to common prayer; a love of Scripture, learning, and the natural world; a strong emphasis on community; the practice of daily prayer and *lectio divina* among the laity; and the election of monks as bishops.[2]

Wide Learning with No Censorship

Bede benefited from the labors of his abbot, Benedict Biscop, who created a substantial library for the monastic community.[3] On his second journey to Rome, Benedict purchased over two hundred books that included Bibles, liturgical texts, classical works, patristic writings, and secular studies ranging from astronomy to medical science as practiced by the ancient Greeks and Romans. On subsequent trips to the Eternal City, he continued to purchase books for the monastic library and, in doing so, created the largest library in Anglo-Saxon England.[4]

[2] In the sixth and seventh centuries, Irish monks traveled from their native island to present-day Scotland, England, and Wales in what historians call the Hiberno-Scottish Mission, establishing monastic houses in Iona, Lindisfarne, Melrose, and Whitby, among others.

[3] Lorraine H. Olley, "Benedict Biscop: Benedictine, Builder, Bibliophile," *Theological Librarianship* 7, no. 1 (January 2014): 34–36.

[4] Michael Lapidge, *The Anglo-Saxon Library* (Oxford: Oxford University Press, 2006), 30.

Contemporary readers do well to pay attention to this collection: it was not a library devoted only to religion. Rather, it included a vast repository of knowledge: in Benedict's mind there was no need to exclude or censure works that did not bear an explicitly Christian stamp. He did not reduce learning to biblical texts (a temptation among some present-day Protestants) or to magisterial texts (a temptation among some present-day Catholics). In this regard, he expressed the Benedictine penchant to learn *widely* from all academic disciplines, allowing secular and religious works to be in conversation with each other.

We should not overlook or diminish the significance of this commitment to expansive learning. As a young monk, Bede lived and studied in a community where biblical texts mingled with scientific texts, something unheard of in various forms of contemporary American religion, especially those that view the Bible as a "scientific" text (something it does not claim for itself). His exposure to wide learning would shape his own study, reflection, and writing. And yet Bede's learning poses something of a challenge to those of us who have been educated in a strictly secular and scientific milieu: as Bede and his confreres studied the natural world with a scientific perspective, they also recognized that same world as a living creation flowing from the hand of the divine Creator—not one without the other. Their attempt at scientific study was thus intended to explore what God continues to create. Bede was possessed of a curious mind eager to study and understand the world in which he lived. What did he say of himself? "It was ever sweet and delightful to me to study, teach, or write."[5]

This "sweet delight" was expressed in various forms of writing. His most famous work is the *Historia Ecclesiastica Gentis Anglorum* (*Ecclesiastical History of the English People*),

[5] Bede, *Ecclesiastical History of the English People*, ed. D. H. Farmer, trans. Leo Sherley-Price, rev. R. E. Latham (London: Penguin, 1991), 329.

completed in 731, in which Bede traced the history of Christianity in England from the third century through the eighth. As a student of the calculation of time, he created two works: *De Temporibus* (*On Time*), completed in 703, an introduction to the calculation of the date of Easter; and a longer work on the same subject, *De Temporum Ratione* (*On the Reckoning of Time*) in 723. Fascinated with the natural world, he created *De Natura Rerum* (*On the Nature of Things*) in 703. Note here that Bede's curiosity led him to write on time and space, two fundamental elements of life. His writings extended to commentaries on biblical books, homilies on the seasons of the liturgical year, Latin and vernacular poetry, instruction for learning Latin, lives of the abbots of Monkwearmouth-Jarrow, and a martyrology. For the ardent student of many disciplines—astronomy, botany, hagiography, history, poetry, and theology—learning widely was a spiritual practice for the glory of God and the enrichment of other human beings. Study and learning were spiritual practices akin to praying the Divine Office or offering assistance to the poor.

In the Midst of Violence, a Benevolent World

Bede lived in a world populated by Angles, Saxons, and Jutes, who had entered and settled in Britain during the fifth century after the Roman legions left the island in the early 400s. Archaeological evidence from the early fifth century indicates the evaporation of Roman culture and the increasing growth of the Anglo-Saxon presence. These northern European tribes brought their religious sensibility to the island named after them,[6] a spiritual tradition frequently at odds with much of ancient and early medieval Christianity.

Consider the Anglo-Saxon gods: Woden, god of war and knowledge; Thunor, god of thunder; and Tiw, god of sky and war. A cousin of the Nordic god Odin, Woden was noted for

[6] England comes from *Ang-land*, "the land of the Angles."

shape-shifting—changing his form into a bird, animal, or reptile in order to observe and sometimes haunt human beings. That the gods could transform themselves into other creatures imbued the natural world with a foreboding energy. Is that eagle just an eagle, or is it a god in hidden form spying on us? And if the gods usually dwelt in the heavens, there were other creatures who contributed to an unsettling experience on earth: mischievous elves, *nicors*—water monsters who lured human beings to death by drowning, and venomous *wyrms*, or worms, who could poison the unsuspecting. Imagine, then, living in a world filled with a chronic fear of supernatural beings. Indeed, fissures, pits, and hollows were thought to be the homes of monsters and wraith-like beings.[7]

When faced with such a threatening presence, the practice of sacrifice emerged as a form of barter with supernatural forces: "We will offer you this animal or human in the hope that our offering will satisfy you and thus curb your threatening presence." Archaeological evidence indicates the pervasive practice of animal sacrifice to placate spirits, monsters, or gods. In his study of horses in pre-Christian Anglo-Saxon society, Chris Fern notes that those animals were killed as offerings to the gods and as companions for dead warlords.[8] Keep in mind that the horse symbolized military violence in Roman Palestine and the humble donkey, ridden by Jesus, served as a sign of peace. There is clear evidence that human sacrifice took place in pre-Christian Ireland and among the Angles and Saxons on the European continent, and there is some evidence of human sacrifice among Anglo-Saxons in Britain, though that claim remains disputed.[9]

[7] Sarah Semple, "In the Open Air," in *Signals of Belief in Early England: Anglo-Saxon Paganism Revisited*, ed. Martin Carver, Alex Sanmark, and Sarah Semple (Oxford: Oxbow Books, 2010), 24.

[8] Chris Fern, "Horses in Mind," in *Signals of Belief*, 130–35.

[9] Hilda E. Davidson, "Human Sacrifice in the Late Pagan Period in North Western Europe," in *The Age of Sutton Hoo: The Seventh Century in North-Western Europe*, ed. Martin Carver (Woodbridge: Boydell Press,

At the same time, there are numerous indications of growing armed conflict as the Anglo-Saxons settled in England. After all, if a community or society worships a punitive or war-like god, such worship will likely shape communal or social practice. In contemporary Western European and North American societies, we find this relationship amply displayed among so-called "Christian Nationalists," who invite people to join an "Army of God," a god of retribution and a movement marked by a belligerent hatred for those who do not conform to the nationalists' notion of what it means to be a "Christian patriot."[10] That the gods of the Anglo-Saxons were war-like inspired a combative regard for others and the ensuing violence of armed aggression. Bloody conflict between these new settlers and the indigenous population as well as among themselves created an atmosphere of dread: with rape, pillaging, and armed conflict came the specter of mutilation and death. Thus, from the fifth century through the seventh, the landscape of Britain was marked by sporadic conflict as Angles, Saxons, and Jutes fought and settled on the island. In light of shape-shifting, harmful monsters, and venomous creatures, the need to placate capricious forces with animal and human sacrifices, and the threat of death due to war, the world seemed to be far from a benevolent and stable home. It was within this chaotic milieu that monastic communities were established and offered another and starkly different vision of life on earth.

In the fifth century BCE, the Sicilian philosopher Empedocles wrote that the world is constituted of four basic "roots"

1992), 338. Davidson notes that sacrificial victims were drawn from criminals, prisoners of war, and slaves, and that human sacrifice as a form of placating the gods took place when natural disasters (e.g., drought, famine, plague) or human disasters (massive deaths during armed conflict) occurred.

[10] Note the description of "patriotic" worship services in Andrew L. Whitehead and Samuel L. Perry, *Taking America Back for God: Christian Nationalism in the United States*, rev. ed. (New York: Oxford University Press, 2020), 1–3.

or elements: fire, earth, water, and air.[11] His claim for these elements was drawn from observation: fire, associated with the sun and lightning; air, breathed by all living things; water surrounding the land and flowing from springs; and the earth and soil, on which humans lived and from which food was collected or cultivated. The Scientific Revolution of the eighteenth century questioned and then expanded exponentially the four elements of life on earth—think of the periodic table as studied in chemistry classes. Yet the four elements, first posited by Empedocles and then commented on by Aristotle, shaped all subsequent thinking about life and the world for centuries to come in Western societies. For Empedocles, the four roots or elements possessed an active and dynamic nature; they were not inert objects.[12] They interact with one another: air and fire produce heat, and water and earth produce cold. They are the active foundations of the natural world and thus of creaturely life, human and otherwise. In time the four elements were associated with the cardinal directions (fire with the north, water with the south, earth with the east, and air with the west), with the four seasons of the year (spring with air and fire for light and warmth; summer with fire and earth for warmth and growth; autumn with earth and water for soil and cooling; winter with water and air for cold and death), and with the stages of human life (spring with birth and childhood, summer with youth, autumn with adulthood, winter with old age and death).[13]

[11] Richard Janko, "Empedocles, *On Nature* I 233–364: A New Reconstruction of *P. Strasb. Gr.* Inv. 1665–6," *Zeitschrift für Papyrologie und Epigraphik* 150 (2005): 1–26.

[12] In his first mention of the roots or elements, Empedocles gives them the names of Greek deities in order to highlight their active nature: Zeus, god of thunder and lightning, with fire; Hera, goddess of women and childbirth, with earth ("Mother Earth"); Aidones or Hades, god of the unseen world, with air; and Nestis or Persephone, daughter of Oceanus, with water.

[13] The relationship between elements, directions, seasons, and stages of life is seen clearly in the diagram created by Byrhtferth, a monk of

For our ancient and medieval ancestors, the four elements of the cosmos were also present in each and every human being: the air we breathe; the water of our tears, sweat, and saliva; the soil of our flesh; and the fire of our intelligence, and our souls. Thus every human being was a microcosm of the cosmos, a living bearer of the world within one's body. No wonder medieval Christians could speak of a *co-natural relationship* between humans and the world. Imagine that: each human being bears the imprint of the cosmos in their body. Indeed, this was a vision of life in which all things—the changing seasons as well as the passages of life—were united and flowing from the benevolent hand of God the Creator.

Bede received this worldview from his study in the monastic library and from his observation of the world in which he lived. Indeed, in his work *On the Nature of Things*, he writes that "the world is the whole universe, which consists of heaven and earth, grouped together by four elements: fire, by which the stars shine; the air in which all living things breathe; with the waters, which are united by encircling and penetrating the earth; and the earth itself, which is the middle and bottom of the world."[14] In contrast to earlier writers who commented only on the four elements, Bede's approach was novel: from the opening chapter of his work on nature, Bede painted "a sophisticated picture of the relationship between the physics of the material universe and God's creative action."[15] The

---

Ramsey Abbey and a student of Bede's *De Natura Rerum*. See Peter Baker, "Byrhtferth of Ramsey, *De Concordia Mensium atque Elementorum* (*On the Concord of the Months and the Elements*)," accessed February 19, 2025, https://www.babelstone.co.uk/Blog/2008/12/byrhtferths-ogham-enigma.html.

[14] Beda Venerabilis, "De Natura Rerum," in *Corpus Christianorum Series Latina*, vol. 123A, ed. Charles W. Jones (Turnhout: Brepols, 1975), 192.

[15] Faith Wallis, "Bede and Science," in *The Cambridge Companion to Bede*, vol. 17, ed. Scott DeGregorio (Cambridge: Cambridge University Press, 2010), 113–26.

two—scientific observation and theological reflection—went hand in hand. Indeed, for Bede, the Word of God revealed in Jesus Christ was and is the agent of creation: not the violence of war or placating sacrifice but rather constant, loving care.

The Springtime of the World

In Bede's Old English, the word for spring was *lencten*, from which we receive the words "lengthen" and "longer" as well as the word Lent, the Christian season of preparation for Easter. Hipparchus of Rhodes, a Greek astronomer in the second century BCE, wrote a detailed account of his discovery of the equinox, that day on which there is an equal (*equi*) amount of light and darkness (*nox*).[16] That is, the amount of daylight in each day in the Northern Hemisphere begins to *lencten* at the spring or vernal equinox, "vernal" from the Latin *ver* for "greening." For millennia, cultures throughout the Northern Hemisphere marked the emergence of daylight from wintry darkness during what we call the month of March.[17] Indeed, the Romans named March after Mars, the god of war, because during this month, a "battle" or "struggle" took place between darkness and daylight. To Bede, this month was known as *Hrethmonath*: the month (*monath*) of Retha (*hretha*), an Anglo-Saxon goddess of fertility.[18]

We should not underestimate what people experienced in Bede's world during the months of February and March: food stored for the winter was beginning to run low; the threat of

[16] Alexander Jones, "Ancient Rejection and Adoption of Ptolemy's Frame of Reference for Longitudes," in *Ptolemy in Perspective*, vol. 36, ed. Alexander Jones (New York: Springer, 2010), 11–44.

[17] The spring equinox can occur on March 19, 20, or 21 because the calendar year does not exactly match the length of time it takes for the earth to travel around the sun.

[18] Bede, *On the Reckoning of Time*, trans. Faith Wallis (Liverpool: Liverpool University Press, 1999), 53.

chronic hunger was real; with little indoor heating, the freezing cold of Northumbria was an incubator for sickness, especially pneumonia; spending more time indoors accelerated the spread of illness; other than herbal remedies, there was limited or no access to medical assistance; with less daylight, the instances of what we call seasonal affective disorder increased; heavy snowfall made communication and transportation difficult if not impossible. Little wonder, then, that the mere thought of spring prompted a deep longing for light, heat, the greening of the land, and the birthing of calves and lambs. The natural world thus offered the promise of life renewed as crops sown in late autumn began to emerge, as greater warmth produced verdant fields, and as flowers and buds on fruit trees began to appear ever so slowly. It should not surprise us, then, that the month of March was considered the beginning of the new year since it coincided with the beginning of spring and its promise of new life. Indeed, the beginning of the new year that we take for granted—January 1—was not adopted in England and the North American colonies until 1752. For centuries, New Year's Day was observed in March.

For Bede and his monastic community, the Christian story of birth and renewal was rooted in the ancient story of the Hebrews in Egypt and their escape from slavery. Their liberation from pharaonic oppression transformed them into a new community, *a new creation*, that enjoyed freedom under the guidance of God.[19] Their passage through the Red Sea was similar to the passage of a newborn through its mother's birth canal: there was struggle, fear, pain, and finally the birth of a free people. This foundational event in the life of Israel was and is commemorated annually in springtime, during the Jewish month of Nisan, at the feast of Passover: "The Lord said to Moses and Aaron in the land of Egypt: This month [Nisan] shall mark for you the beginning of months; it shall be the first

[19] Exod 12:1-2.

month of the year for you" (Exod 12:1-2). As biblical scholars have demonstrated, the earliest celebration of this feast can be traced to the spring barley harvest and the birthing of lambs, the two forming the context in which the passage from slavery to freedom was celebrated with unleavened bread and roasted lamb. "In Israel, this festival of the land, then, was made to be the bearer of the classic story of the people's identity, the Exodus."[20]

The observance of Passover in first-century Jerusalem was the context in which Jesus shared the final meal of his earthly life; was betrayed in a garden; was arrested, accused, and condemned to death; was executed on the wood of a tree; and was raised to new life. To his early followers, the exodus story resonated with their memory of his final days and what had become their story: new life and light, revealed in the risen Christ, emerging out of the nighttime of humiliation and unjust suffering. The Hebrew word for Passover is *pesach*, which in Greek becomes *pascha*, from which we receive the earliest term for the solemnity of the death and resurrection of Jesus: *pascha*, the paschal feast and mystery. Thus Paul writes: "Our paschal lamb, Christ, has been sacrificed. Therefore, let us celebrate the festival" (1 Cor 5:7-8).

We know that by the second century CE, Christians were keeping an annual festival of the resurrection of Jesus Christ. But here we need to pause to correct a view often held by many Christians and their leaders: that the annual celebration of the death and resurrection of Jesus is nothing more than a return to the past, as if Christians are simply keeping the same old thing each year out of a sense of duty or nostalgia, as if the last days of Jesus are an interesting medieval mystery play to be watched at a safe distance. Instead, the Christian sacramental imagination invites one to recognize that through ordinary means—the proclamation of the Word of God, baptism in the

[20] Lathrop, *Holy Things*, 69.

font, communion with bread and wine as Christ's Body and Blood, and in the shared life of his Mystical Body, the church—he comes to his own in the present moment and invites all to live in the power of his risen life: as salt, yeast, and light in the world—not as a return to the past but rather as an encounter with his living presence in the present as he guides his people into the future. Thus, the second-century bishop, Melito of Sardis, in his epic poem on the paschal feast, presented the voice of the risen Christ speaking directly to the gathered assembly: "Come all families of people. . . . For I am your freedom. I am the Passover of salvation, I am the lamb slaughtered for you, I am your ransom, I am your life, I am your light, I am your salvation, I am your resurrection, I am your King. I shall raise you up by my right hand, I will lead you to the heights of heaven, there shall I show you the everlasting father."[21]

Melito was a Quartodeciman, that is, he and his community celebrated *pascha* on the fourteenth day in the first lunar month of the Jewish new year, the month of Nisan. The fourteenth of Nisan was thought to be the date recorded in John 19:14 when Jesus was crucified, the day when lambs were slaughtered in the Jerusalem temple: "I am the lamb slaughtered for you."[22] But note that the fourteenth of Nisan could be any day of the week.[23] This was in keeping with Jewish Christian practice, a practice, said some Quartodecimans, that was embraced by a number of Jesus' first followers.[24]

[21] Melito of Sardis, *On Pascha*, trans. and intro. Alistair Stewart-Sykes (Crestwood, NY: St. Vladimir's Seminary Press, 2001), 65–66.

[22] Melito, *On Pascha*, 65.

[23] *Quarta* = four, *decima* = ten, thus fourteen.

[24] The fourth-century church historian Eusebius of Caesarea quoted Polycrates, bishop of Ephesus, who claimed that the apostle Philip and the apostle John, "the beloved disciple" of the fourth gospel, kept the festival on the fourteenth of Nisan. See his *Church History*, Book V, chap. 24 in *Nicene and Post-Nicene Fathers*, Second Series, vol. 1, ed. Philip Schaff and Henry Wace, trans. Arthur C. McGiffert (Buffalo, NY: Christian Literature, 1890), 242.

On the other hand, Christians in Alexandria, Rome, and other cities of the Latin West celebrated *pascha* on the first Sunday after the first full moon after the spring equinox. This calculation of the date of *pascha* was approved by the bishops gathered at the Council of Nicaea in 325 CE. Western Christians, many of whom were Gentile converts to the faith and unfamiliar with or hostile to Jewish practice, were inspired by the gospel accounts, all of which indicate that the resurrection took place on "the first day of the week," on a Sunday before sunrise (Matt 28:1; John 20:1). It was this latter practice of keeping the paschal feast on a springtime Sunday close to the vernal equinox that eventually held sway among all Christian communities—but not until the eighth century.

Of particular interest to Bede was the dating and significance of *pascha*, or Easter. For modern Christians who can quickly find Easter's date by checking an online or printed calendar, the securing of the date seems quite simple. For Bede, however, there was neither a committee nor a church agency publishing the date of Easter: it was the work of Christian astronomers and clergy each year to secure the date for the keeping of the most significant event in Christian faith and life—the death and resurrection of Jesus Christ—as well as the other Christian feasts whose dates depended upon the *movable* date of Easter,[25] called a movable feast because the date was tied to a changing lunar cycle.

Bede and other medieval Christians knew this: the gospels indicate that Jesus was arrested, accused, crucified, and raised from death on a day close to the spring equinox and the Jewish celebration of Passover. For Bede, the date of the spring equinox was March 21 and the date of Jesus' death at Passover was thought to be March 25. What has only recently come to light is the first-century Jewish conviction that *the great heroes of Israel*

[25] Ash Wednesday, Palm Sunday, Holy Thursday, Good Friday, the Ascension, and Pentecost.

returned to God on the same date they were sent by God into this world: the date of conception—entering the world of flesh—was also the date of their death.[26] Because the date of Jesus' death was well known—a historical event—one could determine the date of his conception. There was in this conviction a symbolic symmetry. It is for this reason that Christians, since at least the fifth century, have kept the feast of the Annunciation—the angel Gabriel announcing to Mary that she would conceive and give birth to a son—on March 25.

A collection of commentaries on the feasts and seasons of the Christian year, compiled in central England between 850 and 890 CE, includes this earthy view connecting conception and death: "On the twenty-fifth day [of March], Gabriel came to St. Mary with God's message, and on that day, St. Mary became pregnant like the trees when they blossom. . . . And then after thirty-two years and three months, Christ was crucified on the cross on the same day. And as soon as he was on the cross, the creation demonstrated that he was true God: the sun grew black and the day was turned into dark night."[27] Note how the anonymous author weaves together significant events in Christ's life with the renewal of the earth at springtime. Filled with growing life, Mary becomes a blossoming spring tree just as the wood of the tree becomes the cross that bears the body of her beloved son. The earth is potently visible in this story of Christ's life.

If the conception in Mary's womb took place on March 25, nine months of pregnancy would lead to giving birth on December 25. Rather than the oft-heard notion that the celebration of Christ's birth in December was, in its origins, nothing more

[26] Thomas J. Talley, *The Origins of the Liturgical Year* (Collegeville, MN: Liturgical Press, 1991), 91–98.

[27] *The Old English Martyrology: Edition, Translation, and Commentary*, ed. Christine Rauer (Cambridge: Cambridge University Press, 2013), 73–75.

than the Christian "baptism" of "pagan" festivities associated with the winter solstice, the knowledge that Jesus died on March 25, so ancient and medieval Christians believed, made it possible to suggest that his conception was on the same date and his birth was nine months later, close to the winter solstice, the emergence of light amid winter's darkness. What came *first* was the normal course of pregnancy leading to birth. What *followed* this biological reality was the Christian use of solstice imagery to complement what was already revealed in the gospels: "In him was life, and the life was the light of all people" (John 1:4).

The study and celebration of Christ's conception, birth, and death led Bede and others to consider the birth of the world through the work of the Word of God: "All things came into being through him, and without him not one thing came into being" (John 1:3). Keep in mind that March heralded the emergence of springtime life from wintry death and that this month was considered the first of the new year. With other medieval Christians, Bede accepted the idea that March 25 was the last day—the eighth day—on which the created the world came to completion: it was the end of the world's very first week. To modern sensibilities, this may sound quite strange! One might smirk at what appears to be fanciful speculation. After all, hasn't modern science informed us that there is no specific date on which the Big Bang occurred some 13.8 billion years ago, followed by the formation of the earth some 4.5 billion years ago?

For Bede, however, it was of great importance to honor what he considered the masterful way in which the divine Creator brought the universe into existence and continues to sustain it through the changing seasons of the year. From March 25, the last of day of creation, one could then count back to March 18, the first day of the world. The Anglo-Saxon monk and scientist Byrhtferth, in his *Enchiridion* or *Handbook* on the seasons of the year, wrote, "In this month almighty God created the whole of creation, visible and invisible. He said, 'Let there be light,' and it was done. That day was March 18."[28] While the modern mind has no idea of a specific date for the world's birth, such was not the case for Bede and other Anglo-Saxon scientists. They were eager to discover when the wondrous creation of the world took place. Why? So that it could be celebrated with thanksgiving to its Creator. No doubt this reckoning of the world's origin—from the darkness of nothing to the creation of light[29]—corresponded with the emergence of new life and light from winter's cold and darkness during March.

The similarity between the order of creation as found in the book of Genesis and the transition from winter to spring in Northumbria was striking to Bede. On the first day of creation, there was darkness and wind,[30] an apt description of winter in Monkwearmouth-Jarrow. On the second and third days, dry land appeared, followed by its greening with vegetation,[31] what Bede and his monks experienced in springtime. And, then, on the fourth day, God created the sun, the moon, and the stars.[32] Of singular importance to Bede was this fourth day, for without sun and moon, it would be impossible to keep time, to have any sense of the passage from day to night, week to week, or month to month. But there was more: in the imagined week of God's creation of the world, this fourth day was March 21, the spring equinox, when daylight began to overcome the darkness of winter. Consider Bede's interpretation of the fourth day:

[28] Byrhtferth of Ramsey, *Byrhtferth's Enchiridion*, ed. Peter S. Baker and Michael Lapidge (Oxford: Oxford University Press, 1995), 70–73.

[29] "Darkness covered the face of the deep. . . . Then God said, 'Let there be light'" (Gen 1:2, 3).

[30] Gen 1:2.

[31] Gen 1:9-13.

[32] Gen 1:14-19.

> It was fitting that just as the Sun at that point in time first assumed power over the day [on the spring equinox], and then the Moon and stars power over the night, so now, to connote the joy of our redemption, day should first equal night in length, and then the full Moon should suffuse [the night] with light. This is for the sake of a certain symbolism, because the created Sun which lights up all the stars signifies *the true and eternal light which enlightens everyone who comes into the world,*[33] while the Moon and stars, which shine, not with their own light, but with an adventitious light borrowed from the Sun, suggest the Body of the Church. In the celebration of the supreme solemnity [of Easter], it was necessary that Christ precede the Church, which cannot shine save through him.[34]

We return again to the conviction held by Bede and early medieval Christians that the earth and its seasons flow from the skillful hand of the Measurer of All Things—a popular Anglo-Saxon name for the Triune God. In his experience of the four seasons, the solstices and equinoxes, and the growth of light and life in springtime, Bede recognized the presence of Christ. The light shines in the darkness, wrote John,[35] the darkness of winter yielding to the light of spring when the "supreme solemnity" of the paschal feast is celebrated, when earth's renewal becomes a sign of that great day when Christ, "the firstborn of all creation," will restore all things,[36] and when night and death shall be no more.[37] "Bede argues that it's fitting that Christ's act of redemption should be linked to the spring equinox . . . and that it should be in the spring, when life returns to the earth. It is, in every sense, the perfect time."[38]

[33] John 1:9.

[34] Bede, *On the Reckoning of Time*, 25–26.

[35] John 1:5.

[36] Col 1:15.

[37] Rev 21:25.

[38] Eleanor Parker, *Winters in the World: A Journey through the Anglo-Saxon World* (London: Reaktion Books, 2022), 119.

The Redeemer of Middle Earth

For those who are familiar with J.R.R. Tolkien, the Oxford professor of Anglo-Saxon and English Language and Literature, and his famous works, *The Hobbit* and *The Lord of the Rings*, the term "Middle Earth" may well ring a bell. Popularized by Peter Jackson's film trilogy, one might assume that Tolkien created the mythical land called Middle Earth. And yet the term appears in early medieval Anglo-Saxon literature and in Bede's history of Christianity in England. At the conclusion of his monumental work, Bede appended the story of an illiterate cowherd named Caedmon who was inspired to sing a song of his own creation in Old English verse. "What should I sing about?" asked Caedmon of the angel who appeared in a dream and invited the young man to sing. "Sing about the Creation of all things," came the reply.[39] In his singing, Caedmon created the earliest recorded poem in the English language:

> Praise we the Fashioner now of Heaven's fabric,
> The majesty of his might and mind's wisdom,
> Work of the world-warden, worker of all wonders,
> How he the Lord of Glory everlasting,
> Created first for the race of men Heaven as a roof tree,
> Then made he Middle Earth to be their mansion.[40]

The Old English word for "creator" is *scyppend*, "the one who shapes things." For Caedmon and Bede, "the Fashioner of Heaven's fabric" created the dwelling place for all creatures—"Middle Earth"—that bears signs of the divine presence, written as it were in sun, moon, stars, seasons, soil, water, air, fire, flora, and fauna. How interesting that the Old English word for poet—*scop*—shares with *scyppend* a common root in *scp*: the Worker of all Wonders seen as a great poet with creation as his

[39] Bede, *Ecclesiastical History*, 248.
[40] Bede, *Ecclesiastical History*, 248–49.

sublime masterpiece. For Bede, the Fashioner, world-warden, wonder worker, and creator of Middle Earth was the Word of God, Jesus Christ. In the Greek of John's gospel, the Word is *logos,* the rational principle through which the creation is ordered and the personified Wisdom of God: "When [the Lord] marked out the foundations of the earth, then I [Wisdom] was beside him, like a master worker" (Prov 8:29-30). No wonder early medieval artists portrayed Christ holding an architect's compass, a gardener's trowel, or a measuring scale as he looks over the earth.

While some popular interpreters view the fourth gospel as a witness to the relationship between God and the individual or Christ and the soul, a closer reading of this text, so prominent in Bede's Christology, says otherwise. For John does not depart from his inspiration—the first chapter of Genesis—but presupposes it when he writes, "In the beginning . . . All things came into being through [the Word]" (John 1:1, 3). John's term for "all things" is the Greek *panta,* the entire creation, not only human souls. John does not circumscribe the activity of the Word of God, for he goes on to write that the Word "was in the world, and the world came into being through him" (John 1:10). John's term for "world" is *cosmos*—"God so loved the *cosmos* that he gave his only Son" (John 3:16). Thus Caedmon's Fashioner of Heaven's fabric and the creator of Middle Earth can rightly be called the cosmic Christ. Of him, Bede wrote: "On seeing the world which Jesus made, and the signs with which he has filled it, we should say that he is truly the [One] who fills the world with his divinity, the world made by him; that he came to his own creation . . . to renew the world which he had made; that he is in the world, by his divine presence, with his own [creatures] for all days."[41]

[41] Bede, "Sermon II.2 in Lent," in *Bede the Venerable, Homilies on the Gospels: From Lent to the Dedication of the Church,* trans. Lawrence T. Martin and David Hurst, OSB (Kalamazoo, MI: Cistercian Publications, 1991), 21.

Bede held the world to be the good creation of the Word and Wisdom of God. At the same time, he believed that the presence of evil in the world diminishes and disfigures creation and its creatures, including humans. In the Night Office, commonly called Compline, sung in monastic houses, one could hear this admonition from Scripture: "Be sober, be watchful. Your adversary the devil prowls around like a roaring lion, seeking someone to devour. Resist him, firm in your faith."[42] The devil, or *diabolus*, from the Greek *diabollein*, is the one who "tears apart" or "breaks into fragments"—an action associated with the lioness felling its prey. In the first letter of Peter, we find the presence of disfigurement and death symbolized by a predator.

Bede knew of this large and muscular cat from his study of Scripture and early Christian writings: the lion is associated with the house of Judah[43] and in one instance with Jesus Christ.[44] In the second century CE, it was associated with the evangelist Mark, whose gospel begins with the "crying out" of John the Baptist like a "roaring" lion in the wilderness.[45] In Anglo-Saxon and Norman churches, the lion was depicted as a fearsome animal ready to devour its victim: indeed, at some church entrances, the lion is holding a victim in its jaws! Carved lions at church doors depict martyrdom or the sacrifices experienced by those who are faithful to Christ and his nonviolent manner of life.[46] One is mindful of the early Chris-

[42] 1 Pet 5:8-9a, in "An Order for Compline," in *The Book of Common Prayer* (New York: Oxford University Press, 1979), 132.

[43] Gen 49:9.

[44] Rev 5:5.

[45] Jerome, *Commentary on Matthew*, trans. Thomas P. Scheck (Washington, DC: Catholic University of America Press, 2008), 55.

[46] *The Symbolism of Churches and Church Ornaments: A Translation of the First Book of the Rationale Divinorum Officiorum of William Durandus*, intro. and trans. John M. Neale and Benjamin Webb (London: Gibbings, 1906), ci. Richard Strake, "The Lion in Christian Iconography," in *A Guide to Christian Iconography: Images, Symbols, and Texts*, accessed September 11, 2024, https://www.christianiconography.info/lions.html.

tian martyr, Ignatius of Antioch, who pleaded with the Christians in Rome not to intervene on his behalf as he prepared to die in the imperial coliseum for his refusal to abandon his loyalty to Jesus Christ: "Let me be fodder for wild beasts—that is how I can get to God. I am God's wheat and I am [about to be] ground by the teeth of wild beasts to make a pure loaf for Christ."[47] In his homily for the Easter Vigil, Bede speaks of evil as the lion, a menacing force "who brought sin into the world" and "whose roaring surrounded us and sought out from among us someone it might cause to perish."[48]

In the Night Office, Christians have prayed this promise for centuries: "[The Most High] will command his angels concerning you / to guard you in all your ways. / On their hands they will bear you up, / so that you will not dash your foot against a stone. / You will tread on the lion and the adder, / the young lion and the serpent you will trample under foot" (Ps 91:11-13). The promise to tread on the lion was fulfilled, said Bede, in the public ministry, death, and resurrection of Jesus Christ: he began the process of dismantling the disfiguring and death-dealing power of evil in the world. An early artistic depiction of Christ treading the lion is found in the archbishop's chapel at Ravenna, in which a clean-shaven Jesus, holding a cross over his shoulder, has planted his feet on the heads of a lion and a dragon. In the tenth-century Anglo-Saxon gospel book of the Duke of Arenberg, we find the same image in a miniature painting.[49]

In counterpoint to the fragmenting power of evil in life, Bede preached that "the unspotted Lamb came among us and for us."[50] Let us pause and ask: Isn't this an odd image? A lamb,

[47] Ignatius of Antioch, "Letter to the Romans," in *Early Christian Fathers*, ed. Cyril Richardson (New York: Simon and Schuster, 1995), 104.

[48] Bede, "Sermon II.7 The Easter Vigil," in *Bede the Venerable, Homilies on the Gospels*, 66.

[49] E. Baldwin Smith, *Early Christian Iconography and the School of Ivory Carvers in Provence* (Princeton: Princeton University Press, 1918), 154–55.

[50] Bede, "Sermon II.7 The Easter Vigil," 66.

less than a year old, as the redeemer of Middle Earth? One might rightly expect an Anglo-Saxon warrior to lead the heavenly host into battle, but a lamb? Of course Bede knew well the story of the escape from Egyptian slavery, an exodus that was marked by the killing of lambs so as to sprinkle their blood, a sign of God's protection, on Hebrew doorposts and lintels. And he knew that the springtime commemoration of that escape was kept with the killing of lambs and their consumption by the children of Israel in the Promised Land during the festival of Passover. He knew that in John's gospel, John the Baptist refers to Jesus as the Lamb of God and that the wounded and slain yet living Lamb is at the heart of the book of Revelation, the center of its worship. But a young lamb as the One who undoes the damage inflicted on earth's creatures by a ravaging lion? How could the apparent weakness of a lamb overcome the fierce power of a predator?

In her remarkable study of contemporary American fundamentalist interpretations of the book of Revelation, Barbara Rossing makes clear that this apocalypse, this unveiling, has nothing to do with predicting future events, with discerning who's in and who's out in God's future, or with weapons of war.[51] Rather, her engaging and careful discussion reveals that the lamb embodies something quite different than the stereotype of the fierce alpha male ready to crush his enemies in combat. Instead of this conventional and pervasive view, so prominent in much of American culture, Revelation invites the Christian to consider an alternative: the power of nonviolence and self-giving love that marked the attitude of Jesus, the Lamb of God, in his public ministry toward those who were most vulnerable in society, those who were considered powerless or inferior by religious leaders and the lords of em-

[51] Barbara R. Rossing, "Lamb Power," in *The Rapture Exposed: The Message of Hope in the Book of Revelation* (New York: Basic Books, 2004), 107–13.

pires. It is the slain lamb who is raised by God into new life, a new life that makes possible nonviolent and loving lives for those who follow the Lamb of God. "We have to look at *the subversive heart* of this book—the redefinition of victory—to understand how it subverts violence itself. Just like the Lamb, God's people are called to 'conquer' not by fighting but by remaining faithful, by testifying to God's victory in self-giving love."[52]

In his homily for the Paschal Vigil, Bede welcomed the paradox of God's power manifested in weakness: "It was the unspotted Lamb who gave his blood . . . and by undergoing death he condemned the sovereignty of death forever. . . . The Lamb brought to naught the lion that had brought sins into the world. It was the Lamb who restored us . . . and put the sign of his death on our foreheads in order to ward off the weapons of the death-bearing enemy."[53] In this Easter homily, Bede clearly offered an alternative to a culture that normalized armed aggression, disfigurement, and death. Those who follow the Lamb do not take away life: they accept the call to support and renew life with self-giving love. Thus he preached that the Lamb of God is the One who "cast down the opponent of our freedom and peace."[54]

But there is more: "He, the Lamb of God, consecrated for us, even before we were created, the spiritual food of life in which we are refreshed."[55] What does the Lamb of God offer in the Mass but his very presence and his power to live as people who reject violence and pursue peace, as people whose lives are marked by self-giving love, by sacrifice for the sake of others? "Let us strive, dearly beloved, to lay hold of these

[52] Rossing, "Lamb Power," 111.

[53] "On our foreheads," a reference to baptismal anointing, in Bede, "Sermon II.7 The Easter Vigil," 66.

[54] Bede, "Sermon II.7 The Easter Vigil," 66.

[55] Bede, "Sermon II.7 The Easter Vigil," 67.

mysteries by the interior love of our mind, and always to grasp them by living them."[56] Here Bede does more than present a lovely idea: he offers a challenging way of living in the world from day to day, a way of living nourished by Christ's Body and Blood. Here, then, the Redeemer of Middle Earth is the One who renews the whole creation with his blood, what all Jews at the time of Jesus understood to be the life force animating all creatures. Indeed, where there is blood, there is life.

In the ninth century, a monastic scholar of St. Gall with the unusual name of Notker the Stammerer wrote admirably of Bede using solar symbolism: "God, the orderer of natures, who raised the Sun from the East on the fourth day of Creation, has made Bede rise from the West as a new Sun to illuminate the whole Earth."[57] Although Notker's praise of Bede may tend toward the hyperbolic, it nonetheless suggests that Bede was known in monastic circles on the European continent some two hundred years after his death. Notker used the image of the sun to describe a monk who spent considerable time reflecting on the four elements of the natural world, the changing seasons of the year, the lunar and solar calendars, and how all of these revealed the world-warden, the worker of wonders, the redeemer of Middle Earth: Jesus Christ. In a regional culture that was marked by armed aggression between rival rulers and would soon suffer the imprecations of marauding Vikings, Bede offered an alternative to the violence that stalked the earth: the renewal of life through the refusal of retribution and the offering of self-giving love as seen in the death and resurrection of the Paschal Lamb.

[56] Bede, "Sermon II.7 The Easter Vigil," 67.

[57] As quoted in James Campbell, "Bede," in *The Oxford Dictionary of National Biography* (Oxford: Oxford University Press, 2004), 85. See also Erwin Rauner, "Notkers des Stammlers 'Notati de illustribus uiris,'" Teil I: Kritische Edition, *Mittellateinisches Jahrbuch* 21 (1986): 34–69.

One is then compelled to ask: is this not the springtime for which so many yearn today, the end of retribution as an accepted practice and the birth of forgiveness and enlightened peace?

Bede wrote that the creating Word of God "fills the world with his divinity . . . comes to his own creation . . . and renews the world."[58] At first glance such praise might sound like wishful thinking. In a largely secularized and scientific view of the earth, where do we recognize the signs of his divinity? But Bede encourages us to consider his conviction that the world was and is the wondrous work of "the firstborn of all creation."[59] In the signs of springtime in the Northern Hemisphere, signs planted by the Word of God, one can discern in earth's release from the bonds of winter and the greening of the land the story of Christ's liberation from the darkness of death and his enlightening presence available to all creatures.

[58] Bede, "Sermon II.2 in Lent," 21.
[59] Col 1:15.

5

Walafrid Strabo: God's Gardener

The COVID-19 pandemic forced the vast majority of North Americans into lockdown for a number of months, when only essential workers were allowed to venture out to their jobs. Forced to stay home, many people were inspired to take up gardening. Indeed, seventy-one million households have been counted as gardening households since the pandemic lockdown began in spring 2020, making the United States one of three nations in the world to boast such a statistic, along with Australia and China.[1] Of that number, just half engage in gardening to create a pleasing or beautiful space, while 45 percent—and that number is increasing—grow vegetables, fruits, edible flowers, and herbs. The National Institute of Food and Agriculture reports that there are over eighty-four thousand certified master gardeners in the nation, who offer advice and assistance to the millions of amateurs.[2] Whether for aesthetic or culinary purposes, gardens thrive on apartment balconies, in tiny plots behind townhouses, in house yards, and in the growing number of community gardens throughout North America. Indeed, one could say that gardens and gardening are growing, a claim that rarely makes the headlines, yet one that points to the hard work and rewards of cultivating the soil.

[1] Anthony Mariotti, "Gardening Statistics," accessed October 31, 2024, https://www.rubyhome.com/blog/gardening-stats/.

[2] U.S. Department of Agriculture, accessed October 31, 2024, https://www.nifa.usda.gov/.

A Garden in Eden

Jews and Christians are no strangers to gardens. After all, the first creation story speaks of the earth as God's garden: "God said, 'Let the earth put forth vegetation: plants yielding seed, and fruit trees of every kind on earth that bear fruit with the seed in it.' And it was so. The earth brought forth vegetation: plants yielding seed of every kind, and trees of every kind bearing fruit with the seed in it. And God saw that it was good" (Gen 1:11-12). Reflecting on this global garden, the psalmist praises God the gardener: "You cause the grass to grow for the cattle, / and plants for people to use, / to bring forth food from the earth, / and wine to gladden the human heart, / oil to make the face shine, / and bread to strengthen the human heart" (Ps 104:14-15).

The second creation story describes the home of the primal parents: "The Lord God planted a garden in Eden, in the east; and there he put the man whom he had formed. Out of the ground the Lord God made to grow every tree that is pleasant to the sight and good for food, the tree of life also in the midst of the garden, and the tree of the knowledge of good and evil" (Gen 2:8-9). From this garden there flowed a river, which divided into four streams that watered the earth. The story continues with the call of the primal parents to tend the garden, only to end with their banishment from this idyllic setting for eating what was forbidden: "By the sweat of your face you shall eat bread until you return to the ground, for out of it you were taken; you are dust, and to dust you shall return" (Gen 3:19). While some might be tempted to view gardens solely as places of beauty and retreat, the biblical witness is more realistic: evil seduction and betrayal can readily slither into Paradise.

As he oversaw the construction of the temple in Jerusalem, Solomon created a garden-like structure. The entrance doors were made of cypress wood and carved with palm trees and flowers, while the doors to the inner sanctuary were made of olive wood and carved with botanical images. The inner walls were decorated with cherubim, trees, and many flowers: lilies and pomegranates abounded in the adornment of the temple. In all of this, Solomon intended to construct a new Eden in which God and God's people would meet.[3]

The author of the Gospel of John, reflecting on the second creation story in Genesis, points to Jesus as the vine or tree of life: "I am the true vine, and my Father is the vinegrower. He removes every branch in me that bears no fruit. Every branch that bears fruit he prunes to make it bear more fruit. . . . I am the vine, you are the branches. Those who abide in me and I in them bear much fruit, because apart from me you can do nothing" (John 15:1-2, 5). Note that in this I AM saying of John's, Jesus includes the gardener's labor: God the master gardener prunes and cuts so that more fruit might abound. While this saying offers a metaphor of the relationship between Jesus and his followers, it nonetheless could not be known apart from the careful observation of how one tends to fruit-bearing vines and trees.

Two other gardens became prominent in the Christian tradition. The first was a place of testing, prayer, and trial. Gethsemane comes from the Hebrew term for olive press (*gat shemanim*). In this grove or garden of olive trees, Jesus, Peter, James, and John retreated after their Passover meal, the Last Supper. "[Jesus] said to them, 'I am deeply grieved, even to death; remain here, and keep awake.' And going a little farther, he threw himself on the ground and prayed that, if it were possible, the hour might pass from him" (Mark 14:34-35). It was in this garden that Jesus was betrayed and arrested. And it was in this garden that he rejected any form of violence intended to save his life. Here there was to be no recrimination. At the same time, his desire to pray alone in anticipation of a plot against

[3] See 1 Kgs 6. On the Jerusalem temple as the paradisial garden, see Carol Meyers, "The Temple, Jerusalem" in *Anchor Bible Dictionary* 6, ed. Freedman, 360.

him recapitulated his common practice of seeking a place of solitude to pray before he made a significant decision.

The second garden witnessed his burial and resurrection: "Now there was a garden in the place where he was crucified, and in the garden there was a new tomb in which no one had ever been laid. And so, because it was the Jewish day of Preparation, and the tomb was nearby, they laid Jesus there" (John 19:41-42). Alone among the evangelists, John refers to the place of burial as a garden, a place of cultivation and growth, of life emerging from the darkness of the soil. It is in this garden that Mary Magdalene, grieving the death of Jesus, encounters a stranger: "Jesus said to her, 'Woman, why are you weeping? Whom are you looking for?' Supposing him to be the gardener, she said to him, 'Sir, if you have carried him away, tell me where you have laid him, and I will take him away.' Jesus said to her, 'Mary!' She turned and said to him in Hebrew, 'Rabbouni!' (which means Teacher)" (John 20:15-16). Here the garden is a place of surprising and joyful encounter, a counterpoint to Gethsemane. But there is more: in her meeting with the risen Christ, Mary is commissioned to proclaim the astonishing news of Jesus' resurrection, of his new life, to the other disciples. Little wonder that the early church called her the apostle to the apostles. Thus we can see that the garden becomes a place of both meeting and mission.

We encounter another garden, this one in a dream. In the year 203, Perpetua, a young mother and newly baptized Christian, was arrested for refusing to abandon her loyalty to Jesus Christ. She and her companion, Felicity, were jailed by the imperial magistrate as they awaited death in the arena of Carthage, their home in North Africa. In her autobiographical account, the first extant writing by a Christian woman, she narrates this dream: "I went up [a ladder], and I saw a very great space of garden, and in the midst of it a man sitting, white-headed, in shepherd's clothing, milking his sheep; and standing around in white were many thousands. He said to me: 'Welcome, child.' "[4] This and Perpetua's other dreams served as visions of what would come. In this case, she would be welcomed at death by the risen Christ into a beautiful garden reminiscent of the first Paradise and the garden in which Jesus was raised from death into life.

In these gardens we encounter God the gardener tending the earth at its creation; the home of the primal parents who were instructed to care for Eden; a temple adorned with botanical carvings reminiscent of the first Paradise; the image of Jesus as a fertile vine and tree of life; an olive grove that witnesses prayer and testing; a cemetery garden from which the one who was thought to be dead is raised to new life; and a dream-like paradise that promised union for the martyrs with the shepherd of souls. It would seem that the garden—a place of work and of rest—continued to exert its influence in Jewish and Christian practice, offering a space to grow food and to commune with the divine gardener. Neither of these impulses was lost on monastic communities that, in the early Middle Ages, were known for their gardening expertise.

The Garden in the Rule

In his instruction concerning the monastery's porter, the monk who greets visitors, Benedict also includes this encouragement: "The monastery should, if possible, be so constructed that within it all necessities, such as water, mill and garden are contained, and the various crafts are practiced."[5] As noted earlier, Benedict conceived of the monastery as a place marked by self-sufficiency. It was the monks and nuns who built their shelter; cultivated vegetables, grain, and grapes; and designed water channels for irrigation, bathing, drinking, and cooking.

[4] Jennifer A. Rea and Liz Clarke, "The Passion of Perpetua and Felicity," in *Perpetua's Journey: Faith, Gender, and Power in the Roman Empire* (Oxford: Oxford University Press, 2018), 16.

[5] RB 66.6.

Though Benedict preferred a garden inside the walled community, we know that Benedictine communities were active in the cultivation of fruit orchards, hillside vineyards, vast grain fields, and vegetable and herb gardens. There was in all this a certain pragmatism: a garden was needed to supply produce and medicinal herbs for the community. And this, too: grain for bread and grapes for wine were needed for the celebration of the Eucharist, in addition to serving as staples in the monastic diet.[6]

The well-known ninth-century plan for the monastic complex at St. Gall in northeastern Switzerland presents a number of gardens: an herbal plot set next to a physician's house and pharmacy, a fruit orchard in the monastic cemetery, a large vegetable garden, and cloister gardens.[7] What we discern in this horticultural plan are diverse needs in the monastic community: medicinal herbs used to treat monks and laypeople who were sick; the juxtaposition of monastic graves—the portal to union with the Triune God—and fruit trees, expressing the Christian conviction that out of death, new life bursts forth; vegetable gardens that provided produce for a largely vegetarian diet; and the enclosed cloister garden—the *hortus conclusus*—marked by a flowing water fountain and abundant flowers, with other foliage that served as a symbol of Paradise restored, the flowing water reminiscent of the river in Eden, the Jordan, and waters of the baptismal font: a site devoted to meditation and prayer.

[6] "Two kinds of cooked food, therefore, should suffice for all the brothers, and if fruit or fresh vegetables are available, a third dish may also be added. A generous pound of bread is enough for a day whether for only one meal or for both dinner and supper" (RB 39.3-4); "We believe that a half bottle of wine a day is sufficient for each" (RB 40.3).

[7] For the most comprehensive study to date of the plan for the monastic complex, see Walter Horn and Ernest Born, *The Plan of St. Gall: A Study of the Architecture and Economy of, and Life in, a Paradigmatic Carolingian Monastery*, trans. Charles W. Jones, 3 vols. (Berkeley: University of California Press, 1979).

As a place of food production, monastic gardens grew a wide range of vegetables and fruits, depending on location and climate. These included apples, beans, beets, blackberries, cabbage, carrots, cauliflower, cherries, fennel, garlic, green peas, leeks, lemons, onions, parsnips, pears, plums, radishes, shallots, and turnips. The primary text for the herbal medicines used in early medieval monasteries was the five-volume work *De materia medica* written by the Greek physician, Dioscorides, who served in the Roman imperial army during the first century CE.[8] Translated into Latin, Dioscorides's compendium was used for a thousand years in monastic communities to care for monks and nuns as well as the many laypeople who sought medical attention in a monastery's public infirmary. Among the many herbs and flowers cultivated for medical purposes were betony, chamomile, chervil, lavender, lemon balm, poppy, rose, rosemary, sage, thyme, and yarrow.

Keep in mind that for close to one thousand years, monastic infirmaries were the health centers of medieval Western Europe, hospices where monarchs and farmers alike received medical assistance from nuns and monks who served as infirmarians, nurses, and pharmacists. In these "hospitals," the monastics used herbal, floral, and alcohol remedies to treat sickness, wounds, and disease, and they produced new therapies through experimentation. While the use of herbal medicines went into decline in Western Europe and North America with the creation of synthetic drugs and antibiotics in the late nineteenth and twentieth centuries, there has been a renaissance of their use, albeit with modern scientific analysis. In contrast to the United States, herbal medicines are prescribed frequently in China, France, and Germany, where they undergo strict analysis and testing. That they are still used today in Europe is a testament to their pervasive presence in medieval monastic communities.

[8] Dioscorides, *De materia medica*, trans. Lily Y. Beck (Hildesheim: Olms-Weidman, 2005).

Walafrid Strabo

One of the best-known monastic gardeners was Walafrid, a Swabian from southern Germany, born in 808. He was educated at Reichenau Abbey, a monastery founded in 724 on Reichenau Island in Lake Constance. His Benedictine education led him into monastic life at the island monastery. He then studied at the Abbey of Fulda under the gifted teacher Rabanus Maurus. After spending nine years as tutor to Charles, the son of Louis the Pious, emperor of the Holy Roman Empire, Walafrid returned to Reichenau, where he was elected abbot of the community. It was as abbot and gardener that he wrote *De cultura hortorum*, "On the Cultivation of Gardens," commonly referred to as *Hortulus*, Latin for "a little garden."[9] As abbot, Walafrid did not refrain from working with the soil: he appears to have been an avid gardener. Indeed, his comments on becoming soiled with labor suggest a measure of criticism for his monastic brothers who disdained such "ordinary" work:

> Whatever property one is given in the country, whether it is soft ground or a sandy beach where gravel still lies, or if it has brought about abundant fruits with its fertile moisture, whether set high on steep hills or open to the level plains below or rough with slopes and valleys, it does not refuse to bring forth native produce if only your care is not hindered by heavy lethargy. . . . You must not decline to *blacken your hands* calloused by a hard hoe, nor refuse to *spread dung* from full baskets on the dry dust.[10]

[9] For a helpful introduction to the life of Walafrid, see Wilfrid Blunt's biographical statement in Walahfrid Strabo, *Hortulus*, trans. Raef Payne (Pittsburgh: Hunt Botanical Library, 1966), 1–11. The Payne translation includes the Latin text.

[10] "Walafrid Strabo," in Ronald E. Pepin, trans., *A Benedictine Reader: 530–1530*, ed. Hugh Feiss, OSB, Ronald E. Pepin, and Maureen M. O'Brien (Collegeville, MN: Liturgical Press, 2019), 117; emphasis mine.

We find genuine delight in his commentary on blackening one's hands in the garden, a real affection for growing herbs, fruits, vegetables, and flowers. As a keen observer of nature's seasons, Walafrid notes that when winter, "the savage devourer of our ample toil," is banished by the arrival of spring, the garden, indeed the earth itself, appears restored in its "ancient splendor."[11] With his monastic brother Bede, Walafrid recognized that the coming of spring brought to mind the first life of the world, the celebration of the new year with the spring equinox: herbs and flowers put forth their roots in the earth's bosom, forests display abundant leaves, mountainsides are clothed in grass, and meadows flourish with bright greenness. In what he calls his *parvus campus*, his "little field," Walafrid notes that he must attack nettles and weeds with his hoe so that they do not suffocate the tender, emerging growth.[12] If you are a gardener, does your heart not go out to Walafrid's struggle with the nettles and weeds that choke the life out of the tender shoots? He is no absent supervisor of the garden as was Virgil whose *Georgics* served as some inspiration for *De cultura hortorum*.[13] Walafrid dirtied his hands with soil and dung. He describes the labor of bringing fresh water and dispersing it gently with his palms so that the seeds and sprouts are not washed away by a stronger force. He carefully separates plants that need very little sunlight from those that need an abundance.

The majority of *De cultura hortorum* is devoted to affectionate descriptions of the plants found in Walafrid's small field: sage, an herb rich in virtue; rue, the antidote to toxins and an effective laxative; melon, a luscious delicacy; fennel, mixed with

[11] "Walafrid Strabo," 118.

[12] "Walafrid Strabo," 118.

[13] The classical Roman writer Virgil composed his work on agriculture—*georgica*, or "agricultural things"—during the civil war that witnessed the triumph of Octavian and his accession as Emperor Caesar Augustus just prior to the birth of Jesus in the first century CE.

wine to treat a rasping cough; iris, used to sweetly scent the laundry; chervil, an inhibitor of internal bleeding; the poppy, helpful for stomach ulcers; celery, taken with wine and vinegar for a troubled stomach; and the root of the radish, for controlling a nasty cough. Walafrid writes of herbs mixed with wine, highlighting the ancient and medieval conviction that wine possesses medicinal virtues. His garden included wormwood, otherwise known as absinthe, an herbaceous plant that, when mixed with wine, was believed to aid digestion. Rose wine was used to diminish muscular pain and inflammation.

Toward the conclusion of *De cultura hortorum*, Walafrid speaks of the rose, the lily, and the tender shoot:

> This Germany of ours . . . revives the rose-colored growth of red flowers copiously every year. The blossom [of the rose] is said to surpass all the foliage of the plants in vigor and fragrance so much so that it is deservedly declared to be the Flower of flowers. . . . The renowned lilies oppose their flowers to this plant, and their fragrant scent fills the air even a long way off. . . . Since blessed virginity shines in this flower . . . the lily emits its fragrant scent. Truly, these two illustrious kinds of pleasing flowers signify the greatest victories of the church throughout the ages; the church gathering the offerings of roses in the blood of martyrdom and carries lilies in the splendor of flourishing faith.
>
> O Virgin Mother, in your fertile seed a mother, in your undefiled faith a virgin, a bride for the sake of the Bridegroom; Bride, Dove, House, Queen, Faithful Friend. . . . To you came a flower from the scepter-bearing offspring of Jesse, the sole restorer and founder of ancient stock. He consecrated the pleasing lilies in his words and way of life, coloring the roses by his death. . . . He embraced the virtue of each flower.[14]

We encounter similar imagery in the New Testament in which Jesus identifies himself with an element of creation: "[Jesus]

[14] "Walafrid Strabo," 123–24.

took a cup, and after giving thanks he gave it to them, saying, 'Drink from it, all of you, for this is my blood of the covenant. . . . I will never again drink of *this fruit of the vine* until that day when I drink it new with you in my Father's kingdom" (Matt 26:27-29); "The hour has come for the Son of Man to be glorified. Very truly, I tell you, unless *a grain of wheat* falls into the earth and dies, it remains just a single grain; but if it dies it bears much fruit" (John 12:23-24); "I am *the true vine,* and my Father is the vinegrower" (John 15:1); "Christ has been raised from the dead, *the first fruits* of those who have died" (1 Cor 15:20). Other botanical images cluster around the figure of Jesus: *frankincense* and *myrrh,* the gifts of visitors at his birth (Matt 2:11); the tiny *mustard seed* (Matt 13:31-32); an *imperishable seed* (1 Pet 1:23); *palm branches* (John 12:13; Rev 7:9); the oil of the *olive tree* (Matt 21:1; 26:30); *thorns* and a *reed* (Matt 27:27-30); wine vinegar sprinkled on *hyssop* (John 19:29); the *root* and offspring of David (Rev 22:16); and the *tree of life* (Rev 22:2).

Inspired by scriptural metaphors, Walafrid speaks of the rose and its redness associated with blood and the death of Jesus, the "first" martyr, and the company of Christian martyrs; he speaks of the fragrance of the lily spreading the aroma of faith. As a gardener who carefully observed and cultivated annual plantings, he was clearly familiar with the fertile seed—the image he uses to describe the fertile womb of the Virgin Mary. In this regard, Walafrid does not shy away from speaking about Mary's physicality, drawing a comparison between the nurturing soil of the earth and a mother's womb. There is an earthiness in his writing about Mary and Jesus, something we should expect from a monastic gardener who worked regularly with soil and dung. He does not describe Mary and Jesus as exalted, royal persons, protected from ordinary dirt by dwelling in a faraway heaven. He is not overly concerned with purity and immaculate lives as were later generations. No, this is a mother and a son rooted in earth's soil. Indeed, the comparison of the two wombs—the earth's and Mary's—was not made in a monastic scriptorium, a hall dedicated to creating texts, but rather in close contact with the four elements of water, soil, light, and air; in close observation of the processes of conception, growth, birth, maturation, diminishment, and death shared by all living creatures: humans, animals, and plants.

"To you came a flower from the scepter-bearing offspring of Jesse."[15] One wonders if Walafrid was familiar with the O Antiphons of Advent, refrains that surround the singing of the Magnificat, Mary's Song, from December 17 to 23. On December 19, we hear this antiphon: *O Radix Jesse*, "O Root of Jesse, you stand for an ensign of humankind; before you kings shall keep silence, and to you all nations shall have recourse: Come, save us, and do not delay."[16] Historians of church music suspect that the antiphons originated in Italy during the sixth century while Benedict was alive. The Carolingian cleric Amalarius of Metz, a contemporary of Walafrid's in the ninth century, noted their use during the latter half of the season of Advent.[17]

Step into a good number of European churches today, and one will find the genealogical "tree" of Jesus depicted in stained glass, beginning with Jesse, the father of David, usually positioned in the lowest section, with a number of figures—patriarchs, matriarchs, or prophets—above him, culminating in the Virgin Mary and Jesus Christ. Frequently, Jesse is depicted sleeping with a tree trunk or vine emerging from his side, growing upward: "A shoot shall come out from the stump of Jesse, and a branch shall grow out of his roots" (Isa 11:1). Concerning the spiritual significance of this arboreal image, the contemporary medievalist, Eleanor Parker, writes: "*O radix Jesse* plays with the plant imagery of the 'root,' asking Christ

[15] Walafrid Strabo," 124.

[16] *Benedictine Daily Prayer*, ed. Johnson, 1337.

[17] Fernand Cabrol, OSB, "Avent," in *Dictionnaire d'archéologie chrétienne et de liturgie* I:II, ed. Fernand Cabrol, OSB (Paris: Letouzey et Ane, 1907), 3225.

to help us 'root' and 'ground' our works in him, and talking of how all good things 'spring' from him. . . . Here [the antiphon] refers to the life-giving power of a plant, its healing sap, and the quickening force which runs through all the natural world. It is life in the fullest and most powerful sense—the force of life springing from the stem of Jesse."[18]

"To you came a flower," writes Walafrid, "a flower who embraced the virtue of each flower." To the modern reader, the notion that flowers possess virtues might seem odd if not fantastical. Flowers are used to decorate and enhance birthdays, weddings, anniversaries, and funerals. They may be sweet-smelling and even beautiful, but virtuous? Yet our medieval ancestors remind us that every flower, tree, insect, animal, fish, and bird finds its origin in the benevolent power of God. And thus, as creatures of God, they reflect God's creative genius and serve as signs of God's presence revealed in Jesus Christ, the tender shoot, the rose, and the lily. Close observation of the natural world, something we should expect in an agricultural economy, led medieval Christians to recognize the distinguishing characteristics of flowers, plants, and trees little differently than did Jesus when, in John's gospel, he says: "I am the vine, you are the branches. Those who abide in me and I in them bear much fruit, because apart from me you can do nothing" (John 15:5).

A Botanical Paschal Mystery?

Tucked into a psalm of thanksgiving for God's goodness and steadfast love, we find this comment on the transient nature of life: "As for mortals, their days are like grass; / they flourish

[18] Eleanor Parker, "The O Antiphons as Medieval Carols: O Root of Jesse, O Key of David," *A Clerk of Oxford*, accessed November 25, 2024, https://aclerkofoxford.blogspot.com/2012/12/the-o-antiphons-as-medieval-carols-o.html.

like a flower of the field; / for the wind passes over it, and it is gone, / and its place knows it no more" (Ps 103:15-16). A similar sensibility is found in Job's tense encounter with the Creator: "A mortal, born of woman, few of days and full of trouble, comes up like a flower and withers, flees like a shadow and does not last" (Job 14:1-2). The gardener may spend hours preparing the soil, planting the seed or bulb, keeping predators at bay, and delighting in the growth and beauty of the blossoms, only to see them wither away. The early eighteenth-century hymn "O God, Our Help in Ages Past" captures the same tone: "Time, like an ever-rolling stream, / soon bears us all away; / we fly forgotten, as a dream / dies at the op'ning day."[19] There is loveliness and life as well as diminishment and death in the flower: a realistic view of creaturely life in a culture such as ours that works diligently to deny the reality of diminishment and death.

Walafrid writes, "To you came a flower from the scepter-bearing offspring of Jesse . . . coloring the roses by his death."[20] Close to 85 percent of Americans indicate that the rose is their favorite flower.[21] Indeed, it is the bestseller on Valentine's Day due to the manner in which it is promoted as the flower of romantic love. This notion springs from the ancient Greek myth of Aphrodite, goddess of love, running to assist her lover, Adonis, who was maimed by a boar. In her rush to help him, she pricked her foot on a white rose, which turned red with her blood, the newly red rose now a sign of her ardent devotion to Adonis. If you have ever pricked yourself on the sharp thorn of a rose, you might have a measure of empathy for Aphrodite.

[19] Isaac Watts, "O God, Our Help in Ages Past," in *Gather Comprehensive* (Chicago: GIA Publications, 1994), 614. Watts's hymn is his paraphrase of Psalm 90.

[20] "Walafrid Strabo," 124.

[21] Richard Lutes, "An Enduring American Love Affair," *Produce News*, May 24, 2018, accessed February 19, 2025, https://theproducenews.com/enduring-american-love-affair.

Walafrid takes the reddening of the rose in a different direction when he connects the death of Jesus with the coloring of this flower. In his gospel, John writes that "one of the soldiers pierced [Jesus'] side with a spear, and at once blood and water came out" (John 19:34). For John, the crucifixion was a sign of Jesus' self-giving love for others expressed in the shedding of blood, the color of the red rose. Perhaps Walafrid was also thinking of an early medieval legend that suggested white roses grew at the foot of the cross, roses that turned red when the Savior's blood fell on them. The rose holds together the beauty of the blossom and the danger of its thorns.

In the second letter to Timothy, the author compares the life of faith to a race: "I have finished the race, I have kept the faith. From now on there is reserved for me the crown of righteousness, which the Lord, the righteous judge, will give me" (2 Tim 4:7-8). The race of which the author speaks is an allusion to the Olympic Games of Greece and the crown an allusion to the wreath of laurel leaves that was placed on the head of the victor. The Romans adopted this practice, keeping the laurel crown but also adding a crown of roses. The Roman general who led a great victory in battle received a crown of laurel leaves drawn from the bay laurel tree. During Rome's imperial period when Jesus lived, the emperor, as commander-in-chief of the imperial military forces, reserved for himself a crown or diadem of roses. The emperor was frequently portrayed receiving a crown of roses from the goddess Victoria.[22]

By way of contrast, John narrates the Romans' contempt for Jesus after his arrest and interrogation: "Pilate took Jesus and had him flogged. And the soldiers wove a crown of thorns and put it on his head, and they dressed him in a purple robe. They kept coming up to him, saying, 'Hail, King of the Jews!' and striking him on the face" (John 19:1-3). If we read this passage

[22] A. S. Hooey, "Rosaliae Signorum," *Harvard Theological Review* 30, no. 1 (1937): 15–35.

carefully, we can see that Jesus endured torture at the hands of the Roman army, torture suffused with mockery: although the emperor was crowned with roses, Jesus was crowned with thorns and struck repeatedly on his face. Here, the crown of roses represented the cruelty and injustice of the empire, while the crown of thorns marked Jesus as one who stood in opposition to such violence.

For close to four hundred years, the Christian movement offered a way of life that distinguished its members from the dominant Roman culture: the pursuit of forgiveness and reconciliation in the presence of violence, torture, and retribution; the baptismal welcome into a community of equals in a culture organized into a stratified class structure; abhorrence at the easy and legal taking of life, whether it be a newborn infant, an impoverished and houseless person, or a slave in the coliseum—this disregard for the value of life contrasted with Christian care for abandoned infants, feeding the houseless and elderly infirm, and the incorporation of slaves into the Christian community. Early Christians were regarded with skepticism if not intolerance because of their loyalty to Jesus of Nazareth, crucified by Rome and raised by God to life. By the end of the fourth century, however, the Christian emperor, Theodosius, had transformed this movement into the established religion of the state, and what happened to the image of Jesus? He was crowned with an imperial diadem, his image captured by the establishment.

What, then, is the spiritual significance of this crown of thorns? Is it not that Jesus shares in the suffering of the innocent throughout the world: the millions of migrants forced from their homes due to violence, lack of work, or persecution; the many children born into poverty and hunger; the number of peace-loving civilians caught in wars not of their own making? In his homily on the solemnity of Christ the King, Pope Francis contrasted two ways of life in this world: the use of power to control and conquer others and the exercise of loving action to forgive, restore, and heal: "[Christ's] kingship is paradoxical: his throne is the cross; his crown is made of thorns. . . . The grandeur of his kingdom is not power as defined by this world, but the love of God, a love capable of encountering and healing all things."[23] What does this crown express? Certainly the suffering love of God, but also Christ's alliance with all those who suffer innocently in the world today.

Walafrid inherited another paradoxical image, that of the tree of the cross. Were we to read Mark's account of the death of Jesus, we would hear the anguished cry of loss: "When it was noon, darkness came over the whole land until three in the afternoon. At three o'clock Jesus cried out with a loud voice, 'Eloi, Eloi, lema sabachthani?' which means, 'My God, my God, why have you forsaken me?' . . . Then Jesus gave a loud cry and breathed his last" (Mark 15:33-34, 37). Here we encounter the tree of desolation. John offers a different interpretation: Jesus carries the cross by himself without assistance from a bystander; he offers his beloved disciple as a son to his mother and Mary as mother to that beloved disciple; after receiving a sip of sour wine, he announces that he has completed, "finished," his work as he breathes his spirit into the community of his followers.[24] For John, the tree expresses the victory of Jesus over the powers of evil.

The paradox of the cross—tree of woe and of blessing—was captured in the eighth-century epic poem, "The Dream of the Rood."[25] The rood, or tree, speaks: "I saw the God of hosts sorely stretch out. Darkness covered up with clouds the Creator's corpse, the shining brightness. A shadow went forth,

[23] Pope Francis, "Homily for Solemnity of Christ the King of the Universe and Closing of the Jubilee Holy Year of Mercy," Salt + Light Media, November 20, 2016, accessed February 19, 2025, https://slmedia.org/blog/homily-of-pope-francis-for-solemnity-of-christ-the-king-of-the-universe-and-closing-of-the-jubilee-holy-year-of-mercy.

[24] John 19:30.

[25] Rood comes from the words rod, pole, or crucifix.

wane under the clouds. All creation wept, spoke the king's fall: Christ was on the cross."[26] But then sorrow yields to blissful promise as the tree continues to speak: "On me God's Son suffered a time; thus glorious I now tower under the heavens, and I may heal all."[27] This paradox is captured in the contemporary text created by the Benedictine hymnwriter Delores Dufner: "Faithful cross, O tree of beauty, tree of Eden, tree divine! Not a grove on earth can show us leaf and flow'r and fruit so fine. Gently bearing Jesus' body, tree of life, salvation's sign! . . . Cross of pain transformed to gladness, ever green and shelt'ring tree, symbol once of shame and bondage, now the sign that we are free! Cross of splendor, cross of glory, cross of love's great victory!"[28] There is death and there is life: there is resurrection in the tree.

Medieval Christians knew another story similar to the one we find in medieval dreams and contemporary hymns: the dead wood of the cross becomes a green, life-giving tree when Christ is grafted to it, his blood reviving the wood and transforming it.[29] There is an allusion here to the sign of the cross made on the forehead at baptism and whenever the Holy Trinity is invoked, as well as the chalice of wine-become-blood received during Holy Communion, nourishing and reviving the Christian into greening life, a sign of the resurrection.

A Floral Incarnation

In the early years of the fifteenth century, an anonymous poet created lyrics concerning the rose, a counterpoint to

[26] "The Dream of the Rood," in *Anglo-Saxon Spirituality*, ed. and trans. Robert Boenig (New York: Paulist Press, 2000), 260–61.

[27] "Dream of the Rood," 262.

[28] Delores Dufner, OSB, "Faithful Cross, O Tree of Beauty," in *Pange Lingua Gloriosi: Choral Music for Holy Week* (Portland: Oregon Catholic Press, 2010), no. 22.

[29] George Ferguson, "Tree of Jesse," in *Signs & Symbols in Christian Art* (London: Oxford University Press, 1954), 39.

Walafrid's declaration that a flower came to the Virgin Mary.[30] "There is no rose of such *vertu* / As is the rose that bare Jesu; *Alleluia.* / For in this rose contain-ed was / Heaven and earth in little space; *Res miranda.*"[31] Now keep in mind Walafrid's claim that flowers possess virtues. That word "virtue," *vertu* in Middle English, does not so much signify the purity or pure faith of Mary who entrusted her life to the angel's announcement as it does the power inherent in a flower, plant, or tree. *Vertu* refers to the life-sustaining force or the healing properties within a flower. It can also refer to the divine power present throughout the natural world, as well as in any one of its elements. Eleanor Parker suggests that a better translation would be "There is no rose of such power."[32] Focus your attention on this image in the carol: "In this rose contain-ed was Heaven and earth in little space." Consider, if you will, the tightly arranged petals of a rosebud. The lyric suggests that there is much more than we imagine contained in a very small space. Here, in Mary's womb, heaven and earth meet, the divine and the human commune, the ineffable and the mundane kiss. Now, we might assume that this pertains to Mary alone, and yet the same can be said of each and every Christian, washed in the waters of baptism and nourished with the Body and Blood of Christ: heaven and earth, the divine and human, meet. The tragedy of Christian preaching and catechesis is that they can overlook this conviction: the people of God are the "little space" that contains the presence of the ineffable, the divine.

The use of the rose as a metaphor of the Blessed Virgin Mary dates to the fifth century, if not earlier. Consider the epic poem

[30] "Walafrid Strabo," 124.

[31] Anonymous, "There Is No Rose," in *Carols for Choirs 2*, ed. David Willcocks and John Rutter (London: Oxford University Press, 1970), 190. *Res miranda*: "A marvelous thing."

[32] Eleanor Parker, "Two Carols about Roses," in *A Clerk of Oxford*, December 20, 2012, accessed November 25, 2024, https://aclerkofoxford.blogspot.com/2012/12/two-carols-about-roses.html.

Carmen Paschale ("The Paschal Song"), created by Caelius Sedulius, a Christian Latin poet: "As the tender rose springs up among prickly thorns but does not offend in any way, since its beauty obscures its thorny branches, So holy Mary, the new virgin, descends from the branch of Eve."[33] Perhaps Sedulius was inspired by Ambrose, bishop of Milan, who lived a century earlier: "Mary is the branch, the flower of Mary is Christ, who, like the fruit of a good tree, now flowers [and] bears fruit in us."[34] The floral image becomes a way of speaking about our relationship with Christ, who "flowers" in the lives of the Christian community and "bears fruit in us."

Another medieval lyric speaks of Christ the rose, who appeared as the branch and flower that sprang up in Bethlehem, the place of his birth; who sprang into hell to defeat the fiend's power when he descended to the dead; and who ascended from the tomb into heaven "to be our *bote*," that is, our remedy. The term "remedy" underscores the ability of the flower to contain healing properties. Indeed, the song includes this phrase, "every day [this rose and its remedy] appear in the priest's hand," an allusion to Communion as a source of healing.[35] Every monk and nun who worked with herbs and flowers in a monastic infirmary recognized their medicinal properties: for instance, "[The rose] is a nutrient-rich, astringent, diuretic and anti-inflammatory flower. . . . Roses can be used in tinctures, glycerites, teas, honeys, oxymels, syrups, vinegars and hydrosols, as a flower remedy and an essential oil."[36]

Walafrid's "little field," with flowers and herbs cherished for their aesthetic and medicinal value, serves as an image of

[33] Luigi Gambero, SM, *Mary and the Fathers of the Church: The Blessed Virgin Mary in Patristic Thought*, trans. Thomas Buffer (San Francisco: Ignatius Press, 1999), 284.

[34] Gambero, *Mary and the Fathers*, 199.

[35] Parker, "Two Carols about Roses."

[36] Becky Cole, *The Garden Apothecary* (London: Quadrille, 2022), 114.

the many monastic gardens that were developed in the early and high Middle Ages. His study of Scripture and participation in the Divine Office and Mass led him to recognize a correspondence between the garden and the botanical images in liturgical texts and the Bible. As were Jesus, early Christian communities, Benedict, and Bede, Walafrid was also acutely aware of the changing seasons of the year and their impact on the cultivation of gardens, orchards, vineyards, and fields of grain, as well as the manner in which seasonal changes were mirrored in the liturgical year and the stages of creaturely life.

Of course, the medieval monastics' immersion in an agricultural economy drew them into the natural world in ways that can be difficult to imitate today for those who live in urban areas. Although a majority of people who live in the United States report appreciation for the natural world, over 60 percent spend five hours or less each week outdoors.[37] Indeed, the trend is toward increasing time spent indoors interacting with digital technology. Gardening and hiking appear to be the only ways in which urban dwellers—who comprise 80 percent of the population in Canada and in the United States—encounter the natural world.

But there is more. "One of the worst effects of climate change is its effect on plants and plant life. Climate change is one of the biggest threats to plant species around the world. Rising temperatures and changes in precipitation patterns are making it difficult for many plants to survive in their natural habitats. In some cases, climate change is causing entire populations of plants to disappear."[38] At the same time, Christian and secular

[37] D. J. Case and Associates, "The Nature of Americans," accessed November 30, 2024, https://natureofamericans.org/findings/topic-summary/adults.

[38] Aryeh Brusowankin, "Preventing Plant Extinction Caused by Climate Change," in *The Green Planet*, August 2, 2022, accessed December 1, 2024, https://www.pbs.org/articles/preventing-plant-extinction-caused-by-climate-change#:~:text=One%20of%20the%20worst%20effects,a%20specific%20type%20of%20bee.

communities are creating plant sanctuaries for endangered species. They are working to conserve already-protected terrain and support Indigenous lands where flowers, herbs, and other plants are conserved. Above the Arctic Circle, on the Norwegian island of Spitsbergen, the Svalbard Global Seed Vault holds 1,280,677 flower, herb, grain, and plant seeds, ensuring protection for the world's botanical riches from mismanagement, accidents, armed conflict, disease, and natural disasters.[39] Such efforts by individuals and nations to preserve and protect the floral and arboreal treasures of the earth bear striking resemblance to the work of monastic communities, who for hundreds of years preserved and expanded knowledge and use of plant life amid the collapse of the Roman Empire, Germanic invasions, Viking destruction, pandemics, and global cooling.

Walafrid and other monastics recognized the "virtues" of flower, herb, grape, grain, and fruit. One then wonders if a rebirth of nature consciousness, rooted in arboreal and botanical images and their use in the church's liturgy, might draw Christian worshiping assemblies to give thanks for, cherish, and protect what God gives so abundantly and freely to earth's creatures. Might the recovery of monastic delight in the floral and herbal gifts of the creation, gifts from the One who invites his followers to consider the lilies of the fields, cultivate a commitment not only to appreciate the natural world but also to preserve it?

[39] Cary Fowler, *Seeds on Ice: Svalbard and the Global Seed Vault* (Burlington, VT: Prospecta Press, 2016).

6

Hildegard of Bingen: Witness to Christ's Verdant Energy in the World

In his Rule for monks and nuns, Benedict notes that the child of a noble family can be offered to God in the monastery, a practice that was frowned upon by monastics in the Eastern Mediterranean but common in the West: the Venerable Bede was offered as an oblate at the age of seven.[1] In the year 1106, Hildebert of Bermersheim and Mechthild of Merxheim placed their tenth child, an eight-year-old daughter named Hildegard, into the care of Jutta of Sponheim, a woman of noble birth and an ascetic. As the tenth child, Hildegard was considered a "tithe" to be offered in gratitude to God.[2] More recent research, based on the newly discovered *Vita Jutta*, indicates that Jutta and Hildegard entered the Benedictine monastery at Disibodenberg by the Nahe River in 1112 or 1113.[3]

Hildegard spent the next thirty-five years in this monastery named after Disibod, an Irish monk who settled along the Nahe River in the seventh century and established an anchorage that developed into a loose form of cenobitic monastic life.

[1] RB 59. For a helpful commentary on the practice of child oblation in the Rule, see Kardong, *Benedict's Rule*, 485–92.

[2] A "tithe" is one-tenth of something. The practice of giving one-tenth is mentioned in Gen 14:18-20; Gen 28:16-22; and Neh 10:38.

[3] Anna Silvas, trans., *Jutta and Hildegard: The Biographical Sources* (University Park, PA: Pennsylvania State University Press, 1999), 67.

Fiona Maddocks notes that the monastery was on a confined site: "The abbey church and chapels, refectory, dormitories, and kitchen crammed within the limited area of the mound, with no open space. . . . We see plainly, why, years later, Hildegard left this place where there was not room to expand to found her own monastery. We sense, too, a profound air of claustrophobia."[4]

Little is known of the young Hildegard's cloistered life. Historians suggest that Jutta taught her to sing, chant the psalms, and play a ten-stringed lyre. She may have become proficient in sewing and the adornment of liturgical linens with images. Clearly, she learned a sufficient amount of Latin to read and write in the language of the church. The *Vita Jutta* indicates that Hildegard labored in their small garden and joined her mentor in tending the sick, two experiences that would have significant influence later in Hildegard's life. In the women's cloister of the monastery, Hildegard writes that she often experienced illnesses which placed her in bed.[5] She also notes that from an early age she experienced visions—visions she was reluctant to mention to others: "I had sensed in myself wonderfully the power and mystery of secret and admirable visions from my childhood—that is, from the age of five—up to that time, as I do now. This, however, I showed to no one except a few religious persons who were living in the same manner as I; but meanwhile, until the time when God by His grace wished it to be manifested, I concealed it in quiet silence."[6]

[4] Fiona Maddocks, *Hildegard of Bingen: The Woman of Her Age* (New York: Image Books, 2001), 34.

[5] A number of contemporary neurologists and Hildegard scholars have sought a medical diagnosis for her illnesses. For the contested discussion regarding the application of a modern diagnosis to a medieval monastic, see Katherine Foxhall, "A Shower of Phosphenes: Twentieth-Century Stories and the Medical Uses of History," in *Migraine: A History* (Baltimore: Johns Hopkins University Press, 2019), 135–54.

[6] Hildegard of Bingen, *Scivias*, trans. Mother Columba Hart and Jane Bishop (Mahwah, NJ: Paulist Press, 1990), 59–60. *Scivias* is the shortened version of the Latin phrase, *scito vias Domini*, "know the ways of the Lord."

For twenty-four years, Hildegard lived with Jutta in the Disibodenberg *Frauenklause*, a cloister for nuns. During that period, the community of Benedictine women grew, separate from yet attached to the monastery of monks. In 1136, the beloved Jutta died. After the funeral Mass, Hildegard was elected unanimously by the nuns as *magistra*, or abbess, of the community. It is here that we encounter tension between Hildegard and Abbot Kuno of the men's monastery. He preferred that she be elected as *priorissa*, or prioress, a position which would place Hildegard under his authority. Yet she refused this title, a potent sign of the independence she desired for herself and her nuns. Indeed, this yearning to be free from the claustrophobia of Disibodenberg and dependence on the monks would come to fruition in Hildegard's desire to move the nuns to a new location.

The Sibyl of the Rhine

In 1141, her unwillingness to share her visions came to an end: "It happened that, in the eleven hundred and forty-first year of the Incarnation of the Son of God, Jesus Christ, when I was forty-two years and seven months old: Heaven was opened and a fiery light of exceeding brilliance came and permeated my whole brain, and inflamed my whole heart and my whole breast, not like a burning but like a warming flame, as the sun warms anything its rays touch."[7] Hildegard would come to speak of the source of her initial and ongoing visions as the Living Light who appeared to her first in childhood and then throughout her life. "Though I saw and heard these things, I refused to write for a long time through doubt and [fear of] the bad opinion of others . . . until laid low by the scourge of God, I fell upon a bed of sickness; then compelled at last by many illnesses . . . I set my hand to writing."[8] Her

[7] Hildegard, *Scivias*, 59.
[8] Hildegard, *Scivias*, 60.

first major theological work was *Scivias* (*Know the Ways of the Lord*), a text with vibrant illuminations that was created over a ten-year period.

In 1147, Hildegard and eighteen nuns moved to Rupertsberg near Eibingen, a move filled with risk: they left the security of a stone cloister attached to a community of monks for a temporary shelter at the confluence of the Nahe and Rhine Rivers. Hildegard's confessor and secretary, the Benedictine monk Volmar, was deputed to serve as provost of the new monastery. In 1152, the cloister and church, dedicated to St. Mary the Virgin, were consecrated by Henry, Archbishop of Mainz. Now distant from gloomy Disibodenberg, Hildegard and her nuns lived in the Middle Rhine Valley, a richly green area with terraced vineyards, lush forests, agricultural plots on the plateaus above the river, and abundant sunshine. We should not overlook the topography of the region and its effect on Hildegard and her nuns, who cultivated large gardens filled with flowers, herbs, vegetables, and other plants in keeping with Benedict's desire that every monastic community be self-sufficient in its mill, water source, and garden. Hildegard's care for this garden was expressed in a number of her works, but especially the *Physica*, begun in 1152. A work of medicine, the *Physica* examines the healing properties of herbs, plants, and trees.[9] Indeed, historians have suggested that her work on the therapeutic virtues of plants is the first one written by a woman.[10]

Much has been made of the relationship between her frequent illnesses and her visions. Without moving into a lengthy discussion of contemporary efforts to diagnose her condition, we can say this: her passivity in bedridden illness created in her a receptive mode. This is not an uncommon experience in Christian history: Catherine of Siena, Julian of Norwich, and

[9] Priscilla Throop, trans., *Hildegard of Bingen's Physica* (Rochester, VT: Healing Arts Press, 1998).

[10] Lois N. Magner, *A History of Medicine* (Boca Raton, FL: CRC Press, 1992), 109.

Ignatius Loyola received visions or voices when they were ill or recovering from injury. We do know this: her visions and locutions were not intended for her personal enlightenment but rather for the good of others. The Living Light compelled her to speak and to write so that the people and their ministers might know the will of God: "Explain these things in such a way that the hearer, receiving the words of his instructor, may expound them in those words, according to that will, vision and instruction. Thus therefore, O human, speak these things that you see and hear."[11] She then writes, "I heard a voice from Heaven say to me, 'Cry out, therefore, and thus write!' "[12]

In this command, we hear the echo of the prophetic mission: "I heard the voice of the Lord saying, 'Whom shall I send, and who will go for us?' And I said, 'Here am I; send me!' " (Isa 6:8); "Now the word of the Lord came to me saying, 'Before I formed you in the womb I knew you, and before you were born I consecrated you; I appointed you a prophet to the nations' " (Jer 1:4-5). Hildegard's initial silence—a sign of the reluctant prophet—was interrupted by the voice of the Living Light, who compelled her to "cry out," to serve as the voice who speaks for God. No wonder she was called the sibyl of the Rhine; the term "sibyl" refers to a female prophet. Her visions were not received in a vacuum but rather as messages for lay Christians, monks and nuns, the clergy, and political rulers. Indeed, her first work, *Scivias*, offers a sweeping view of the story of salvation that begins with the creation of the world and ends with the final judgment.

A Vibrant Yet Troubled Creation

In the first book of *Scivias*, Hildegard comments on the visions she has received concerning creation. She sees a great mountain signifying the eternal reign of God, the creator of all

[11] Hildegard, *Scivias*, 59.
[12] Hildegard, *Scivias*, 61.

things. She then considers the creation of humankind: in their original state, the primal parents were filled with light and vitality; they enjoyed the verdant garden prepared for them by the Triune God.[13] They were robust and filled with life-giving moisture. Lucifer, a fallen angel who preferred himself to God, espied these innocent and childlike humans and, distorted by his vice, seduced them. What comes to mind is the predator who offers sweets to the gullible child only to kidnap and then abuse them. In an unusual twist on the story narrated in Genesis 3, Hildegard writes that it was the seducing devil that drew the primal humans out of their first home and into the world of anxiety, fragility, and diminishment: "They lose their original freshness."[14] What remains? The steadfast love of God for God's children who, in their freedom to choose, were led astray: nonetheless, "God was touched by true mercy."[15]

The third vision merits our attention, for it presents us with the universe in the shape of a cosmic egg. The outer edge of the egg is wreathed in a gold and red ring of fire, an edge that breaks out of its rectangular frame: the cosmos is a living thing that cannot be contained by the human imagination! Within the fiery ring of the cosmos, we see winds blowing in many directions and a blue field filled with twinkling stars. Coming closer to the center, there is a watery layer and, above it, a golden disk set next to a crescent. In this illumination, we see the four fundamental elements known to the Venerable Bede: earth, air, fire, and water.

Yet what is seen in a painted illumination should not lead one to think of the cosmos as something static and unchanging. "It is secured but in fire; it moves through the air; it is drenched

[13] Hildegard, *Scivias*, 76.

[14] Heinrich Schipperges, *The World of Hildegard of Bingen: Her Life, Times, and Visions*, trans. John Cumming (Collegeville, MN: Liturgical Press, 1998), 125.

[15] Hildegard, *Scivias*, 87.

in water; it is illuminated by the stars; and it is supported by the winds. . . . Each of these spheres exists in a state of reciprocal tension. . . . There is an interactivity between all creatures."[16] When Hildegard views creation, she sees vitality and growth, no doubt informed by her careful observation of the natural seasons of the year and the seasons of creaturely life.

Concerning the sun, Hildegard writes: "There is a globe of sparkling flame, so great that the whole instrument [of the cosmos] is illuminated by it, which in the splendour of its brightness shows that within God the Father is his ineffable Only-Begotten, the sun of justice, with the brilliance of burning charity, of such great glory that every creature is illuminated by the brightness of His light."[17] Here, then, we see Christ portrayed as the burning sun who illuminates all things physically and spiritually. Here, the Living Light radiates and gives growth to all things.

As did other medieval writers, Hildegard viewed the human being as a microcosm of the cosmos. The four elements that interact throughout the world are present in every human being: earth or soil in one's flesh; water in various forms, from sweat to tears; air that one breathes in and out; and the fire of one's soulful intelligence. "God has adorned the universe with brilliance and beauty. He has filled it with the riches of creation, for the service of humankind."[18] In her study of medicine and healing, Hildegard also recognized that the fundamental elements were allied with cold, heat, dryness, and moisture. Do we usually consider this: that the cosmos is inscribed in the human body, that human beings bear in their flesh and blood the elements of creation? What we have witnessed in the West

[16] Schipperges, *World of Hildegard*, 95.

[17] Hildegard, *Scivias*, 94.

[18] Hildegard of Bingen, *The Book of the Rewards of Life (Liber Vitae Meritorum)*, trans. Bruce W. Hozeski (New York: Oxford University Press, 1997), 134.

since the eighteenth century is the scientific investigation of the creation in all its diversity—all of this admirable work. And yet in that investigation, the human has been and is frequently cast as the observer of creation, in which a distance is created between the analyst and the object of observation.

With Bede, Walafrid, and Hildegard, we discover a *co-natural relationship* between creature and creation, an integral relationship in which the creature is clothed with the fundamental elements created by God: "I, the maker of the world, gave work to be done by my work, of course, by man, with the knowledge that I gave him and by his using the earth and water, air and fire from which he is made."[19] Little wonder that the illumination which appears in Hildegard's *Book of Divine Works* shows a naked human with arms outstretched, surrounded by concentric circles of air, water, soil, and a ring of fire that flows from a fiery, red figure who holds the circles together, the head of a man appearing above the figure: "God bears the great wheel of creation on his breast . . . supported by the figure of flaming Love."[20]

In Hildegard's writing, we hear the voice of this fiery Love: "I flame above the beauty of the fields, and I shine in the waters, and I burn in the sun, the moon, and the stars. . . . I, the fiery force, lie hidden within these things, and they burn because of me."[21] This is not a love removed from the earth, resting in a distant heaven, nor is it an emotional attachment to another being, human or divine. Rather, it is the hidden force that animates all things with life. A modern scientist might say that this sublime force is energy, which many creatures draw from the light of the sun, an energy enlivening cells and molecules. Hildegard might well agree, but she, with Bede

[19] Hildegard, *Rewards of Life*, 286–87.

[20] Schipperges, *World of Hildegard*, 75.

[21] St. Hildegard of Bingen, *The Book of Divine Works*, trans. Nathan M. Campbell (Washington, DC: Catholic University of America Press, 2018), 34.

and Walafrid, would know its name: "All things came into being through [the Word], and without him not one thing came into being. What has come into being in him was life" (John 1:3-4).

Hildegard is insistent in her conviction that after the primal parents were seduced by Satan, they and their offspring, all of humanity, began to experience frailty, the loss of their original freshness, turbulence, and *ariditas* or dryness—images drawn from the land. With Walafrid, she could quote the prophet: "The grass withers, the flower fades" (Isa 40:8). How might modern readers interpret these earthy descriptions of the human condition? Might we not say that a feeling of apathy can rob one of energy? If there is little sense of meaningful purpose in one's life, would this not feel like turbulence: being tossed around with little direction? And who among us has not experienced weakness in body, mind, or spirit at some point in life—what Hildegard refers to as frailty? A dominant voice in the Christian tradition has suggested that this withering and turbulence, otherwise known as sin, is only a *spiritual* reality. Here Hildegard differs. In light of the integral relationship between creatures and the four elements of creation, human actions marked by frailty and disarray actually affect the earth, a *physical* reality: "When humans are entangled in fighting and terror, in hatred and envy, and in other contrary sins, *the* [earth's] *elements are overturned into another, contrary mode*, whether of heat or cold or great downpours and floods."[22]

For a moment, consider the continued growth of desertification, a physical form of aridity or dryness of the land. Desertification is the process in which fertile land used for agriculture is transformed into dusty desert. Agricultural scientists note that the loss of fertile land to aridity is due to human actions: overgrazing, deforestation, and the warming of the climate

[22] *Hildegardis Causae et Curae* (Hildegard, *Causes and Cures*), ed. Paul Kaiser (Leipzig: B.G. Teubneri, 1903), 57; emphasis mine.

with fossil fuels. The drying of land can lead to severe dust storms, food insecurity, and increasing poverty among the two billion people who live in regions of the world susceptible to desertification: western portions of North America, southeastern South America, central and northern Africa, and central Asia. Although Hildegard could not have known the modern peril of growing desertification throughout the world, she was cognizant of how human actions can "overturn the elements" and lead to increasing heat that robs the land of moisture and growth.[23]

But there is more: not only is creation harmed by human action, but the earth also cries out in distress: "The elements bring their complaints to their Creator with great crying aloud . . . so that they may show the significance of their oppression. Caught up by human sins, the elements transgress their proper mode which they received from their Creator. . . . They demonstrate that they cannot keep to the paths and purposes to which they were enjoined by God, because they are subverted by human wickedness."[24] We hear a similar complaint in Isaiah: "The earth dries up and withers, the world languishes and withers; the heavens languish together with the earth. The earth lies polluted under its inhabitants; for they have transgressed laws" (Isa 24:4-5). Let us note here that the refrain, "Cry out!" appears again. The Living Light commanded Hildegard to cry out: to write her visions and to preach.[25] Here

[23] See Helmut Geist, *The Causes and Progression of Desertification* (London: Ashgate/Routledge, 2005), 95–132.

[24] Hildegard of Bingen, *Rewards of Life*, 137.

[25] During a synod gathering in Trier (Germany) in 1147–48, Pope Eugenius III read sections of and approved Hildegard's *Scivias*. He encouraged her to continue writing. His approval of her "crying out" led to four preaching missions between 1158 and 1170. She did not preach at Mass but in public, calling the clergy to abandon corrupt practices and encouraging laypeople to lead lives guided by Christian virtues. Hildegard held that the rise of the Cathars, a lay reform movement critical of church practice, was due to the deplorable state of the clergy. See Beverly M. Kienzie, "Operatrix in vinea domini: Hildegard of Bingen's Preaching

the earth cries out to the Triune God, its creator and healer. With Bede and Walafrid, Hildegard knew well the psalms in which earth rejoices, fields exult, and the trees of the forest sing.[26] To a modern reader, however, the notion that earth's elements "speak" or "cry out" may sound simply romantic if not downright wrong. And yet the forest ecologist Suzanne Simard notes that in light of more recent research, trees, for instance, do speak with each other "through mycorrhizal networks that link tree after tree after tree. They send resources . . . like carbon, nitrogen, phosphorus, water, and defense signals even. They send nutrients to trees that might be struggling under stress."[27] Perhaps, then, the claim that earth's elements sing with joy or cry out with complaint is not so farfetched after all.

A Verdant World

Into this beloved but stressed creation, the Word of God, Jesus Christ, enters, clothed in the four elements. For Hildegard, the hymn prologue of the Gospel of John was of singular importance, for it holds together two creations: "All things came into being through [the Word], and without him not one thing came into being," and "The Word became flesh and lived among us" (John 1:3, 14).[28] It is the creating Word of God who brings the cosmos into existence, and it is the same Word of God who comes in the flesh with verdant and restorative power

and Polemics against the Cathars," *Heresis: Revue d'hérésiologie médiévale* 26–27 (1996): 43–56.

[26] Ps 96:11-12.

[27] "The Secret Language of Trees," in "To the Best of Our Knowledge," aired on Wisconsin Public Radio, April 28, 2018, accessed December 12, 2024, https://www.ttbook.org/show/secret-language-trees#:~:text=The%20way%20that%20communication%20happens,send%20to%20that%20shaded%20tree. See also Wohlleben, *Hidden Life of Trees*, on the ability of trees to communicate with one another.

[28] Sabina Flanagan, *Hildegard of Bingen: A Visionary Life* (New York: Routledge, 1990), 149–50.

where there is dryness, withering, and diminishment. In a responsory for the Creator and Redeemer, Hildegard notes this double creation: "O power within Eternity: All things you held in order in your heart and through your Word were all created according to your will. And then your very Word was clothed within that form of flesh from Adam born."[29]

In the second vision of Book II of *Scivias*, Hildegard describes the figure of the Word made flesh in this manner: "I saw a bright light, and in this light, the figure of a man the color of a sapphire, which was all blazing with a gentle, glowing fire. And that bright light bathed the whole of the glowing fire, and the glowing fire bathed the bright light; and the bright light and the glowing fire poured over the whole human figure, so that the three were one light in power of potential."[30] The placement of the sapphire figure on the disk and the disk on the circular band of white light gives the impression that the figure is moving toward the observer. The sapphire-hued man holds his hands open in front of his body: we can see his palms, a gesture of both prayer and peace—he holds no weapon. Sapphire as a color is mentioned in the initial vision of the prophet Ezekiel: "Above the dome . . . there was something like a throne, in appearance like sapphire; and seated above the likeness of the throne was something that seemed like a human form. . . . I saw . . . something that looked like fire enclosed all around . . . and there was a splendor all around" (Ezek 1: 26, 27). In this sapphire figure, notes Hildegard, there is no trace of aridity, of dryness; there is only "the plentitude of fruition."[31]

Here the Word of God, Jesus Christ, is surrounded by fire and light, the presence of the Spirit and the Father: "The Lord

[29] Hildegard of Bingen, "O vis eternitatis," *International Society of Hildegard von Bingen Studies* (hereafter ISHBS), June 26, 2014, accessed December 11, 2024, https://www.hildegard-society.org/2014/06/o-vis-eternitatis.html.

[30] Hildegard, *Scivias*, 161.

[31] Hildegard, *Scivias*, 161.

is my light" (Ps 27:1). It is an image of the Holy Trinity illuminated by color and form. Having lost their original freshness and thus growing weak and frail in faith, human beings, indeed the whole creation, is in need of restoration, wholeness, balance, and healing. The warmth of fire and the illumination wrought by light play significant roles in the process of restoring creatures and creation. This view is different from a well-known voice in medieval theology which claimed that the first humans and their offspring—all humankind—gave and continue to give offense to their Creator and deserve to be punished for the sin of disobedience. Anselm of Canterbury (1033–1109) proposed that instead of divine punishment (which no human could bear), satisfaction for human sin was made by the sinless Jesus Christ, who willingly died for sinful humans. His death, then, "compensates" for the disobedience of humankind. God is thus "satisfied" with this infinitely valuable act offered by Jesus and, through the ministry of the church, offers forgiveness to humans who are prone to disobedience.[32]

Hildegard does not emphasize the legal and feudal language of owing a debt to God for disobedience. Rather, she writes that the Father expresses his love for creation by sending the Word to restore and heal humans caught in conflict and fear, hatred and envy. The Word of God is clothed in materiality. "The Word is intended to become flesh in this created world, and in fact did so and dwelled among us. This design was part of the Father's will from the beginning. God wanted to reveal himself to the whole world in human form."[33] Note the phrase, "from the beginning." Hildegard did not view the incarnation as a rescue plan after the first humans disobeyed God. Rather, she holds that prior to the creation of the cosmos, God desired to become one with creation out of love. *God always intended to be revealed in human form*. Indeed, Hildegard describes the

[32] Anselm of Canterbury, *Why God Became Man*, trans. Joseph M. Colleran (Albany, NY: Magi Books, 1969).

[33] Schipperges, *World of Hildegard*, 126.

labor of the Sapphire Man in this manner: he comes to his creation and his creatures with gentleness, with nourishment for body and soul, with sweetest charity, and as the one who washes and dries the wounds of life.[34] Do these descriptions of the Word not sound like the qualities one would expect in a nurse?

We do well to keep in mind that Hildegard was a gardener. With Walafrid, she spent time cultivating plants, flowers, and herbs, her hands blackened by the soil. In her field work and in her visions, she recognized the energy that sustains life for all creatures, an energy she calls a "greening power," in Latin, *viriditas*. While a good many commentaries on Hildegard's life and work claim that she originated the term, we know that she may have read it in the works of Pope Gregory the Great, Benedict's biographer. Indeed, Gregory was not the only early medieval author to use the term: "*Viriditas* appears in hundreds of works by many medieval theologians."[35] For instance, in his commentary on the book of Job, Gregory writes: "We understand 'earth' to represent the Church, which puts forth green grass [*herbam virentem*], in that it brings forth fruitful works of mercy from the Word of God. We sometimes understand 'grass' [*herbam*] as the knowledge and doctrine of eternal greenness [*viriditatis*]."[36] For Gregory, the spiritual life without Christ is a "desolate land" that is brought to "greening growth" when the Word of God enters the creation, the life of the baptized, and the church. "Gregory refers to *viriditas* as the 'newness and fecundity of creation.'"[37] While she may have relied

[34] Hildegard, *Scivias*, 161–62.

[35] Jeannette D. Jones, "A Theological Interpretation of *Viriditas* in Hildegard of Bingen and Gregory the Great," *Portfolio of the Department of Musicology and Ethnomusicology* 1 (2012), n. 6, accessed December 13, 2024, https://www.bu.edu/pdme/jeannette-jones/#_edn7.

[36] Gregory the Great, *Moralia in Iob*, ed. Marci Adriaen, *Corpus Christianorum* 143B (Turnhout: Brepols, 1985), 1469.

[37] Almut Furchert, "Cosmic Partnership: Hildegard of Bingen's Vision of an Integral Ecology," *Journal of Social Encounters* 8, no. 2 (2024): 313.

on the works of early medieval theologians in their use of the term *viriditas*, we can say that Hildegard is its greatest champion, as verdant power flows throughout her writings.

We do well, then, to keep in mind that Hildegard views God's greening power and presence as both a physical and a spiritual reality. While she does distinguish one from the other, she is loathe to separate them as do other theologians who assign greater value to the spiritual (the soul) than to the physical (the body). In the natural world, this vitality originates in the four elements of earth, fire, water, and air: it sparkles in the waters, radiates in fire, nourishes the soil, and breathes refreshment in the air. It is sustained by moisture and dryness, heat and cold. Given that human beings bear within themselves the four elements, they, too, are enlivened by *viriditas*, though they are also susceptible to dryness, living lives marked by vice as well as virtue. While Hildegard speaks at length about the vivifying power in nature, we should not assume that everything literally turns green. Rather, *viriditas* is the often-unseen energy that courses through the cosmos, creation, and creatures. Hildegard would agree with modern science: vital energy can transform whatever it touches, but it cannot be created or destroyed—it is the constant in an active cosmos; it is eternal yet present in time and space.[38] "There is a power that has been since all eternity and that force and potentiality is green."[39]

The Greening Word

Hildegard's teaching on the incarnation of the Word of God draws on the annunciation as recorded in the Gospel of Luke: "The angel [Gabriel] said to [Mary], 'The Holy Spirit will come upon you, and the power of the Most High will overshadow

[38] Tamara M. Davis, "Is the Universe Leaking Energy?," *Scientific American* 303, no. 1 (July 1, 2010): 38–47.

[39] Schipperges, *World of Hildegard*, 111.

you; therefore the child to be born will be holy; he will be called Son of God' " (Luke 1:35). In her song, "O greenest virgin," Hildegard expresses this conception with images drawn from the natural world:

> O branch of freshest green,
> O hail! Within the windy gusts of saints
> upon a quest you swayed and sprouted forth.
> When it was time, you blossomed in your boughs—
> "Hail, hail!" you heard, for in you seeped the sunlight's
> warmth
> like balsam's sweet perfume.
> For in you bloomed
> so beautiful a flower, whose fragrance wakened
> all the spices from their dried-out stupor.
> And they all appeared in full viridity.[40]

This is neither the language of Greek philosophy that influenced much of Christian theology nor the rhetoric of Latin canon law that governed most of medieval life. Here we encounter images that have more in common with the poetry of Scripture, inviting the reader or listener to enter the natural world, a world experienced with one's senses. Here the Virgin Mary is *viridissima*, a living branch, from whom a beautiful flower emerged. Given Hildegard's understanding of human beings as "spices," the conception and birth of this flower and its fragrance restores them to full freshness, to vitality. In another song, she speaks of Mary as "the sweetest branch who blooms from Jesse's stock . . . . from whom a bright flower has sprung."[41]

[40] Hildegard of Bingen, "O viridissima virga," ISHBS, October 13, 2014, accessed December 17, 2024, https://www.hildegard-society.org/2014/10/o-viridissima-virga-song.html.

[41] Hildegard of Bingen, "O tu suavissima virga," ISHBS, October 13, 2014, accessed December 17, 2024, https://www.hildegard-society.org/2014/10/o-tu-suavissima-virga-responsory.html.

From the branch, there springs the greening Word, Jesus Christ. "The reality of the Word becomes fruitful in greenness."[42] The mission of this verdant Word encompasses the whole creation. Here, again, Hildegard is critical of the notion, common in contemporary American religion, that there is only one significant relationship: between Christ and the soul. "Too small, too small!" she shouts from the eleventh century. Can you not hear her asking, "Have you read the Gospel of John in which the Savior says, 'God so loved the *world* that he gave his only Son'?" (John 3:16). The "world" is the *kosmon*, the cosmos, the *mundum*, the entire world. "The whole world is called to redemption in the Word."[43]

For Hildegard, Christ's work is exemplified in scenes from the Gospel of John: transforming water into wine at Cana (2:1-12); healing a lame man on the sabbath (5:1-18); feeding five thousand people (6:1-15); inviting people to drink from the Spirit (7:37-39); healing a man born blind (9:1-41); and raising Lazarus from the tomb (11:1-44). In these actions one sees thirst, frailty, dryness, and death transformed by the presence of the verdant Word of God. Mercy, as loving action that benefits others, is a salve, a healing ointment, that restores unto wholeness.

The *magistra* is clear in her understanding that humans are free to cooperate with the greening Word of God or, sadly, to refuse such cooperation. In this she wants to make clear that the Verdant One invites Christians to live into the virtues and allow them to grow within their lives; that living a virtuous life will affect other creatures and creation, both of which participate in the vital presence of *viriditas*. What are the virtues? In Book Three of *Scivias*, she lists five: Celestial Love, Discipline,

[42] *Hildegardis Causae et Curae* (Hildegard, *Causes and Cures*), ed. Paul Kaiser (Leipzig: B.G. Teubneri, 1903), 22.

[43] Schipperges, *World of Hildegard*, 126.

Modesty, Mercy, and Victory.[44] In a slap to the practice of astrology, she writes that humans do not have a special star that decides their fate or way of life "as foolish people believe."[45] Rather, they are invited to enjoy the wholeness that Christ intends for all creatures and creation, a wholeness shaped by the virtues. Hildegard draws on a favored description of the human condition when she writes that "God brought [Jesus Christ] forth as a great fountain so that every faithful throat could drink and never more be dry."[46]

For Hildegard, *viriditas* is an active energy in the cosmos and creation. At the same time, it is mediated through the Redeemer, especially through the Mass, which shares the Body and Blood of the crucified and risen One. In the fifteenth vision of *Scivias*, we see a crowned woman standing next to the crucified Christ. In her hands, she holds a chalice. From the side of Christ, water spills forth on her forehead, and a stream of blood flows into the chalice. This vision is an allusion to John's depiction of the crucifixion: "One of the soldiers pierced his side with a spear, and at once blood and water came out" (John 19:34). In the water issuing from Christ's side, Hildegard sees the sacrament of water and Spirit. She speaks of the blood spilling into the chalice as the "precious wedding present" that Christ, the bridegroom, offers to his beloved spouse, the Christian community, in the Eucharist.

The baptismal sacrament that makes one a Christian is nourished throughout life in the eucharistic sacrament: one receives the life-giving energy of *viriditas*. In the reception of this nuptial gift, a verdant eucharistic energy enters the body and soul of the Christian, nurturing the wholeness God intends for the individual and the whole creation: "Eat and drink the body

[44] Later in Book Three, she speaks of seven virtues: Humility, Charity, Fear, Obedience, Faith, Hope, and Chastity. Her complete list includes thirty-five virtues.

[45] Hildegard, *Scivias*, 100.

[46] Hildegard, *Scivias*, 154.

and blood of my Son," says the voice from heaven, "so that you may be restored to a noble inheritance."[47] What the communicant receives from the Lord is the "gift of fertility,"[48] in which the primary virtues of faith, hope, and love are engendered and strengthened.

Hildegard teaches that humans suffer from frailty, dryness, and turbulence. The "noble inheritance" is the growth of wholeness in spirit, mind, and body. In this regard, the eucharistic energy received in the Mass is a healing balm. It is a "salve of mercy" and a "medicine for your wounds."[49] The Father speaks: "Eat, my friends; drink, and be inebriated, my dearly beloved! What does this mean? Eat in faith, you who through holy baptism have come to my friendship; for the spilled blood of my Son has purged you from Adam's fall, and as you consume the true medicine in the body of my Only-Begotten, the repeated deeds of crime and injustice you have done will be mercifully wiped out for you."[50]

In this regard, Hildegard sees Jesus Christ as a healer. In one of her responsories sung in honor of the Virgin Mary, she writes: "O radiant bright, O mother of a holy medicine, your ointments through your holy Son [are] poured upon the plangent wounds of death. . . . This death you have destroyed."[51] Keep in mind that Hildegard and her nuns were devoted to the art and science of healing, a practice inspired by the healing work of Jesus and its extension in monastic care for the sick.[52] What we find in Hildegardian healing is the conviction that human beings are a unity of body, mind, and spirit. In contrast to modern medicine, which addresses only the body, Hildegard's healing

[47] Hildegard, *Scivias*, 237.

[48] Hildegard, *Scivias*, 238.

[49] Hildegard, *Scivias*, 242.

[50] Hildegard, *Scivias*, 249.

[51] Hildegard of Bingen, "O clarissima mater," ISHBS, September 4, 2014, accessed December 18, 2024, https://www.hildegard-society.org/2014/09/o-clarissima-responsory.html.

[52] RB 36.

practice treated the whole person, a treatment that included the reception of Holy Communion, spiritual counsel, natural medicines, and music therapy to calm anxiety and fear.

A Surplus of Earthy Images

In 1146, Hildegard wrote a letter to Bernard of Clairvaux, in which she asked the famous Cistercian abbot to listen carefully to her plea: "I beseech you . . . through the Word that gave birth to the world, through the sublimity of the Father whose sweet *viriditas* released the Word in the Virgin's womb, where it took on flesh like a honeycomb built from honey: may this same sound descend on your heart so that you do not remain idly numb to this person's words."[53] Hildegard delighted in a diversity of images when speaking of Jesus Christ: the Word, *viriditas*, and the sweetly surprising honeycomb!

In her explication of the creation of the world and the first humans, she speaks of Christ as a bright light in human form: "In the earth there appeared a radiance like the dawn . . . and in the radiance of that dawn, the Supreme Will was enkindled. . . . And I saw a serene Man coming forth from this radiant dawn; and it drove the [darkness of the serpent] back with great force . . . and so the serene Man who had come out of the dawn shone more brightly than human tongue can tell."[54]

As we know, Hildegard's use of light is both physical and spiritual; she distinguishes between the two but views them as one because she observes the manner in which light energizes creation and enlightens the mind and soul of humankind. She notes that this supernal light blazes *within* human beings, unaware in the eleventh century of what modern science dis-

[53] Hildegard of Bingen, *The Letters of Hildegard of Bingen*, trans. Joseph L. Baird and Radd K. Ehrman (Oxford: Oxford University Press, 1994), 27–28.

[54] Hildegard, *Scivias*, 149–50.

covered in the late twentieth century: that in the process of earth's creation some 4.5 billion years ago and in the subsequent evolution of life on earth, all creatures, human and otherwise, hold in their bodies traces of starlight in the trillions of molecules that make each life possible. Thus all living things—from fireflies to human beings—emit measures of light, light unseen to the human eye but nonetheless present in particles of light.[55] No doubt, the daughter of the Living Light would be delighted by this discovery.

She holds that Christ is suffused with the energy of *viriditas*: he embodies and diffuses the greening power that heals, restores, and vivifies human beings who suffer from diminishment, physical frailty, and spiritual withering. For those who have been wounded in life, he is a healing salve: "He was born of the Virgin, and so has the sweetest savor and the strongest [ointment], which He distills like balsam; which is the resurrection of life, by which the dead have been raised. And that ointment has healing in it that . . . cleanses the wounds of sin; for the Incarnation is full of wholeness and sweetness."[56] Hildegard extends this image of spiritual healing to include those who suffer with physical infirmity: Jesus Christ is their healer who, through human agents, offers medicine for body and soul. For those who are thirsty, he is a fountain who transforms physical and spiritual withering into life-giving moisture.

Modern readers do well to recognize that farming in early medieval Europe had more to do with gardening than the large-scale and mechanized crop farming present in contemporary, developed nations. The medieval gardener, working with the soil throughout the year, had an intimate relationship with the

[55] Jacob Berkowitz, *The Stardust Revolution: The New Story of Our Origin in the Stars* (Lanham, MD: Prometheus Books, 2022), 87–113; Bennet Daviss, "Body Talk," *New Scientist*, February 23, 2002, accessed February 5, 2024, https://www.newscientist.com/article/mg17323314-800-body-talk/.

[56] Hildegard, *Scivias*, 440.

land little different from that of the farmers, fishers, and vintners of first-century Palestine.[57] Hildegard, the monastic gardener, may well have been inspired by the *Hortulus* of Walafrid Strabo[58] when she speaks of Christ using the garden images of a flower, a blossom, and a fruit that grew from the branch or vine of the Virgin Mary. The flower offers the fragrance of Christ, while the fruit of the vine becomes the wine transformed into his Blood received by the faithful in the Mass. One can actually smell fragrance and taste crushed grape. In contrast to Anselm, Abelard, and Bernard, who debated the relationship between faith and reason, Hildegard offers earthy images that are more experiential and mystical, Christological images that highlight the path of salvation informed by Scripture, the natural world, and monastic virtues.

As an abbess who worked in the garden and lived in a richly fertile region along the Rhine, Hildegard offers a vision of Christian faith and life discerned in the Books of Scripture and Nature, two of the primary sources of monastic spirituality. Hers is the language of image, metaphor, and vision. She does not participate in the philosophical analysis that would come to dominate the scholastic method of the twelfth and thirteenth centuries, a method that prized dialectical reasoning and abstraction.[59] As the abbess and teacher of her nuns, Hildegard

[57] Victoria Sweet, "Hildegard of Bingen and the Greening of Medieval Medicine," *Bulletin of the History of Medicine* 73, no. 3 (Fall 1999): 388.

[58] Mariano Bizzari, "Lessons from the Past: Hildegard of Bingen," *Organisms: Journal of Biological Sciences* 2, no. 1 (2018): 114; Gertrude M. Engbring, "Saint Hildegard, Twelfth Century Physician," *Bulletin of the History of Medicine* 8, no. 6 (1940): 777.

[59] James Ginther, "Hildegard of Bingen's Theology," in *The Cambridge Companion to Hildegard of Bingen*, ed. Jennifer Bain (Cambridge: Cambridge University Press, 2021), 85–104. Ginther suggests that Hildegard's three major works—*Scivias*, *The Book of Life's Merits*, and *The Book of Divine Works*—form a structured theological system that served as the foundation for the spiritual and theological formation of her nuns, a view of Hildegard's theology that, Ginther claims, has been impeded by her status as a mystic and a visionary.

was concerned with their spiritual welfare and growth, a growth rooted in the marriage of Christ and his spouse: Christian women and men. This relationship, which includes the earth, is sustained by the Holy Spirit:

> O fire of the Spirit and Defender,
> the life of every life created:
> Holy are you—giving life to every form.
> O mighty course that runs within and through
> all things—up in the heights, upon the earth,
> and in the very depths—
> you bind and gather all together.
> From you the clouds flow forth, the wind takes flight,
> the stones their moisture hold,
> the waters rivers spring,
> and earth viridity exudes.[60]

In her last great work, *The Book of Divine Works*, completed in 1173, Hildegard wrote that the fundamental vocation of every Christian is to understand oneself and all of creation as the marvelous work of God. The Christian who grows in this understanding, she writes, is a flourishing garden, a fruitful orchard. But there is more: "God gathered together the world out of the elements . . . stitched it together . . . and filled it with creatures. . . . He surrounded and fortified humankind and everywhere imbued them with the greatest strength, so that creation might assist them in all things and so that [humans] might do their work *with* creation."[61] Here Hildegard points to an interdependent relationship between humans and creation, one in which Christians are called to care for and work with creation, rather than dominate or abuse it.

[60] Hildegard of Bingen, "O ignis Spiritus paracliti," ISHBS, November 18, 2014, accessed December 18, 2024, https://www.hildegard-society.org/2014/11/o-ignis-spiritus-paracliti-sequence.html.

[61] Hildegard, *Book of Divine Works*, 54; emphasis mine.

One wonders: does this vocation not ring true in our own age, in which the earth and its creatures call out in great urgency for protection and restoration? Hildegard writes that bright flowers adorn the body of the Son of God. Let's be clear: this is not medieval hyperbole. The flowers adorning the wounded and risen body of Christ are those women and men in whom the green virtues flower.

7

Monastic Mentors

In 1945, a teenager named Muhammad Ali al-Samman discovered a trove of ancient manuscripts in a jar buried at Nag Hammadi, a town by the Nile River in Upper Egypt. The texts were written in Coptic and eventually found their way to the Egyptian Department of Antiquities. These ancient manuscripts came to be called the Nag Hammadi Library, a collection dated to the second and third centuries of the common era. One of the best known texts is the Gospel of Thomas, a gathering of sayings allegedly made by Jesus. This "gospel" begins with a short announcement: "These are the hidden words that the living Jesus spoke and Didymos Judas Thomas wrote them down."[1]

Let us note a curious juxtaposition in this introduction to the Thomas collection: "hidden" and "words." The Gospel of Thomas is a collection of sayings, nothing else. With other writings in the Nag Hammadi Library, we find no historical context, no locations, and no times mentioned. "There are no stories of Jesus. . . . The content of the books is largely knowledge of technique, of *askesis*, to enable the self to escape the fleshly conditions of life."[2] The majority of texts in the Nag Hammadi Library are considered gnostic, a diverse religious

[1] Stephen J. Peterson, James M. Robinson, and Hans-Gebhard Bethge, *The Fifth Gospel: The Gospel of Thomas Comes of Age* (Harrisburg, PA: Trinity Press International, 1998), 7.

[2] Lathrop, *Holy Ground*, 129–30.

and philosophical movement that arose in the Eastern Mediterranean and flourished in the second century.

Proponents of a gnostic worldview claimed that "human souls or spiritual principles do not belong in this material world (which is often described as evil and ignorant); they can be saved only by receiving the revelation that they belong in a heavenly realm where there is a hierarchy of emanations from the true God. . . . Many gnostic authors thought that Jesus brought the revelation enabling a return to the divine world."[3] The gnostics taught that Jesus offered a secret revelation, "hidden words," that would enable the individual soul to transcend the world of matter, to escape what they considered the prison of materiality. The gnostic worldview was *sarcophobic*, fearful of and opposed to bodily existence, and by extension, *ecophobic*, disdainful of the creation and creaturely existence. In fact, the gnostics taught that a lesser divine being, the *demiurge*, created the world. What Jesus taught, they said, was an esoteric knowledge for a spiritual elite that would lead its adherents into an immaterial existence in another world, a spiritual realm divided into a hierarchical structure with the "purer" adherents at the top and "lesser" adherents at the bottom.

Now we might imagine that any discussion of gnosticism is an artifact from the past, of little consequence for contemporary life. And yet its worldview persists in some forms of American religion and culture. For instance, in the robust, aggressive individualism of American life, the self alone matters—a persistent theme in gnostic beliefs. Given the triumph of the therapeutic in much of American rhetoric, the search for personal fulfillment, for discovering "my personal bliss," continues to animate privileged portions of the American public.[4]

[3] Raymond E. Brown, SS, *An Introduction to the New Testament* (New York: Doubleday, 1997), 92.

[4] This refers to the proliferation of self-help gurus and "life coaches," who market their "skill" in personal development. It does not refer to trained and licensed therapists, who treat patients who have been wounded by themselves, others, or the culture in which they live.

Given the preaching of individual immortality—"being saved for heaven"—as the primary goal of the spiritual life that is found in many American churches, it is not difficult to see traces of gnostic concern in this rhetoric. Indeed, the claim to hold "secret knowledge" that will lead the individual to freedom from past "psychic blockage" continues to animate various movements, with Scientology as a prime example.

Some sociologists have claimed that by the 1980s, American society had become focused primarily on the self and the search for personal fulfillment, losing its earlier communitarian sensibility shaped by biblical and republican commitments.[5] It should not surprise us, then, that Vivek Murthy, a former surgeon general of the United States, issued a lengthy report which warned of the pervasive and growing sense of loneliness among Americans, an epidemic of isolation and disconnection from others that *preceded* the coronavirus pandemic. The study's view of the future? "Instead of coming together to take on the great challenges before us, we will further retreat to our corners—angry, sick, and alone."[6]

Earthbound Practice

What stands in contrast to a gnostic worldview are the four canonical gospels of the New Testament, in which we find stories about Jesus, his community of followers, and the natural world. Rather than a selection of isolated sayings on how to flee from this world, we find interactions with other human beings and their surroundings. We read about towns, a river and a lake, vineyards, grain fields, and the wilderness. We hear Jesus speak about the community's relationship with God, one

[5] Robert N. Bellah et al., *Habits of the Heart: Individualism and Commitment in American Life* (Berkeley: University of California Press, 1983/1996), 55–84, 142–66.

[6] *Our Epidemic of Loneliness and Isolation: The U.S. Surgeon General's Advisory on the Healing Effects of Social Connection and Community* (Washington, DC: Office of the Surgeon General, 2023), 4.

another, and the world in which they live. There is a consistent cultivation of a common life. Indeed, when Jesus speaks in parables or sayings, he frequently if not exclusively uses the second person plural: *you all together*, not *you alone*. We are drawn into an awareness of the changing arc of each day, from sunrise to sunset, and of the seasons of the year, from summer heat to winter rains. We sense that the manner of his life—his eating with others, his healing others, his forgiving others, his criticism of religious elites—drew enmity and ultimately his death. In the gospels, there is no escaping mortality into a netherworld. Rather, there is a real death and the resurrection of his body, a glorified body. What does he say to an incredulous Thomas as he shows him his wounds? "Put your finger here and see my hands. Reach out your hand and put it in my side" (John 20:27).

In contrast to the hyperindividualism and attendant loneliness in much of contemporary American culture is the practice of Jesus' first followers, who welcomed the gifts of creation into their common worship: flowing water, scented olive oil, leavened bread, Galilean wine, burning tapers, fish, milk, and honey. Gathered on the first day of the week, the day of his resurrection, they prayed "Our Father," not "my father," not "my God." They spoke these words over wine and bread: "We thank you, our Father, for the holy vine of David your servant which you have revealed to us through Jesus your child. . . . You created all things and you have given food and drink to [your] children for their enjoyment."[7]

Rather than searching for personal bliss, they focused their communal energy on care for those in need among them: "Those who are prosperous and who desire to do so, give what they wish, according to each one's choice, and the collection is deposited with the presider. He aids orphans and widows, those who are in want through disease or through another

[7] Deiss, "The Didache," in *Springtime of the Liturgy*, 74, 75.

cause, those who are in prison, and foreigners who are sojourning here. In short, the presider is a guardian to all those who are in need."[8] In this second-century description of the early Christian liturgy, we recognize an intrinsic relationship between communal worship and social commitments in the world of daily life, what the Eastern Orthodox refer to as "the liturgy after the liturgy."

Thus the gathering on Sunday oriented the worshiping assembly toward its care of others and did so by employing the gifts of the earth that were welcomed by Jesus in his public ministry. Early Christians fed the hungry poor with bread, wine, and fish. They anointed the sick with olive oil and used water to clean and refresh them. They placed wreaths of greens and flowers around the heads of their beloved dead. They traced the sign of the cross, the tree of life, over their bodies. In doing so, they honored the elements of creation given to them by God and extended the social ministry of Jesus to their sisters and brothers in need.

Monastic Delight in the Earth

We find a similar pattern or impulse in the Rule of Benedict: the monastic community is anchored in the work of God, common prayer, and the presence of Jesus Christ, the Lord,[9] the Light of life,[10] the Workman who calls to his workers,[11] the Rock,[12] and the Suffering One.[13] In the midst of social collapse, armed conflict, economic turbulence, and degraded communication, Benedict set forth the strength of sharing life in an assembly that prayed the psalms, meditated on the gospels,

[8] Justin Martyr, "1 Apology 67," in Lathrop, *Holy Ground*, 138.
[9] RB Prol. 3.
[10] RB Prol. 13.
[11] RB Prol. 14.
[12] RB Prol. 28.
[13] RB Prol. 50.

and sang hymns that greeted the first light of dawn, the sun at its zenith, and the stars as night descended. Such grounding in common prayer led to serving members of the community, guests, and the poor and sick, who found in the monastery a refuge from the vicissitudes of a culture marked by strife. Here we encounter the image of Christ the selfless leader, who came to serve rather than be served: he eschewed any hint of privilege.[14] In such a setting, the gnostic dream of the individual's escape from the earth would be mitigated though the temptation to see the monastic community as a spiritual elite, which would be ever-present and, in time, would lead to waves of reform.

In this monastic milieu, we encounter diverse Christological images that were shaped by the closeness of monastic communities to the earth. The Venerable Bede, marveling at the natural seasons of the year and the changes wrought in the sunlit and starry heavens, recognized Jesus Christ as the world-warden and wonder worker. In his inclusion of Caedmon's lyrics, we read of the Fashioner of Heaven and the creator of Middle Earth. In a land marked by armed conflict and the normalization of blood feuds, Bede turned the attention of his monastic colleagues and lay Christians to the peace-loving Lamb, who challenged the evil of retribution and "put the sign of his death on our foreheads in order to ward off the weapons of the death-bearing enemy."[15]

Walafrid Strabo, the great Benedictine gardener, reminds us of Jesus' presence in gardens at his arrest and death and resurrection. Guided by Benedict's Rule that called for a garden to be cultivated in every monastic community, Walafrid labored in the soil, blackening his hands as he spread dung among the flowers and herbs he grew for meals and medicine in the mon-

[14] Mark 10:45.

[15] "On our foreheads," a reference to baptismal anointing, in Bede, "Sermon II.7 The Easter Vigil," 66.

astery. In his *De cultura hortorum*, we read of herbs and flowers used in the monastic infirmary to treat sickness and wounds. He then leads the reader to recognize the presence of Christ the gardener, who continues to animate the growth of earth's flora and arbors. In a hymn of praise to the Virgin Mary, he says, "to you came a flower from the scepter-bearing offspring of Jesse . . . coloring the roses by his death . . . He embraced the virtue of each flower."[16]

While some might hold to a more nostalgic reading of a floral text or dismiss it as a gardener's fantasy, Walafrid does not hesitate to speak about childbirth and death. The deep red of the rose is the color of the martyr's blood. In "The Dream of the Rood," the blood of Christ colors the wood of the tree and the floral growth at its base. By way of contrast, the rose became an enchanting image of the Virgin Mary, who gave birth to Jesus, the "flower" filled with virtues. This is to say that the Mystery of the Incarnation and the Paschal Mystery were discerned in the Books of Scripture and Nature. In this, Walafrid and other gardeners exceled, as evidenced in the floral and arboreal poems and lyrics which flourished throughout this period.

The mystic gardener and Benedictine abbess Hildegard of Bingen received visions of the cosmos, creation, and creatures both human and otherwise. The Living Light urged her, indeed commanded her, to cry out, write, and preach what she witnessed in the visions that appeared throughout most of her life. Her work was *umbra viventis lucis*, a reflection of the Living Light. At the creation of world, she saw a serene man suffused with light pushing back the darkness of deception and evil. In a circle of white and red-tinged gold, there appeared a Sapphire Man who comes with gentleness to the creation. She sings of a flower, Jesus Christ, whose fragrance awakens all the spices, Christians, from their dried-out stupor. The dynamic energy

[16] "Walafrid Strabo," 123–24.

which animates all things, giving them light and life, is *viriditas*, the greening power that flows freely and abundantly from the Green One throughout the cosmos. To those who are withering or wounded in life and faith, he is the healer who treats the whole person—body, mind, and spirit—with herbal and floral medicine, with music, prayer, spiritual counsel, and the sacrament of healing. To those who humbly welcome him into their lives, the divine honeybee creates within them a sweet and nourishing honeycomb.

The many Christological images witnessed in her visions tumble forth, sharing one thing in common: the visionary world of Jesus in nature. Hildegard does not delve into dialectics, ontological arguments, or the compatibility of divine attributes—subjects treated by other medieval theologians. Hers is the language of garden and vision, of poetry and musical lyric, of the struggle between vice and virtue. Yet what she says of the creating Word of God is intended for Christians in their daily lives. For instance, she encourages frequent Communion at Mass so that the people of God, the Body of Christ, might receive the Lord's greening energy and so serve his life-giving presence in daily life. One dimension of their vocation is to cherish and protect the creation.

Benedictine closeness to the earth—at least for the first five hundred years of the order's existence—encouraged delight in creation as well as the challenging work of cultivating crops, orchards, herbs, and flowers for meals and medicines.[17] In this,

[17] From Benedict's desire that every monastic engage in spiritual reading, there emerged monastic libraries, which led to the establishment of monastic schools. The shift from agricultural labor to educational work was prompted in part by Charlemagne's edicts in the late eighth century concerning the establishment of schools in all monasteries and abbeys. "As monks became unintentionally wealthy through their success in crafts and agriculture, they became increasingly religious professionals, scholars, and economic stewards. As they spent increasing amounts of time in prayer, study, and bookkeeping, the monks ceased to participate in the holy work of manual labour that had been prescribed in the original

the monastic sons and daughters of Benedict and Scholastica labored as did the agricultural workers who surrounded Jesus. He honored them in his observations of the natural world, his incorporation of nature's gifts in his sayings and parables, and his use of natural elements in his public life. What we discern in the work of monks and nuns in field and garden, infirmary and kitchen, is an *ecophilic* sensibility so different from the *ecophobia* present in some strains of Christian spirituality. With Benedict, Bede, Walafrid, and Hildegard, we discern that all five senses—touch, taste, smell, sight, and hearing—are the means through which a person encounters the Word of God, Jesus Christ. These senses serve as the ordinary means through which the risen Christ enters into the lives of his followers.

Here is one challenge in exploring early medieval monastics: the vast majority of university students enrolled in my courses on monastic history have been tutored in the "catechism" of American culture. They have been taught to believe that the past is of little value in their lives. What matters is the present moment and perhaps tomorrow or the end of the academic term. Indeed, more than one student has wondered why anyone would spend time—"waste time"—studying the lives and works of dead people. This attitude presents a challenge but also an opportunity: the chance to listen to voices from the past who might have wisdom to share with those who live in the present, voices that have been overlooked by those who have controlled the "curriculum" of church and academy. We might then view the evangelists, the first Christians, and early medieval monastics as mentors, who offer a portrait of Jesus infrequently heard in the preaching, liturgies, catechesis, agencies, and schools of the church. What, then, might they offer us?

---

rules of Columba and Benedict . . . the decline of such labour among the monks led to the corruption of the monasteries." Michael S. Northcott, *Place, Ecology, and the Sacred: The Moral Geography of Sustainable Communities* (London: Bloomsbury, 2015), 33.

The First Language of Faith

The first and primordial language of religion is story, symbol, and ritual.[18] This is the language of metaphor and image that captures the imagination and can prompt a transformation in one's view of God, life, and the world. Indeed, this is the language of the gospels, in which Jesus tells stories and parables that surprise and orient his listeners toward a particular vision: living in the reign of God. As we have noted earlier, the primordial event in Israel's history—the journey from slavery to freedom—was enacted in the Passover ritual with the telling of the story and the "consuming" of the story in bread, wine, salt, olive oil, and lamb—elements of creation that made present the past event as hope for the future.

But then one wonders if this is the language that marks contemporary preaching, teaching, and sung lyric. Philosophy and theology—whose languages prize categorization, analogy, and systematic interpretation—can overwhelm the primordial awe and replace this wonder with dry analysis or repetition of doctrine or, in the hands of some preachers and teachers, a dull "explanation" that flattens the richness of image or parable into an easily consumable product. Our monastic mentors drank deeply of the first language, with images of Jesus Christ that cohered with his use of story, symbol, and ritual, expanding their understanding and experience of the central figure in Christian faith and life.

The Book of Scripture and the Book of Nature

In the early seventeenth century, the Florentine astronomer Galileo Galilei popularized the term the "Book of Nature" as

[18] Gail Ramshaw, *Reviving Sacred Speech: The Meaning of Liturgical Language* (Akron, OH: OSL Publications, 2000), 1–40; Thomas Fawcett, *The Symbolic Language of Religion* (Minneapolis: Augsburg, 1971), 26–38, 48–68, and 95–114.

a way to suggest that the natural world can be "read" and thus known by scientists.[19] In his use of the term, however, Galileo was building upon a much earlier biblical tradition: "The heavens are telling the glory of God; / and the firmament proclaims his handiwork. / Day to day pours forth speech, / and night to night declares knowledge" (Ps 19:1-2). In the natural world, one can discern the creative work of God. In his letter to Christ's followers in Rome, the apostle Paul wrote that "Ever since the creation of the world [God's] eternal power and divine nature, invisible though they are, have been understood and seen through the things he has made" (Rom 1:20). Here we suggest that Jesus was adept at "reading" the Book of Nature as his parables and sayings overflow with images drawn from the natural world.

And yet he was not a "nature lover," for whom the natural world was a closed system in which one worshiped nature alone. Rather, he was adept at reading the Book of Scripture and the Book of Nature: "Look at the birds of the air; they neither sow nor reap nor gather into barns, and yet your heavenly Father feeds them" (Matt 6:26). Note that the birds of the air are connected to the heavenly Father who feeds them. Indeed, we can see that Jesus' view of the natural world was informed by his grasp of Scripture, by the stories his people read, proclaimed, interpreted, and ritualized. Holding the two "books" together and thus allowing them to be in conversation with each other is much different than reading the Bible without observing nature (the source of much anthropocentric thinking in the Christian tradition) or studying the natural world without reading the Bible (a practice common even among some earth-friendly Christians). Given the increasing number of people living in urban areas and attending urban churches, one has to wonder if the holding of the two books

[19] Lorne L. Evernden, *The Social Creation of Nature* (Baltimore: Johns Hopkins University Press, 1992), 52.

together will be lost in coming generations. One wonders: are seminarians—future homilists—trained in the Book of Nature? Or does the education of future leaders in the church focus solely on the Book of Scripture with an anthropocentric lens, in which the Scriptures set forth the plan of salvation for humankind alone? Bede, Walafrid, and Hildegard were adept at reading both books; their scientific curiosity about the natural world never prevented them from recognizing that the Scriptures reveal the source and sustainer of the natural world.

Word Becomes Flesh

The canon of the New Testament holds together two images: "The Word became flesh and lived among us" (John 1:14): the creating Word of God and the flesh of Jesus of Nazareth. The search for the historical Jesus attempts to discover the Jesus *behind* the gospel accounts that were written decades after his death and resurrection. Indeed, those who search for the "authentic" Jesus of history have remained skeptical of any attribution of divinity to him: the flesh of Jesus, yes, but not the incarnation of the Word of God in him. It can be easier to hold exclusively to one or the other viewpoint: the humanity of Jesus or the divinity of Jesus. Yet Christian practice holds the two together, asking how each informs the other.

In this study, we have attempted to see Jesus through an "ecological lens," looking for continuity between his immersion in the natural world during his public ministry and the natural images used by New Testament authors to describe his significance: a fish, the sign of Jonah (Matt 12:38-40); the hen and her chicks (Luke 13:34); "the Lamb of God" (John 1:29); the lion of Judah (Rev 5:5); the serpent lifted up (John 3:14-15); "the bread of life" (John 6:35); the vine with branches (John 15:1-8); the water of life (John 4:14); the wine of the kingdom (Mark 14:23-25); "the light of the world" (John 8:12); and "the bright morning star" (Rev 22:16). Such earthly metaphors are complemented by others: he is the new Adam or new earth creature (1 Cor 15:22); the creating Word of God (John 1:1-3); "the firstborn of all creation" (Col 1:15-16); the gatherer of all things in heaven and earth (Eph 1:10); "the great shepherd of the sheep" (Heb 13:20); and the sustainer of all things (Heb 1:3). It was after they experienced his risen presence that his followers began to recognize his more-than-local presence, his presence throughout the cosmos. It was this recognition that led early Christian communities to worship him as God's agent of creation through whom "all things came into being" (John 1:3) and as the One in whom "all things hold together" (Col 1:17).

Let us be clear: it is no easy thing to hold two apparently different or conflicting images together at the same time: the creating Word of God and human flesh, Jesus and the Lamb of God, Christians and the salt of the earth. Yet that is the function of a paradox and rich metaphor, the function of the primordial language of religion: to prompt a question, to push one to ask how *this* is related to *that*, to expand one's awareness rather than delimit it. In this regard, Bede's juxtaposition of the birth of the new year in springtime with the conception and death of Jesus pushes one to ask how one is related to the other. How might holding the two together expand one's understanding of Jesus Christ and what he offers the world? Walafrid's holding together the figure of Jesus and a flower filled with virtues pushes one to ask how flowers can be virtuous and how this metaphor sheds light on the person and work of Jesus Christ.[20] Hildegard taught that the Word of God is clothed in soil, water, air, and fire, the four elements of creation. Does the juxtaposition of those elements with Jesus Christ not shed light on his relationship with the creation and thus

[20] Readers do well to obtain and study Gail Ramshaw's *Liturgical Language: Keeping It Metaphoric, Making It Inclusive* (Collegeville, MN: Liturgical Press, 1996), for a helpful introduction to metaphor.

diminish our tendency to see ourselves as the primary center of God's concern?

The Gifts of the Earth

An older but still reliable understanding suggests that a sacrament is an outward sign instituted by Christ to bestow grace. Here we suggest that, in the history of Christianity, considerable attention has been given to the grace given by Christ: the inner, invisible dimension of a sacrament. Much less attention has been given to the outward sign. And yet the outward signs, gifts of creation given by God, deserve our consideration in and of themselves: water, scented olive oil (chrism), bread, wine, oil of the sick, oil of catechumens—as well as the gospel book, crucifix, paschal candle, baptismal candles, incense, branches (palm or otherwise), ashes, and vesture.

The early followers of Jesus welcomed the gifts of the earth in their worship as signs of his crucified and risen presence with them. The liturgical and sacramental reforms of the twentieth century placed particular emphasis on the central and primary things of the liturgy, stripping away baroque excess and cumbersome ethnic or national additions, restoring what our ancestors in the faith experienced in the early centuries of Christian life and worship. The church holds that the sacraments flow from Christ and his Body under the inspiration of the Holy Spirit.[21] How, then, do we understand the outward, visible signs of creation before discussing their spiritual significance as the means of grace? This is not to suggest the displacement of the theological and salvific significance of the sacraments. Rather, it is to suggest that a mystagogical reflection on these earthy gifts can assist in recognizing the presence of Christ throughout creation.[22]

[21] *Catechism of the Catholic Church*, no. 290.

[22] See Benjamin M. Stewart, *A Watered Garden: Christian Worship and Earth's Ecology* (Minneapolis: Augsburg Fortress, 2015).

But, then, we rightly ask if the gifts of the earth are truly central and primary in the actual practice of the church or if ancillary devotions and artifacts displace them. If we hold that the Word of God, Jesus Christ, is the agent of creation, then one can draw out the relationship between Christ and the many gifts of creation. Are the worshiping assemblies of the church drawn to recognize that the waters used to wash new members into the Body of Christ are local waters? Is there homiletical or catechetical reflection on the origin of bread and wine in one's practice or region?[23] There is to be no gnostic myth in the life of the church that disparages the goodness of what God continues to create for the well-being of God's creatures, human and otherwise. There is to be only this: thanksgiving that leads to care for others.

Care for Others

In his request for a garden in each monastery, Benedict underscored the need to provide food and drink for the monastic community. At the same time, he considered of particular importance care of the sick and the poor stranger. "Care of the sick must rank above and before all else, so that they may truly be served as Christ."[24] "Great care and concern are to be shown in receiving poor people and pilgrims, because in them more particularly Christ is received."[25] The request for a garden expanded quickly into what we read in Walafrid and Hildegard: large beds devoted to the cultivation of medicinal herbs and flowers, fields of grain, orchards, and vineyards. Very quickly the Benedictine monastery became a refuge for people fleeing armed conflict and a center of health and healing.

[23] See Gilbert Ostdiek, OFM, *Mystagogy of the Eucharist: A Resource for Faith Formation* (Collegeville, MN: Liturgical Press, 2015).

[24] RB 36.1.

[25] RB 53.15.

Consequently, the produce of garden and field was used to feed the hungry poor and treat the sick and wounded—a continuation of the public ministry of Jesus, who fed hungry crowds, healed the sick, calmed the tormented, and washed the feet of his disciples. Rather than guarding or hoarding food and medicine for the monastic community, Benedict opened its doors to welcome those who were challenged by poverty and sickness. Do we not recognize in this hospitality the presence of Christ the host and healer, the One who served others rather than himself alone?

We live in a time when the earth is in danger of diminishment and continued wounding: this is the diagnosis of modern science and of many Christian leaders, including Pope Francis. Consequently, he called upon Catholics, other Christians, and people of goodwill to work diligently in protecting and conserving the riches of creation that flow from the hands of God. And, at the same time, Pope Francis pointed out that "saving the earth" is insufficient if those who suffer from environmental degradation are overlooked. The two must be joined: care for the earth and care of those who suffer: "The deterioration of the environment and of society affects the most vulnerable people on the planet."[26]

It is hard to imagine that a priest would baptize an infant or adult in waters drawn from a polluted river or a deteriorating aquifer. One would expect clean water. And would it not be tragic to sip eucharistic wine whose grapes had been harvested by migrant laborers denied a living wage by their managers, ignoring their God-given dignity? Does the presence of beeswax in the towering paschal candle not prompt one to ask why bee colonies are dying at such high rates? Is it possible that overdevelopment and the resulting loss of habitat contribute to this high death rate? And what of the use of harmful pesticides? Are parishes and monastic communities called to

[26] Pope Francis, *Laudato Si': On Care for Our Common Home*, no. 48.

be attentive supervisors of the natural elements essential to their sacramental and social ministries?

Encounter with Energy, Natural and Spiritual

We have already noted that North Americans continue to spend more and more time indoors using digital technology. This does not bode well for cultivating a sense of responsibility for our common home. Walafrid speaks to us from the ninth century: "Go outside! Work in a garden. Take a walk or go on a hike. Discover your local ecology." In doing so, one encounters God's love of diversity and the radiant presence of the risen Christ in, with, and through "the things God has made." It goes without saying that the ability to read the Book of Nature requires familiarity with the natural world. "Do not shy away from blackening your hands in the soil," Walafrid counsels.

Though they did not know one another, Bede, Walafrid, and Hildegard shared a common conviction: creation is charged with a vibrant energy that animates all growth, an energy that courses through and sustains the lives of all creatures. This energy appeared to Hildegard as the Living Light, visible to her bodily eyes. Indeed, in one of her visions, we see this fiery energy surrounding the cosmos and the earth. From a scientific perspective, the primary source of energy for the earth is the sun. At the same time, light radiates from stars, fireflies, lightning, and luminous organisms in the ocean. The *aurora borealis*, named after Aurora, the Roman goddess of the dawn, and Boreas, the god of the cold north wind, glimmers with iridescent colors in the Northern Hemisphere.

Hildegard referred to this enlightening energy, a scientific and a spiritual reality that courses through the cosmos, as *viriditas*. Walafrid counseled his monks and nuns to come outside and work in the garden. Hildegard claimed that all humans are called to work with Christ's greening energy and so participate with him in rescuing all things from frailty, withering, and drying up. That is a compelling way to think of one's purpose in life.

Salvation as Flourishing

The word "salvation," so embedded in Christian thought and practice, is similar to the term "salve," a derivative of the Latin *salvus*, meaning safe, healthy, or wholesome. Indeed, a salve is the ointment one applies to a rash or wound to heal it. In her understanding of the human condition, Hildegard claims that human beings are wounded and prone to frailty, to a spiritual aridity which affects body, mind, and soul. She recognizes clearly that human actions can diminish and destroy life: she does not shy away from this conviction into a naïve optimism about the human condition. Indeed, the Living Light revealed to the *magistra* that human actions can cause terrible damage to the earth, an inconvenient truth that we understand today.

Into this experience comes Jesus Christ, the verdant energy of God in human form who brings wholeness and healing, *salvus*. Yet he bears in his glorified body the wounds suffered in his crucifixion: his solidarity with all who suffer in this world. He is attentive to all who yearn for safety, health, and wholeness. This verdant energy courses through the cosmos and creation as light that sustains life: "What has come into being in him was life, and the life was the light of all people" (John 1:3-4). Where there is light, there is life, a scientific and spiritual truth. In the presence of this Living Light, humans, other creatures, and creation are called to flourish: *this* is the will of God. But is it our will, our desire?

The Gardener

In these few pages, we have suggested that early medieval monastics, inspired by their reflection on Jesus in nature in his homeland, offer a perspective on the central figure in the Christian story that is rarely found in the many theological works produced during the two millennia of Christian history. Here we have offered a historical and quite earthy view, one small chapter in the history of the images of Jesus. Located in places distant from urban life, monastic communities have cared for their parcels of the earth for fifteen hundred years with sustainable agriculture and, when such labor was not possible, with gardens for meditation and the cultivation of herbs, flowers, and trees: reflections of the first Paradise and the one to come at the end of the ages.

Is it any wonder that in these cultivated spaces, reflection on the One who was mistaken as a gardener would take place? Many medieval and renaissance paintings depict the encounter between Mary Magdalene and the risen Christ in which he is often portrayed with gardening tools as he leans on his shovel, wearing a floppy gardener's hat. "Jesus is the gardener of the human soul, eradicating noxious vegetation, and planting the flourishing seeds of virtue."[27] Here, then, from the great store of monastic life is one more gift: the gardener who desires but one thing—the flourishing of life.

[27] Debra Rienstra, *Refugia Faith: Seeking Hidden Shelters, Ordinary Wonders, and the Healing of the Earth* (Minneapolis: Fortress Press, 2022), 155.

Bibliography

Primary Sources

Anselm of Canterbury. *Why God Became Man*, translated by Joseph M. Colleran. Albany, NY: Magi Books, 1969.

Apostolic Tradition. In Lucien Deiss, *Springtime of the Liturgy: Liturgical Texts of the First Four Centuries*, translated by Matthew J. O'Connell. Collegeville, MN: Liturgical Press, 1979.

"Bava Batra 58b." In *The William Davidson Babylonian Talmud*. Accessed February 15, 2024. https://www.sefaria.org/Bava_Batra.58b?lang=bi.

Beda Venerabilis. "De Natura Rerum." In *Corpus Christianorum Series Latina*, vol. 123A, edited by Charles W. Jones, 192. Turnhout: Brepols, 1975.

Bede. *Bede the Venerable, Homilies on the Gospels: From Lent to the Dedication of the Church*. Translated by Lawrence T. Martin and David Hurst. Kalamazoo, MI: Cistercian Publications, 1991.

Bede. *Ecclesiastical History of the English People*. Edited by D. H. Farmer, translated by Leo Sherley-Price, and revised by R. E. Latham. London: Penguin, 1991.

Bede. *On the Reckoning of Time*. Translated by Faith Wallis. Liverpool: Liverpool University Press, 1999.

Bede. "Sermon II.2 In Lent." In *Bede the Venerable, Homilies on the Gospels: From Lent to the Dedication of the Church*, translated by Lawrence T. Martin and David Hurst, OSB, 21. Kalamazoo, MI: Cistercian Publications, 1991.

Bede. "Sermon II.7 The Easter Vigil." In *Bede the Venerable, Homilies on the Gospels: From Lent to the Dedication of the Church*, translated by Lawrence T. Martin and David Hurst, OSB, 66. Kalamazoo, MI: Cistercian Publications, 1991.

"Berakhot 33a:35." In *The William Davidson Babylonian Talmud*. Accessed February 16, 2024. https://www.sefaria.org/Berakhot.33a.35?lang=bi&with=all&lang2=en.

Bernard of Clairvaux. *Sermons on the Song of Songs*, 4 vols. Translated by Kilian Walsh, OCSO, and Irene M. Edmonds. Collegeville, MN: Liturgical Press, 1971–80.

Bernard of Clairvaux. *The Voice of My Beloved: The Song of Songs in Western Medieval Christianity* by E. Ann Matter. Philadelphia: University of Pennsylvania Press, 1992.

Byrhtferth of Ramsey. *Byrhtferth's Enchiridion*. Edited by Peter S. Baker and Michael Lapidge. Oxford: Oxford University Press, 1995.

Clement of Alexandria. "Hymn to Christ the Teacher." In Lucien Deiss, *Springtime of the Liturgy: Liturgical Texts of the First Four Centuries*, translated by Matthew J. O'Connell. Collegeville, MN: Liturgical Press, 1979.

"The Didache or Teaching of the Twelve Apostles." In Lucien Deiss, *Springtime of the Liturgy: Liturgical Texts of the First Four Centuries*, translated by Matthew J. O'Connell. Collegeville, MN: Liturgical Press, 1979.

Dioscorides. *De materia medica*. Translated by Lily Y. Beck. Hildesheim: Olms-Weidman, 2005.

"The Dream of the Rood." In *Anglo-Saxon Spirituality*, edited and translated by Robert Boenig. New York: Paulist Press, 2000.

Egeria. *The Pilgrimage of Egeria*. Translated by Paul F. Bradshaw and Anne McGowan. Collegeville, MN: Liturgical Press, 2018.

Eusebius of Caesarea. *Church History*, Book V, chap. 24. In *Nicene and Post-Nicene Fathers*, Second Series, vol. 1, edited by Philip Schaff and Henry Wace, translated by Arthur C. McGiffert, 242. Buffalo, NY: Christian Literature, 1890.

Fry, Timothy, OSB, ed. *The Rule of Saint Benedict in Latin and English with Notes*. Collegeville, MN: Liturgical Press, 1981.

Gregory the Great. *Dialogues: Tome II*. Edited by Adalbert de Vogüé, OSB, and translated by Paul Antin, OSB. Vol. 260 in *Sources Chrétiennes*. Paris: Éditions du Cerf, 1979.

Gregory the Great. *Moralia in Iob*. Edited by Marci Adriaen. Vol. 143B in *Corpus Christianorum, Series Latina*. Turnhout: Brepols, 1985.

Hildegard of Bingen. *The Book of Divine Works*. Translated by Nathan M. Campbell. Washington, DC: Catholic University of America Press, 2018.

Hildegard of Bingen. *The Book of the Rewards of Life (Liber Vitae Meritorum)*. Translated by Bruce W. Hozeski. New York: Oxford University Press, 1997.

Hildegard of Bingen. *Hildegardis Causae et Curae* (*Hildegard, Causes and Cures*). Edited by Paul Kaiser. Leipzig: B.G. Teubneri, 1903.

Hildegard of Bingen. *The Letters of Hildegard of Bingen*. Translated by Joseph L. Baird and Radd K. Ehrman. Oxford: Oxford University Press, 1994.

Hildegard of Bingen. "O clarissima mater." International Society of Hildegard von Bingen Studies (hereafter ISHBS), September 4, 2014. Accessed December 18, 2024. https://www.hildegard-society.org/2014/09/o-clarissima-responsory.html.

Hildegard of Bingen. "O ignis Spiritus paracliti." ISHBS, November 18, 2014. Accessed December 18, 2024. https://www.hildegard-society.org/2014/11/o-ignis-spiritus-paracliti-sequence.html.

Hildegard of Bingen. "O tu suavissima virga." ISHBS, October 13, 2014. Accessed December 17, 2024. https://www.hildegard-society.org/2014/10/o-tu-suavissima-virga-responsory.html.

Hildegard of Bingen. "O viridissima virga." ISHBS, October 13, 2014. Accessed December 17, 2024. https://www.hildegard-society.org/2014/10/o-viridissima-virga-song.html.

Hildegard of Bingen. "O vis eternitatis." ISHBS, June 26, 2014. Accessed December 11, 2024. https://www.hildegard-society.org/2014/06/o-vis-eternitatis.html.

Hildegard of Bingen. *Scivias*. Translated by Mother Columba Hart and Jane Bishop. Mahwah, NJ: Paulist Press, 1990.

Ignatius of Antioch. "Letter to the Romans." In *Early Christian Fathers*, edited by Cyril Richardson. New York: Simon and Schuster, 1995.

Jerome. *Commentary on Matthew*. Translated by Thomas P. Scheck. Washington, DC: Catholic University of America Press, 2008.

Josephus, Flavius. *The Jewish War: Books III–IV*. Translated by H. St. J. Thackeray. Loeb Classical Library. Cambridge: Harvard University Press, 1927.

Justin Martyr. "1 Apology 67." In Gordon Lathrop, *Holy Ground: A Liturgical Cosmology*. Minneapolis: Fortress Press, 2003.

"The *Kiddush* for Sabbath and Feast Days." In Lucien Deiss, *Springtime of the Liturgy: Liturgical Texts of the First Four Centuries*, translated by Matthew J. O'Connell. Collegeville, MN: Liturgical Press, 1979.

Melito of Sardis. *On Pascha*. Translation and Introduction by Alistair Stewart-Sykes. Crestwood, NY: St. Vladimir's Seminary Press, 2001.

Mishneh Torah, Prayer and the Priestly Blessing. Chap. 7. Accessed February 19, 2024. https://www.sefaria.org/Mishneh_Torah%2C_Prayer_and_the_Priestly_Blessing.7?lang=bi.

The Old English Martyrology: Edition, Translation, and Commentary. Edited by Christine Rauer. Cambridge: Cambridge University Press, 2013.

RB 1980: The Rule of St. Benedict in Latin and English with Notes. Edited by Timothy Fry, OSB. Collegeville, MN: Liturgical Press, 1981.

Rea, Jennifer A., and Liz Clarke. "The Passion of Perpetua and Felicity." In *Perpetua's Journey: Faith, Gender, and Power in the Roman Empire*. Oxford: Oxford University Press, 2018.

Siddur Tehillat Hashem. Translated by Nissen Mangel. New York: Kehot Publication Society, 2004.

Strabo, Walahfrid. *Hortulus*. Translated by Raef Payne. Pittsburgh: Hunt Botanical Library, 1966.

Strabo, Walafrid. "Hortulus: On the Cultivation of Gardens." In *A Benedictine Reader: 530–1530*, translated by Ronald E. Pepin, edited by Hugh Feiss, OSB, Ronald E. Pepin, and Maureen M. O'Brien. Collegeville, MN: Liturgical Press, 2019.

Tertullian. *On Baptism*. Edited and translated with introduction and commentary by Ernest Evans. London: SPCK, 1964.

Tertullian. "On Repentance." In *The Ante-Nicene Fathers: Fathers of the Second Century*, edited by Alexander Roberts, James Donaldson, and A. Cleveland Coxe, and translated by Sydney Thelwall. Buffalo, NY: Christian Literature Publishing, 1885.

Tertullian. "On the Crown." In *The Ante-Nicene Fathers: Fathers of the Second Century*, edited by Alexander Roberts, James Donaldson, and A. Cleveland Coxe, and translated by Sydney Thelwall. Buffalo, NY: Christian Literature Publishing, 1885.

Theodosius. "Theodosius I (379–395) on Catholic and Heretic." In *Documents of the Christian Church*, 4th ed., edited by Henry Bettenson and Chris Maunder, 23. Oxford: Oxford University Press, 2011.

Scripture and Ritual Texts

Benedictine Daily Prayer: A Short Breviary. 2nd ed. Edited by Maxwell Johnson, OblSB. Collegeville, MN: Liturgical Press, 2015.

The Holy Bible. The New Revised Standard Version Bible. National Council of the Churches of Christ in the United States of America, 1989.

The Roman Missal. Third Typical Edition. Totowa, NJ: Catholic Book Publishing, 2011.

Secondary Sources

1 Pet 5:8-9a. In "An Order for Compline," in *The Book of Common Prayer*, 132. New York: Oxford University Press, 1979.

Adkins, Frankie. "Boops, Hums and Farts: The Mysterious World of Fish Communication," April 19, 2024. Accessed April 19, 2024. https://www.bbc.com/future/article/20240418-boops-hums-and-farts-the-mysterious-world-of-fish-communication.

Anonymous. "There Is No Rose." In *Carols for Choirs 2*, edited by David Willcocks and John Rutter, 190. London: Oxford University Press, 1970.

Athanasius. *The Life of St. Antony*. Translated by Robert T. Meyer. Westminster, MD: Newman Press, 1950.

Bagatti, Bellarmino. *Ancient Christian Villages of Galilee*. Translated by Paul Rotondi. Jerusalem: Franciscan Printing Press, 2001.

Baker, Peter. "Byrhtferth of Ramsey, *De Concordia Mensium atque Elementorum* (*On the Concord of the Months and the Elements*)." Accessed February 19, 2025. https://www.babelstone.co.uk/Blog/2008/12/byrhtferths-ogham-enigma.html.

Bar-Ilan, Meir. "Illiteracy in the Land of Israel in the First Centuries C.E." In *Essays in the Social Scientific Study of Judaism and Jewish Society*, edited by Simcha Fishbane, Alain Goldschläger, and Stuart Schoenfeld, 46–61. New York: Ktav, 1992.

Bauckham, Richard. *The Bible and Ecology: Rediscovering the Community of Creation*. Waco, TX: Baylor University Press, 2010.

Bellah, Robert N., Richard Madsen, William M. Sullivan, Ann Swidler, and Steven M. Tipton. *Habits of the Heart: Individualism and Commitment in American Life*. Berkeley: University of California Press, 1983/1996.

Berkowitz, Jacob. *The Stardust Revolution: The New Story of Our Origin in the Stars*. Lanham, MD: Prometheus Books, 2022.

Binns, John. "John the Baptist: Desert and Diet." *Theology* 127, no. 1 (2007): 13–21.

Bizzari, Mariano. "Lessons from the Past: Hildegard of Bingen." *Organisms: Journal of Biological Sciences* 2, no. 1 (2018): 114.

Borias, André, OSB. "Le Christ dans la Règle de Saint Benoit." *Revue Bénédictine* 82 (1972): 122.

Borowski, Oded. *Every Living Thing: Daily Use of Animals in Ancient Israel*. Walnut Creek, CA: AltaMira Press, 1998.

Brown, Raymond E., SS. *An Introduction to the New Testament*. New York: Doubleday, 1997.

Brusowankin, Aryeh. "Preventing Plant Extinction Caused by Climate Change." In *The Green Planet*, August 2, 2022. Accessed December 1, 2024. https://www.pbs.org/articles/preventing-plant-extinction-caused-by-climate-change#:~:text=One%20 of%20the%20worst%20effects,a%20specific%20type%20of%20bee.

Bulmer, Ralph. "The Uncleanness of the Birds of Leviticus and Deuteronomy." *Man* 24, no. 2 (June 1989): 304–21.

Cabié, Robert. "The Coptic and Ethiopian Rites." In *The Sacraments*, vol. III in *The Church at Prayer*, edited by A. G. Martimort and translated by Matthew J. O'Connell, 83. Collegeville, MN: Liturgical Press, 1988.

Cabié, Robert. *The Eucharist*. Edited by A. G. Martimort and translated by Matthew J. O'Connell. Collegeville, MN: Liturgical Press, 1986.

Cabrol, Fernand, OSB. "Avent." In *Dictionnaire d'archéologie chrétienne et de liturgie* I:II, edited by Fernand Cabrol, OSB, 3225. Paris: Letouzey et Ane, 1907.

Cahill, Michael, trans. and ed. *The First Commentary on Mark: An Annotated Translation*. New York: Oxford University Press, 1998.

Campbell, James. "Bede." In *The Oxford Dictionary of National Biography*, 85. Oxford: Oxford University Press, 2004.

Canadian Drought Monitor, Government of Canada. Accessed February 11, 2024. https://agriculture.canada.ca/en/agricultural-production/weather/canadian-drought-monitor/current-drought-conditions.

Carletti, Sandro. *The Catacombs of Priscilla*. Translated by Alice Mulhern. Vatican City: Pontifical Commission for Sacred Archaeology, 1982.

Carson, Rachel. *Silent Spring*. New York: Houghton Mifflin, 1962.

Catechism of the Catholic Church. 2nd ed. United States Catholic Conference—Libreria Editrice Vaticana, 1997.

Centers for Disease Control and Prevention, "Only 1 in 10 Adults Get Enough Fruits or Vegetables." Accessed February 17, 2024. https://archive.cdc.gov/#/details?q=https://www.cdc.gov/nccdphp/dnpao/division-information/media-tools/adults-fruits-vegetables.html&start=0&rows=10&url=

https://www.cdc.gov/nccdphp/dnpao/division-information/media-tools/adults-fruits-vegetables.html.

The Century of the Self. 2002 BBC documentary, June 20, 2016. Accessed April 17, 2024. https://www.youtube.com/watch?v=DnPmg0R1M04.

Chavkin, Sasha. "How an American Meat Broker Is Fueling Amazon Deforestation." *Associated Press*, November 3, 2023. Accessed April 26, 2024. https://apnews.com/article/brazil-china-amazon-deforestation-beef-climate-trade-2a7a9a4310b6abca727dabb596e2e84d.

Claiborne, Robert. *The Roots of English: A Reader's Handbook*. New York: Times Books, 1989.

Cole, Becky. *The Garden Apothecary*. London: Quadrille, 2022.

Colombàs, García M. "Bibbia e monachesimo." In *Dizionario degli Istituti di Perfezione*, vol. I, edited by Guerrino Pelliccia and Giancarlo Rocca, 1448–58. Rome: Edizioni Paoline, 1974.

Danin, Avinoam. "Flora and Vegetation of Israel and Adjacent Areas." *Bocconea* 3 (1992): 18.

Davidson, Hilda E. "Human Sacrifice in the Late Pagan Period in North Western Europe." In *The Age of Sutton Hoo: The Seventh Century in North-Western Europe*, edited by Martin Carver, 338. Woodbridge: Boydell Press, 1992.

Davis, Tamara M. "Is the Universe Leaking Energy?" *Scientific American* 303, no. 1 (July 1, 2010): 38–47.

Daviss, Bennet. "Body Talk." *New Scientist*, February 23, 2002. Accessed February 5, 2024. https://www.newscientist.com/article/mg17323314-800-body-talk/.

Deiss, Lucien. *Springtime of the Liturgy: Liturgical Texts of the First Four Centuries*. Translated by Matthew J. O'Connell. Collegeville, MN: Liturgical Press, 1979.

D. J. Case and Associates, "The Nature of Americans." Accessed November 30, 2024. https://natureofamericans.org/findings/topic-summary/adults.

"Dolphin Communication 2024." Accessed March 17, 2024. https://dolphins.org/communication.

Dufner, Delores, OSB. "Faithful Cross, O Tree of Beauty." In *Pange Lingua Gloriosi: Choral Music for Holy Week*, no. 22. Portland: Oregon Catholic Press, 2010.

Dunkle, Brian P., SJ. *Enchantment and Creed in the Hymns of Ambrose of Milan*. Oxford: Oxford University Press, 2016.

Engbring, Gertrude M. "Saint Hildegard, Twelfth Century Physician." *Bulletin of the History of Medicine* 8, no. 6 (1940): 777.

Evenou, Jean. "The East: The Rite of Crowning." In *The Sacraments*, vol. III in *The Church at Prayer*, edited by A. G. Martimort, 192–95. Collegeville, MN: Liturgical Press, 1988.

Evernden, Lorne L. *The Social Creation of Nature*. Baltimore: Johns Hopkins University Press, 1992.

Fawcett, Thomas. *The Symbolic Language of Religion*. Minneapolis: Augsburg, 1971.

Ferguson, George. "Tree of Jesse." In *Signs & Symbols in Christian Art*, 39. London: Oxford University Press, 1954.

Fern, Chris. "Horses in Mind." In *Signals of Belief in Early England: Anglo-Saxon Paganism Revisited*, edited by Martin Carver, Alex Sanmark, and Sarah Semple, 130–35. Oxford: Oxbow Books, 2010.

Firmage, Edwin. "Birds." In *The Anchor Bible Dictionary* 6, edited by David Noel Freedman, 1144. New York: Doubleday, 1992.

Flanagan, Sabina. *Hildegard of Bingen: A Visionary Life*. New York: Routledge, 1990.

Fowler, Cary. *Seeds on Ice: Svalbard and the Global Seed Vault*. Burlington, VT: Prospecta Press, 2016.

Foxhall, Katherine. "A Shower of Phosphenes: Twentieth-Century Stories and the Medical Uses of History." In *Migraine: A History*, 135–54. Baltimore: Johns Hopkins University Press, 2019.

"Fresh Fish Availability." Accessed February 18, 2024. https://www.chefs-resources.com/seafood/fresh-fish-availability-chart/.

Furchert, Almut. "Cosmic Partnership: Hildegard of Bingen's Vision of an Integral Ecology." *Journal of Social Encounters* 8, no. 2 (2024): 310–27.

Gambero, Luigi, SM. *Mary and the Fathers of the Church: The Blessed Virgin Mary in Patristic Thought*. Translated by Thomas Buffer. San Francisco: Ignatius Press, 1999.

Geist, Helmut. *The Causes and Progression of Desertification*. London: Ashgate/Routledge, 2005.

Ginther, James. "Hildegard of Bingen's Theology." In *The Cambridge Companion to Hildegard of Bingen*, edited by Jennifer Bain, 85–104. Cambridge: Cambridge University Press, 2021.

Hanson, K. C., and Douglas E. Oakman. *Palestine in the Time of Jesus: Social Structures and Social Conflicts*. Minneapolis: Fortress Press, 1998.

Havlíceki, Filip, and Miroslav Morcinek. "Waste and Pollution in the Ancient Rome Empire." *Journal of Landscape Ecology* 9, no. 3 (2016): 33–49.

Herren, Michael W., and Shirley Ann Brown. *Christ in Celtic Christianity: Britain and Ireland from the Fifth to the Tenth Century*. Woodbridge, England: Boydell Press, 2002.

Hooey, A. S. "Rosaliae Signorum." *Harvard Theological Review* 30, no. 1 (1937): 15–35.

Horn, Walter, and Ernest Born. *The Plan of St. Gall: A Study of the Architecture and Economy of, and Life in, a Paradigmatic Carolingian Monastery*. Translated by Charles W. Jones. 3 vols. Berkeley: University of California Press, 1979.

Israeli Red List of Threatened Breeding Birds. https://redlist.parks.org.il/en/aves/.

Jacob, Irene and Walter. "Flora." In *The Anchor Bible Dictionary* 2, edited by David Noel Freedman, 803. New York: Doubleday, 1992.

Janko, Richard. "Empedocles, *On Nature* I 233–364: A New Reconstruction of *P. Strasb. Gr.* Inv. 1665–6." *Zeitschrift für Papyrologie und Epigraphik* 150 (2004): 1–26.

Jensen, Morten. "Climate, Droughts, Wars, and Famines in Galilee as a Background for Understanding the Historical Jesus." *Journal of Biblical Literature* 131, no. 2 (2012): 307–24.

Jensen, Robin M. *Baptismal Imagery in Early Christianity: Ritual, Visual, and Theological Dimensions*. Grand Rapids, MI: Baker Academic, 2012.

Jeong, Dong Hyeon. *Embracing the Nonhuman in the Gospel of Mark*. Atlanta: SBL Press, 2023.

John, V. G. "Kingdom of God and Ecology: A Parabolic Perspective." *Bangalore Theological Forum* 34, no. 1 (June 2002): 91–123.

Jones, Alexander. "Ancient Rejection and Adoption of Ptolemy's Frame of Reference for Longitudes." In *Ptolemy in Perspective*, vol. 36, edited by Alexander Jones, 11–44. New York: Springer, 2010.

Jones, Jeannette D. "A Theological Interpretation of *Viriditas* in Hildegard of Bingen and Gregory the Great." *Portfolio of the Department of Musicology and Ethnomusicology* 1 (2012). Accessed December 13, 2024. https://www.bu.edu/pdme/jeannette-jones/#_edn7.

Kardong, Terence, OSB. *Benedict's Rule: A Translation and Commentary*. Collegeville, MN: Liturgical Press, 1996.

Kasper, Cardinal Walter. "The Symbol of Water in the Biblical, Patristic, and Liturgical Tradition." In *The Adriatic Sea: A Sea at Risk, A Unity of Purpose*, edited by Neal Ascherson and Andrew Marshall, 159. Athens: Religion, Science and the Environment, 2003.

Kasprzak, Dariusz, OFM Cap. "Monastic Exegesis and the Biblical Typology of Monasticism in the Patristic Period." *Theological Research* 2, no. 1 (2014): 85–103.

Kiel, Micah. *Apocalyptic Ecology: The Book of Revelation, the Earth, and the Future*. Collegeville, MN: Liturgical Press, 2017.

Kienzie, Beverly M. "Operatrix in vinea domini: Hildegard of Bingen's Preaching and Polemics Against the Cathars." *Heresis: Revue d'hérésiologie médiévale* 26–27 (1996): 43–56.

Krautheimer, Richard. *Rome: Profile of a City, 312–1308*. Princeton: Princeton University Press, 2000.

Kreglinger, Gisela H. *The Spirituality of Wine*. Grand Rapids, MI: Eerdmans, 2016.

Lapidge, Michael. *The Anglo-Saxon Library*. Oxford: Oxford University Press, 2006.

Lathrop, Gordon. *Holy Ground: A Liturgical Cosmology*. Minneapolis: Fortress Press, 2003.

Lathrop, Gordon. *Holy Things: A Liturgical Theology*. Minneapolis: Fortress Press, 1993.

Lear, Linda. *Rachel Carson: Witness for Nature*. New York: Houghton Mifflin, 1997.

Llewellyn, Peter. *Rome in the Dark Ages*. New York: Praeger, 1971.

Lutes, Richard. "An Enduring American Love Affair." *Produce News*, May 24, 2018. Accessed February 19, 2025. https://theproducenews.com/endurIng-american-love-affair.

MacCulloch, Diarmaid. "The Triumph of Monastic Silence." In *Silence: A Christian History*, 53–104. New York: Penguin, 2013.

Maddocks, Fiona. *Hildegard of Bingen: The Woman of Her Age*. New York: Image Books, 2001.

Magnan, Celine. "Jesus in His Environment." *Today's Good News*. Accessed April 14, 2024. https://www.goodnews.ie/environment.shtml#.

Magner, Lois N. *A History of Medicine*. Boca Raton, FL: CRC Press, 1992.

"Magnificat Antiphon for December 21" (the Winter Solstice). In *Benedictine Daily Prayer: A Short Breviary*, 2nd ed., edited by Maxwell Johnson, OblSB, 1337. Collegeville, MN: Liturgical Press, 2015.

Magnusson, Roberta J. *Water Technology in the Middle Ages: Cities, Monasteries, and Waterworks after the Roman Empire*. Baltimore: Johns Hopkins University Press, 2001.

Malina, Bruce J., and Richard L. Rohrbaugh. *Social-Science Commentary on the Synoptic Gospels*. 2nd ed. Minneapolis: Fortress Press, 2003.

Mariotti, Anthony. "Gardening Statistics." Accessed October 31, 2024. https://www.rubyhome.com/blog/gardening-stats/.

Marmion, Columba, OSB. "The Following of Christ." In *Christ: The Ideal of the Monk*, 23–24. Brewster, MA: Paraclete Press, 2014; 1926.

Maron, Nimrod. "Faunal Remains from Nazareth." *'Atiqot* 98 (2020): 93–102.

McDonnell, Kilian, OSB. *The Baptism of Jesus in the Jordan: The Trinitarian and Cosmic Order of Salvation*. Collegeville, MN: Liturgical Press, 1996.

McGann, Mary, RSCJ. "The Corporate Industrial Food System: Origin, Goals, Outcomes." In *The Meal That Reconnects: Eucharistic Eating and the Global Food Crisis*, 59–76. Collegeville, MN: Liturgical Press, 2020.

McGowan, Andrew. "Food and Drink in Early Christian Rituals." In *Ascetic Eucharists: Food and Drink in Early Christian Ritual Meals*, 95–106, 115–17. Oxford: Oxford University Press, 1999.

Meyers, Carol. "The Temple, Jerusalem." In *Anchor Bible Dictionary* 6, edited by David Noel Freedman, 360. New York: Doubleday, 1992.

Miller, Susan. " 'I Came That They May Have Life, and Have It Abundantly' (John 10:10): An Ecological Reading of John's Gospel." *Expository Times* 124, no. 2 (2012): 64–71.

Minear, Paul S. *Images of the Church in the New Testament*. Louisville: Westminster John Knox Press, 1960.

Mullinix, Nayiri. *Michigan News*, University of Michigan, February 14, 2024. Accessed April 17, 2024. https://news.umich.edu/nearly-15-of-americans-deny-climate-change-is-real-ai-study-finds/.

Nadel, Dani, •••et al. "New Evidence for the Processing of Wild Cereal Grains at Ohalo II, a 23,000-Year-Old Campsite on the Shore of the Sea of Galilee, Israel." *Antiquity* 86 (December 2012): 990–1003.

Newberg, Andrew B., •••et al. "Effect of a One-Week Spiritual Retreat on Dopamine and Serotonin Transporter Binding: A Preliminary Study." *Religion, Brain & Behavior* 8, no. 3 (March 2017): 265–78.

North American Bird Conservation Initiative Committee (NABCI). *State of the Birds Report: United States 2022*. Edited by Gus Axelson. Cornell, NY: Cornell University, 2022.

Northcott, Michael S. *Place, Ecology, and the Sacred: The Moral Geography of Sustainable Communities*. London: Bloomsbury, 2015.

Olley, Lorraine H. "Benedict Biscop: Benedictine, Builder, Bibliophile." *Theological Librarianship* 7, no. 1 (January 2014): 34–36.

Ostdiek, Gilbert, OFM. *Mystagogy of the Eucharist: A Resource for Faith Formation*. Collegeville, MN: Liturgical Press, 2015.

Our Epidemic of Loneliness and Isolation: The U.S. Surgeon General's Advisory on the Healing Effects of Social Connection and Community. Washington, DC: Office of the Surgeon General, 2023.

Parker, Eleanor. "The O Antiphons as Medieval Carols: O Root of Jesse, O Key of David." In *A Clerk of Oxford*, December 20, 2012. Accessed November 25, 2024. https://aclerkofoxford.blogspot.com/2012/12/the-o-antiphons-as-medieval-carols-o.html.

Parker, Eleanor. "Two Carols about Roses." In *A Clerk of Oxford*, December 20, 2012. Accessed November 25, 2024. https://aclerkofoxford.blogspot.com/2012/12/two-carols-about-roses.html.

Parker, Eleanor. *Winters in the World: A Journey through the Anglo-Saxon World*. London: Reaktion Books, 2022.

Pelikan, Jaroslav. "The Monk Who Rules the World." In *Jesus Through the Centuries: His Place in the History of Culture*. New Haven: Yale University Press, 1985.

Peterson, Stephen J., James M. Robinson, and Hans-Gebhard Bethge. *The Fifth Gospel: The Gospel of Thomas Comes of Age*. Harrisburg, PA: Trinity Press International, 1998.

Pfann, Stephen, Ross Voss, and Yehuda Rapuano. "Surveys and Excavations at the Nazareth Village Farm (1997–2002): Final Report." *Bulletin of the Anglo-Israel Archaeological Society* 25 (2007).

Pilch, John. *The Cultural Dictionary of the Bible*. Collegeville, MN: Liturgical Press, 1999.

Pope Francis. "Greeting of His Holiness Pope Francis to the Participants in the Convention Organized by Vinitaly on the Theme, 'The Economy of Francis and the World of Italian Wine,'" January 22, 2024. Accessed February 15, 2024. https://www.vatican.va/content/francesco/en/speeches/2024/january/documents/20240122-vinitaly.html.

Pope Francis. "Homily for Solemnity of Christ the King of the Universe and Closing of the Jubilee Holy Year of Mercy." Salt + Light Media, November 20, 2016. Accessed February 19, 2025. https://slmedia.org/blog/homily-of-pope-francis-for-solemnity-of-christ-the-king-of-the-universe-and-closing-of-the-jubilee-holy-year-of-mercy.

Pope Francis. *Laudato Si': On Care for Our Common Home*. Rome: Libreria Editrice Vaticana, 2015.

Ramshaw, Gail. *Liturgical Language: Keeping It Metaphoric, Making It Inclusive*. Collegeville, MN: Liturgical Press, 1996.

Ramshaw, Gail. *Reviving Sacred Speech: The Meaning of Liturgical Language*. Akron, OH: OSL Publications, 2000.

Rauner, Erwin. "Notkers des Stammlers 'Notati de illustribus uiris.'" In Teil I: Kritische Edition, *Mittellateinisches Jahrbuch* 21 (1986): 34–69.

Rea, Anne W., and Wayne R. Munns Jr. "The Value of Nature: Economic, Intrinsic, or Both?" *Integrated Environmental Assessment and Management* 13, no. 5 (2017): 953–55.

Richards, Jeffrey. *The Popes and the Papacy in the Early Middle Ages, 476–752*. London: Routledge and Kegan Paul, 1979.

Rienstra, Debra. *Refugia Faith: Seeking Hidden Shelters, Ordinary Wonders, and the Healing of the Earth*. Minneapolis: Fortress Press, 2022.

Rossing, Barbara R. "Lamb Power." In *The Rapture Exposed: The Message of Hope in the Book of Revelation*, 107–13. New York: Basic Books, 2004.

Sanders, E. P. *Judaism: Practice and Belief, 63 BCE–66 CE*. Norwich: SCM Canterbury, 1992.

Schedl, Barbara. *Der Plan von St. Gallen: Ein Modell europäischer Klosterkultur*. Vienna: Böhlau Wien, 2014.

Schipperges, Heinrich. *The World of Hildegard of Bingen: Her Life, Times, and Visions*. Translated by John Cumming. Collegeville, MN: Liturgical Press, 1998.

"The Secret Language of Trees." In "To the Best of Our Knowledge," aired on Wisconsin Public Radio, April 28, 2018. Accessed December 12, 2024. https://www.ttbook.org/show/secret-language-trees#:~:text=The%20way%20that%20communication%20happens,send%20to%20that%20shaded%20tree.

Semple, Sarah. "In the Open Air." In *Signals of Belief in Early England: Anglo-Saxon Paganism Revisited*, edited by Martin Carver, Alex Sanmark, and Sarah Semple, 24. Oxford: Oxbow Books, 2010.

Shire, Michael. *The Illuminated Haggadah*. New York: Stewart, Tabori, and Chang, 1998.

Silberner, Joanna. "A Healthy Dose of Quiet." *Scientific American* 330, no. 5 (May 2024): 58–65.

Silvas, Anna, trans. *Jutta and Hildegard: The Biographical Sources*. University Park, PA: Pennsylvania State University Press, 1999.

Smith, E. Baldwin. *Early Christian Iconography and the School of Ivory Carvers in Provence*. Princeton: Princeton University Press, 1918.

Snir, Ainit, Dani Nadel, Iris Groman-Yaroslavski, Yoel Melamed, Marcelo Sternberg, Ofer Bar-Yosef, and Ehud Weiss. "The Origin of Cultivation and Proto-Weeds, Long Before Neolithic Farming." *PLoS One* 10, no. 7 (July 2015). Accessed July 4, 2024. https://journals.plos.org/plosone/article?id=10.1371/journal.pone.0131422.

Snyder, Graydon F. *Inculturation of the Jesus Tradition: The Impact of Jesus on Jewish and Roman Cultures*. Harrisburg, PA: Trinity Press International, 1999.

Squatriti, Paolo. *Water and Society in Early Medieval Italy, AD 400–1000*. Cambridge: Cambridge University Press, 1998.

Stewart, Benjamin M. *A Watered Garden: Christian Worship and Earth's Ecology*. Minneapolis: Augsburg Fortress, 2015.

Strake, Richard. "The Lion in Christian Iconography." In *A Guide to Christian Iconography: Images, Symbols, and Texts*. Accessed September 11, 2024. https://www.christianiconography.info/lions.html.

Strange, James F. "Magdala." In *The Anchor Bible Dictionary* 4, edited by David Noel Freedman, 463–64. New York: Doubleday, 1992.

Suzuki, Toshitaka N. "Wild Birds Use an Ordering Rule to Decode Novel Call Sequences." *Current Biology* 27, no. 15 (August 2017): 2331–36.

Sweet, Victoria. "Hildegard of Bingen and the Greening of Medieval Medicine." *Bulletin of the History of Medicine* 73, no. 3 (Fall 1999): 381–403.

The Symbolism of Churches and Church Ornaments: A Translation of the First Book of the Rationale Divinorum Officiorum of William Durandus. Introduction and translation by John M. Neale and Benjamin Webb. London: Gibbings, 1906.

Talley, Thomas J. *The Origins of the Liturgical Year*. Collegeville, MN: Liturgical Press, 1991.

Throop, Priscilla, trans. *Hildegard of Bingen's Physica*. Rochester, VT: Healing Arts Press, 1998.

Torvend, Samuel, OblSB. *Monastic Ecological Wisdom: A Living Tradition*. Collegeville, MN: Liturgical Press, 2023.

Toussaint-Samat, Maguelonne. *A History of Food*. Translated by Anthea Bell. Oxford: Wiley-Blackwell, 2009.

Trainor, Michael. *About Earth's Child: An Ecological Listening to the Gospel of Luke*. Sheffield, UK: Sheffield Phoenix Press, 2017.

Tyson, Alec, Cary Funk, and Brian Kennedy. "What the Data Says about Americans' Views of Climate Change." Accessed February 19, 2025. https://www.pewresearch.org/short-reads/2023/08/09/what-the-data-says-about-americans-views-of-climate-change/.

U.S. Department of Agriculture. Accessed October 31, 2024. https://www.nifa.usda.gov/.

U.S. Drought Monitor. Accessed February 11, 2024. https://droughtmonitor.unl.edu/.

U.S. Fish and Wildlife Service. "FWS-Listed U.S. Species by Taxonomic Group—Fishes." Accessed February 20, 2024. https://ecos.fws.gov/ecp/report/species-listings-by-tax-group?statusCategory=Listed&groupName=Fishes.

U.S. Fish and Wildlife Service. "Threats to Birds." Accessed February 21, 2024. https://www.fws.gov/library/collections/threats-birds.

Wainwright, Elaine M. *Habitat, Human, and Holy: An Eco-Rhetorical Reading of the Gospel of Matthew*. Sheffield, UK: Sheffield Phoenix Press, 2016.

Wallis, Faith. "Bede and Science." In *The Cambridge Companion to Bede*, vol. 17, edited by Scott DeGregorio, 113–26. Cambridge: Cambridge University Press, 2010.

Wang, Weiqiao, and Jiang Feng. "Water as a Common Reference for Monastic Lives and Spaces in Cistercian and Han Buddhist Monasteries." *Frontiers of Architectural Research* 12, no. 1 (February 2023): 85–103.

Watts, Isaac. "O God, Our Help in Ages Past." In *Gather Comprehensive*, 614. Chicago: GIA Publications, 1994.

Weiss, Zeev. "Sepphoris." In *Oxford Classical Dictionary*. Accessed February 27, 2024. https://doi.org/10.1093/acrefore/9780199381135.013.8039.

Whitehead, Andrew L., and Samuel L. Perry. *Taking America Back for God: Christian Nationalism in the United States*. Rev. ed. New York: Oxford University Press, 2020.

Wohlleben, Peter. *The Hidden Life of Trees: What They Feel, How They Communicate: Discoveries from a Secret World*. Translated by Jane Billinghurst. Vancouver, BC: Greystone Books, 2016.

Wohlleben, Peter. *The Inner Life of Animals: Love, Grief, and Compassion: Surprising Observations of a Hidden World*. Translated by Jane Billinghurst. Vancouver, BC: Greystone Books, 2017.

Wright, KC. "The Benefits of Adding a Drizzle of Olive Oil to Your Diet." *American Heart Association News*, September 28, 2022. Accessed February 14, 2024. https://www.heart.org/en/news/2022/09/28/the-benefits-of-adding-a-drizzle-of-olive-oil-to-your-diet.

Wright, Lawrence. *Clean and Decent: The Fascinating History of the Bathroom and the Water Closet*. New York: Viking Press, 1960.

Index